TAGORE

A Life

National Biography

TAGORE

A Life

KRISHNA KRIPALANI

एकः सूते सकलम्

NATIONAL BOOK TRUST, INDIA

This book was published by the author himself in 1961 and distributed through Orient Longmans, New Delhi and reprinted in 1971.

All quotations at the beginning of each chapter are from Tagore's own writings.

ISBN 978-81-237-1959-7

First NBT Edition 1986
Reprints 1997, 2001, 2005, 2008, 2011 (twice) (*Saka* 1933)

₹ 110.00

Published by the Director, National Book Trust, India
Nehru Bhawan, 5 Institutional Area, Phase-II
Vasant Kunj, New Delhi-110 070

To
Sruja
with love,
[illegible]
30-06-2017

to

what once was

Contents

Ancestry

Thy centuries follow one another,
perfecting a small wild flower.

HISTORY and legend, fact and myth are so inextricably blended in Indian tradition that it is not always easy to say where the one ends and the other begins. And so when we trace the genealogy of even such a remarkable family as the Tagores we are soon lost in the mists of popular tradition and family lore through which we have to pick our way gingerly backwards.

By the middle of the 8th century, after a long period of political unrest and religious and social chaos, Bengal was consolidated as a powerful Hindu kingdom. This much is history well corroborated by text books. Now the legend. To restore the "purity" of Hindu society corrupted by Buddhist anarchy, five Brahmins were imported from the western Kingdom of Kanauj which was a stronghold of Brahminic culture. The progeny of these five Brahmins whose names are remembered to this day made the new racial aristocracy of Bengal which has continued since then. Historians have little to say of this interesting and colossal eugenic experiment which has made Bengal what it is. However, one of the five Brahmins was named Daksha and is reputed to be an ancestor of the Tagores.

History is full of ironies. At the end of the 12th century Bengal was overrun by Turko-Afghans from the west and in course of time came to be ruled as a province of the Muslim Emperor in Delhi. Many Hindus were converted to Islam, some by force, some lured by greed to share the power of the new masters. A Brahmin adventurer in love with a Muslim girl was clever enough to kill two birds with one stone. By voluntarily adopting the new religion he got the woman he desired and rose to be an influential dignitary, the Dewan of the Muslim Governor of Jessore in South

Bengal. His new name was Pir Ali Khan. Two of his trusted officers were the Brahmin brothers, Kamadev and Jayadev, descendants in direct line, after many generations and vicissitudes unrecorded by history, of the legendary ancestor Daksha.

One day—so the story goes—during the observance of Ramazan fast, seeing Pir Ali Khan smell a lemon Kamadev jestingly remarked, "According to our religious code smelling is half-eating. You have therefore violated your fast." Pir Ali Khan said nothing, but having been born a Hindu the words rankled in his mind. Some days later he invited the Brahmin brothers, with several other Hindus, to a music concert in the Governor's palace. In a room adjoining the hall where the audience was listening to music, a feast of choice Muslim dishes which included beef was laid on the table. When the smell penetrated the concert hall the Hindus began to feel uneasy. Pir Ali Khan smilingly remarked, "If smelling is half-eating, as your religious code enjoins, you have all tasted of the forbidden food and have lost your caste." A panic ensued and the Hindus fled, covering their noses. But the stigma remained. Since then the Tagore family is said to have fallen in the hierarchy of caste and is referred to derogatively as Pirali Brahmins.

Having lost the "purity" of caste the family found it difficult to live in a community which gave it little quarter. The predicament was particularly galling when it came to finding suitable husbands for the daughters. And so the family, hounded from their ancestral home, wandered from place to place, each member seeking fortune for himself and husbands for the daughters. He would be a bold Brahmin who accepted the daughter of such a family. Such a bold fellow was one Jagannath Kushari who married a niece of the ill-fated brothers Kamadev and Jayadev whose indiscreet jest had caused all the trouble. Jagannath Kushari had to pay a heavy price for this temerity, for he too was obliged to leave his home. It was a descendant in the male line of this bold and rash man who is said to have founded the Tagore family.

His name was Panchanan Kushari. Exile and social persecution had made the descendants defiant and adventurous. Having lost the pride of caste, they lost their fear too, for not much else was left to lose. Since they could not be more holy they decided to be more human and seek the other good things that life and the times made possible. Adventure was in the air. Unheard-of things were happening in the country. White men from across the seas had opened a factory and trading centre on the banks of the holy Ganges and such was their power and prestige that even the Muslim rulers thought it prudent to keep on good terms with them. So Panchanan and his uncle Sukhdev left home in the last decade of the 17th century, as their forefathers had done earlier, and settled down in a village called Govindpur on the bank of the Ganges, not far from the British settlement.

Govindpur was at that time a small fishing village whose inhabitants were all of the so-called low caste. Seeing a Brahmin family settle in their midst they felt elated and gave the uncle and his nephew all the honour due to their caste. Panchanan was always addressed by them as Panchanan Thakur, as the Brahmins are often addressed even to this day. He had found a lucrative occupation in supplying provisions to the foreign ships that sailed up the river. The British and other foreigners had thus ample opportunities of dealing with him and naturally assumed, as most foreigners would still do, that Thakur was Panchanan's surname or family name. So they referred to him as Mr Thakur and unable to articulate the unfamiliar name, pronounced it as Tagore.

The family prospered. Its fortunes were from the beginning linked with the rise of the British power in India. As this power and commerce grew, what was originally a group of fishing villages became the rich and prosperous city of Calcutta, and the fortune of the Tagore family grew with it. The descendants of Panchanan Thakur became merchant princes and landed aristocrats.

The family fortune reached its peak in the life and career of Dwarkanath Tagore, the grandfather of poet Rabindranath. Born in 1794, Dwarkanath was only thirteen years old when his father died. Handsome, versatile and enterprising, he was a romantic figure who in an earlier age would probably have carved out a kingdom for himself and become a prince. Prince, however, he came to be called because of his magnificent way of living and his large public charities. His extensive business covered many fields, indigo factories, saltpetre, sugar, tea, coalmines, etc. He owned large agricultural estates in Bengal and Orissa, a fleet of cargo boats that plied to the British coast and founded the first modern bank with Indian capital, known as the Union Bank. All these multifarious concerns he controlled through his firm, Carr, Tagore and Co.

He lived lavishly and entertained regally. The aristocrats of those days lived a double life. At home in the joint family the orthodox and traditional ways of life were maintained and the household deity was scrupulously worshipped morning and evening. Outside the family quarters were spacious reception rooms and banquet halls hung with chandeliers where the master of the family entertained his friends and visitors, where wine flowed freely, where the ornamented hookah was always ready with fragrant tobacco, where famous musicians vied with one another in displaying their virtuosity and the professional dancing girls their charms. In the heart of Calcutta in the quarter known as Jorasanko the family mansion of the Tagores still stands, now a seat of learning, a grateful nation's monument to Dwarkanath's illustrious grandson. What no longer stands is the stately edifice which Dwarkanath had built on the adjoining land where he entertained friends and guests and all the leading lions of the then ruling society of Calcutta.

No less lavish and extravagant were his charities. There was hardly an institution or cause to which he did not give generously. He helped in the founding of the National Library in Calcutta as also of the first centre of modern education in India, the Hindu College, in 1816, which later grew into what is now known as the Presidency College of Calcutta. He was actively associated with the establishment in 1835 of the first medical college and hospital in Calcutta which is today a vast network of hospitals and a major centre of medical education in the country. He gave free scholarships to encourage students to take up the study of medicine and in order to break down the Hindu prejudice against dissection of dead bodies, he would himself be present in the room when the dissection took place.

He was the first Indian member and patron of the Asiatic Society of Bengal founded in 1784 by Sir William Jones. Many of the leading scientific institutions of today, like the Archaeological Survey of India, the Zoological Survey of India, the Botanical and Geological Surveys of India as well as the Indian Museum in Calcutta, the oldest and biggest in India, owe their origin to this Society. On the eve of his departure for England a contemporary English journal published in Calcutta wrote, "To describe Dwarkanath's public charities would be to enumerate every charitable institution in Calcutta, for from which of them has he withheld his most liberal donations?"

It was not only that he gave of his wealth generously and wisely. He stood up bravely, in the teeth of popular opposition, for every social reform and progressive movement of his day, religious, social and political. He was a faithful friend and staunch supporter of Raja Rammohun Roy, that remarkable religious and social reformer and visionary whom Indian historians have described unanimously as the Father of modern India. The Prince had a shrewd political sense and though he recognised in the establishment of the British rule in India a historical necessity for the consolidation of his country into a modern nation, he was one of the first to organise public opinion and bring the influence of the new rising interests to bear on the good government of the country.

To cross the seas in those days was for the Hindu much more than a mere adventurous voyage. It meant a revolutionary act of defiance against society, for there was a taboo against sea-voyage and severe penalties were prescribed for the culprits. Dwarkanath went to England twice, in 1842 and again in 1844. The well-known orientalist, Friedrich Max Müller, was then a young student in Paris, studying the Rig Veda under Prof. Burnouf. In his Autobiography Max Müller has borne testimony to the vivid impression left on his mind by his chance encounter with the lively and versatile personality of Dwarkanath in Paris, and has described the splendid party given by Dwarkanath to Louis Philippe of France when the room was hung with Kashmir shawls, afterwards distributed among the most distinguished guests.

Dwarkanath did not return home from his second visit to Europe. Like his friend and senior contemporary Raja Rammohun Roy who had died in Bristel, thirteen years earlier, Dwarkanath died, away from his home, in London on 1st August 1846, at the age of fifty-two. In a full column obituary notice in its issue of August 3, 1846, *The Times* (London) said : "Perhaps there is no individual in India, be his rank or position what it may, who has more largely patronized the advancement and fortunes of the many around him, and we believe there are not a few now in India and England who owe entirely to Dwarkanath Tagore the blessing of their present success and independence."

He left behind three sons of whom the eldest was Debendranath, father of the poet. In his own way Debendranath was even more remarkable than his fabulous father. As the father had come to be known popularly as Prince, the son came to be known as the Maharshi, for he was both saint and sage. Though born of Dwarkanath he was truly the moral heir and spiritual successor to Raja Rammohun Roy whose mission he continued and made fruitful. His personality left a deep impact on the intellectual development of Rabindranath.

Born in 1817 Debendranath was brought up in circumstances of increasing luxury which reached its peak when he attained his youth. The pampered darling of a wealthy father and a doting mother and a still more doting grandmother, he grew up as a wilful young man and for some time gave himself up to a life of luxury. But not for long, for the crisis came early and suddenly, when he was only eighteen. His grandmother was on death-bed and had to be removed to a tiled shed on the bank of the ganges, for to die near the holy river was what every pious Hindu desired. For three nights the grandmother lingered on, during which Debendranath was with her almost all the time, spending lonely, weird hours of the dark in the imminent presence of death. On the night before her death, as he was sitting alone by the river he was suddenly seized by an intense spiritual elation and he lost his normal consciousness. When he recovered it, "I was as if no longer the same man. A strong aversion to wealth arose within me. The coarse bamboo mat on which I sat seemed to be my fitting seat, carpets and costly spreadings seemed hateful, in my mind was awakened a joy unfelt before."

In his Autobiography which he wrote many years later he has described vividly his spiritual hunger, his search for truth and the birth and growth of his faith. It is a remarkable document which Evelyn Underhill has described as "one more amongst the small number of authentic histories of the soul." On his return home he gave away many of his personal possessions to friends and others. But merely divesting himself of material possessions brought him neither joy nor understanding. He studied the sacred books of his religion as well as books of Western philosophy, but found no satisfaction. "Great grief was in my heart. Darkness was all around me. The temptations of the world had ceased, but the sense of God was no nearer; earthly and heavenly happiness were alike withdrawn. Life was dreary, the world was like a graveyard." In this state of mind, "one day all of a sudden I saw a page from some Sanskrit book flutter past me. Out of curiosity I picked it up but found I could understand nothing of what was written on it." He sent for a well-known Sanskrit scholar, who identified the text as the first verse of the *Isopanishad* and explained its meaning: "All this whatever moves in this moving world, is enveloped by God. Therefore find your enjoyment in renunciation; do not covet what belongs to others."

This came as a revelation to the young devotee groping in the dark. "My faith in God took deep root; in lieu of worldly pleasures I tasted divine joy. . . When I had thoroughly entered into the Upanishads, and when my intellect began to be daily illumined by the gift of truth, I felt a strong desire to spread the true religion." And so on the very day of the year 1839 when the Hindus of Bengal celebrate the annual festival of the goddess Durga, Debendranath called his friends and followers together and formally inaugurated a purely theistic association, dedicated to the worship of a universal and formless Divinity that informs all life and being, in accordance with the teaching of the Upanishads. This faith, at once old and new, was a challenge to the current Hindu dogma and ritual which centred round the worship of a deity's image. Indeed, even as Debendranath was invoking the new faith, the gongs and cymbals were sounding in his own family mansion where the worship of the goddess Durga was in full swing. He was powerless to stop it.

Raja Rammohun Roy had founded in 1825 the Brahma Sabha as a meeting place for all people, irrespective of caste or race, for the worship of One True God, without the use of any images or symbols or any sectarian ritual. But the movement had languished until this young intrepid mystic, with the sure instinct of a religious reformer, amalgamated in 1843 his new-born Sabha with the older organisation and renaming it Brahma Samaj turned the meeting place into a movement and what was little more than an intellectual club into a vigorous centre of a dynamic faith.

While Debendranath, God-intoxicated, was laying the foundation of a reformed church, the father continued to dazzle his countrymen with his ostentatious ways. He would have liked his son to share his glory and to continue the family tradition of making and spending wealth, but the son was occupied with an altogether different mission. The father was naturally disappointed and annoyed. "As it is he has very little head for business," he remarked at one time, "now he neglects business altogether; it is nothing but Brahma, Brahma, the whole day."

Nevertheless, the feelings between the two were not estranged, for the son continued to work in his father's bank, while giving more and more of his time, resources and zeal to what he felt was his life's goal. One shrewd precaution the father did take. Not knowing how his vast and fast expanding business delicately poised on credit would fare in his son's hands after his death, he made a trust of some of his landed estates making the sons beneficiaries, to ensure that they would always have an assured income, whatever ill-luck might overtake the business. A superb gambler, he knew that fortune was an uncertain mistress.

And so it proved to be. Soon after Dwarkanath's death in London, it was discovered that the firm's liabilities far exceeded its ready assets. There was a rush on the bank and the famous House of Carr, Tagore & Co. had to close its doors. This crisis showed the mettle the son was made of. He called the creditors together, placed all the cards before them and announced that though in law the creditors had no rights over the trust property, he and his brothers voluntarily renounced their claims to the benefit of the trust until the last rupee of the liabilities had been paid. Having thus reduced himself and his family to utter penury, he felt the strange joy that comes of renunciation. "What I had desired came to pass. I wanted to renounce the world and the world left me of its own accord. What a singular coincidence!"

He was not, however, reduced to penury. The creditors were impressed with his integrity and allowed him and the brothers a fair monthly allowance and after some time handed over the management of the entire property into Debendranath's hands. It took him many years of judicious management and frugal living to pay off all the compounded debts. Not only he succeeded in paying off the debts with interest, but he even made good all the charities and donations which the Prince had hastily and too generously promised before he left for England.

The Maharshi travelled widely in India in those days when journeying was full of hazards and was a real adventure. Almost every year he left his home and travelled over the western plains to the Himalayas. Like the Rishis of old he loved the lofty, snowcapped mountains. He was a keen observer of nature and men and his Autobiography is full of vivid descriptions of nature and shrewd observations on men and events.

Before one such visit undertaken at the end of 1856, he had for some time been overcome by a persistent and morbid sense of world weariness and had longed to retire for good to his beloved Himalayas. He had intended not to return to his family but to spend the remaining years in quiet contemplation. It is worth relating why he failed to keep to his resolve. One day in September 1858 he was walking over the mountains, as was his wont, and stopped to enjoy the sight of a waterfall. He was led to muse on the blind destiny of the waters, so clear, cool and beautiful there!—but as they entered the plains they would soon become muddy, dark and soiled. And yet muddied and bereft of their pride, they will fertilise the land and help mankind. Suddenly he heard a voice within say, "Give up thy pride and be lowly like this river. The truth thou hast gained, the devotion and trustfulness that thou hast learnt here, go, make them known to the world."

Escapism was alien to his robust nature and philosophy. He obeyed the command and returned to the world of his duties in Calcutta. Though he continued to travel and visit the Himalayas, he never again thought of escaping. He lived to a ripe old age, lived to see the sunset of the last century and the sunrise of the new, lived to see the religious and social movement he had started gain such momentum that it left him far behind—a solitary peak on the frontier between the old and the new.

A Wonder-Eyed Child

The steps that I heard in my childhood's play,
their music resounds in all the music of this world.

IT was fortunate that the Maharshi came down to earth from his lofty perch in the Himalayas where he at one time threatened to spend the rest of his life in divine contemplation, for within three years after the Himalayan interlude was born, on 7th May 1861, Rabindranath Tagore. Great as were the Maharshi's many other gifts to his people, the greatest was his fourteenth child.

However, when the child was born the event seemed of little significance. His mother Sarada Devi had already borne her husband thirteen children and was to bear him one more son two years later (who, however, died soon after). Perhaps in no family would the fourteenth child be particularly welcome and much less so in a family where all the elder brothers and sisters and their families lived together in one joint household. The huge and rambling mansion at Jorasanko swarmed with children and grandchildren and the birth of an additional member could not have been an event of any special importance. The child was named Rabindranath, or Rabi for short. He was a healthy and fair baby but perhaps not as fair as some of his elder brothers and sisters, for his eldest sister Saudamini used to remark playfully as she bathed the child, "My Rabi may be dark and not so fair but he'll outshine all the others."

When the child grew up into a little boy he was relegated, along with nephews and nieces of more or less the same age, to the care of servants. The mother, whose health had broken down after the birth of the fifteenth child, had a vast household to supervise, with many daughters and daughters-in-law, sons and sons-in-law and their children. To the many normal complications of a joint Hindu family the Tagores had added some new ones by the practice of enlisting the sons-in-law as regular members of the household. Sarada Devi must have been a woman of uncommon character, tact and patience to keep such a household together and in harmony. It is a pity that not more is known of this remarkable woman who made possible others' greatness while leaving little trace of her own.

Her husband was a truly remarkable man and no doubt the wife was proud of him; but being a religious reformer possessed by a sense of mission, he could hardly have been an easy husband to live with. Herself the daughter of an orthodox caste Hindu family, she must have needed considerable flexibility of mind to suffer his iconoclastic zeal. Her numerous progeny, robust, handsome and talented, overflowed with vitality and presented problems of their own. Some of them were geniuses or near-geniuses and some were mental cases. Her eldest son Dwijendranath was a man of gigantic intellect, poet, musician, philosopher and mathematician. In whatever he did he revealed a mind of great originality, an imagination, fertile and inventive. His experiments in poetic composition, ingenious and daring, left a deep impress on the development of his youngest brother. Nor is he less distinguished as a thinker and writer of philosophic prose. He invented the shorthand in Bengali and wrote a manual on it in verse which has been described by a discerning critic as "a monument of ingeniousness as well as a metrical wonder."

Her second son Satyendranath was the first Indian to break into the stronghold of the Indian Civil Service. But he has other and better claims to distinction. He was a fine scholar of Sanskrit and wielded an excellent pen in Bengali and in English. In the former he published verse translations of the *Gita* and *Meghaduta,* a book on Buddhism and his own reminiscences which are of considerable interest. He was also the first writer to introduce Marathi religious poetry to Bengali readers. In English he translated the Maharshi's Autobiography which was later published by Macmillans, London. His young wife was a girl of considerable beauty and intelligence but like most women of that period more or less illiterate and in purdah. He succeeded in educating her, not only in Bengali and English, but in all the accomplishments of the age. It is said that when Satyendranath first took her out, unveiled, in an open horse-carriage through the streets of Calcutta, the city was dumbfounded and the incident was long remembered as a major scandal. But Satyendranath was undaunted and later took her with him to England. Their son Surendranath and daughter Indira, both handsome and versatile, were favourite playmates of Rabindranath when he first went to England for studies. Indira Devi lived to be a grand old dame of Bengali letters and a recognised authority on her uncle's music—a handsome and gracious figure who carried her years as lightly as she carried her many accomplishments until her death in August 1960, at the age of eighty-seven.

Sarada Devi's third son Hemendranath died comparatively young, at the age of forty. He is chiefly remembered for the tribute which his youngest brother paid him while recalling the education of his early years. Hemendranath who was in charge of directing the studies of little Rabi and his companions had insisted that the children should be taught in the mother tongue and not in English. Commenting on this little mercy the poet wrote many years later: "Learning should as far as possible follow the process of eating. When the taste begins from the first bite, the stomach is awakened to its function before it is loaded, so that its digestive juices get full play. Nothing like this happens, however, when the Bengali boy is taught in English . . . While one is choking and spluttering over the spelling and grammar, the inside remains starved, and when at length the taste is felt, the appetite has vanished, while all around was the cry for English teaching, my third brother was brave enough to keep us to our Bengali course. To him in heaven my grateful reverence."

The fifth son Jyotirindranath was, indeed, a genius of uncommon versatility and one of the most accomplished men of his age. Musician, composer, poet, dramatist and artist of remarkable sensibility, his overflowing energy and ardent nationalism led him into many adventures far beyond the range of the arts and letters. He strove to break the British monopoly of shipping and industry and nearly ruined himself financially in the process. His influnce on the intellectual and poetic development of his younger and more famous brother was considerable.

Of the other children of Sarada Devi, the most noteworthy, apart from the youngest son, were the two daughters, the eldest, Saudamini, who looked after the infant poet and was later the devoted companion and caretaker of the aged Maharshi, and the fifth daughter, Swarnakumari, who was a distinguished musician and writer and is remembered as the first woman novelist of Bengal. Swarnakumari's two daughters also achieved notable distinction, Hiranmayi as a social worker, and Sarala as a writer, musician and an active participant in the political struggle for national freedom.

To keep such a progeny, brilliant, headstrong and wayward, together and in peace was no small achievement. If Sarada Devi had little time or inclination to look after her youngest son, it is not surprising. Her motherliness had been taxed to the utmost and she had perhaps little surplus left to spare. But the hunger for mother's affection, never appeased in childhood, was to survive in the son as a recurring longing for feminine affection and care. Its haunting echoes can be heard in the exquisite child poems he wrote in the peak of his manhood, some of which were later published in English as *The Crescent Moon.*

And yet years later when he recalled his childhood there was no trace of self-pity. Rather he congratulated himself on his good luck at having been spared the dangerous luxury of being petted and spoiled by parental solicitude. "While the process of looking after," he commented, "may be an occasional treat for the guardians, to the children it is always an unmitigated nuisance." Nor was the child pampered in any other respect. Though the family had the reputation of an aristocratic way of life, the children were brought up more or less austerely. "Our food had nothing to do with delicacies. A list of our articles of clothing would only invite the modern boy's scorn. On no pretext did we wear socks or shoes till we had passed our tenth year. In the cold weather a second cotton tunic sufficed. It never entered our heads to consider ourselves ill-off for that reason. It was only when old Niyamat, the tailor, would forget to put a pocket into our tunic that we complained, for no boy has yet been born so poor as not to have the wherewithal to stuff his pockets."

The period of childhood and early boyhood which was spent under the tutelage of family servants was later dubbed by him as servocracy. The child was restless and, as ever after, "a thirst for the far-away". To save himself the botheration of chaperoning the child on his sprees, one of the servants hit upon an easy stratagem. He would stand Rabi in a convenient spot and tracing a chalk line all around it warned him with a solemn face of the deadly peril of stepping outside the magic circle. The child had been told the story of *Ramayana* and knew of the fearful calamity which Sita had courted when she transgressed the ring which Lakshmana had drawn round her. So the child remained rooted to the spot and dared not step out, though the servant had disappeared. Fortunately the chalk circle was near a window which overlooked the outer grounds where shimmered a bathing pool with a large banyan tree on one side and a fringe of coconut palms on the other. Through the venetian shutters of the window he would gaze below and be absorbed in watching the antics of the various bathers, each with his peculiar ritual, and the giant banyan tree and the play of shadows round its base. Years later he was to recall this childhood companion:

> With tangled roots hanging down from your branches,
> O ancient banyan,
> You stand day and night like an ascetic wrapt in meditation.
> Do you recall the child whose fancy played with your shadows?

If the child submitted to the rigours of "servocracy" it was not because he was unduly docile but because of his boundless curiosity in his surroundings which invested even the most trivial object with interest. "Looking back on childhood's days the thing that recurs most often is the mystery which used to fill both life and world . . . It was as if Nature shut her hands and laughingly asked, 'What have I got inside?' and nothing seemed impossible."

The painful experience of a circumscribed childhood was also to survive as a lasting impression and to mould his ideal of education in later years. The child's curiosity and longing for the big and mysterious world of men and nature beyond the confines of home and the school became for him symbolical of the soul's yearning for "the great beyond". In his play *Dak Ghar* (later published in English as *The Post Office)* which he wrote in 1911 he dramatised this longing in the character of the little boy Amal. Amal is a delicate and sensitive child who is confined to his bed in a dark room because his over-solicitous guardian and the ignorant family physician fear that he will catch all kinds of ailments if exposed to "the elements". From his sick bed Amal watches the procession of life in the street outside and longs to participate in it. The village postman jokingly assures him that he will bring him a letter from the King. Amal dies in the hope and as he closes his eyes the Herald announces the coming of the King. Death brings deliverance and innocent faith its final reward.

But the child Rabi was more robust than Amal and survived the neglect of his parents and the tyranny of the servants. In fact he was none the worse for it. The first nursery rhyme he learnt sent a thrill of joy through his being. It was a common jingle in Bengali meaning "The rain patters, the leaf quivers," but to the child it was a first revelation of the magic of poetry—the first poem of the Arch Poet, as he described it later. "Whenever the joy of that day comes back to me even now, I realise why rhyme is so needful in poetry. Because of it the words come to an end, and yet do not end; the utterance is over, but not its ring; and the ear and the mind can go on and on with their game of tossing the rhyme to each other. Thus did the rain patter and the leaves quiver again and again, the livelong day in my consciousness."

His school–going began earlier than it need have. A tutor had been engaged to teach him elementary reading and writing at home but the arrangement came to a premature end. When the child found that his elder brother and a nephew were going to school in a carriage, he started to howl for the same privilege. The exasperated tutor gave him "a resounding slap" and said, "You're crying to go to school now; you'll have to cry a lot more to be let off later." The child had his way but it did not take him long to discover that no truer prophecy was ever uttered.

The first school he thus went to was known as the Oriental Seminary. What he learnt there he was never able to recall but the ingenious methods of punishment practised to drill learning into the children left a vivid impression on his mind and on his limbs. Returning home he would work off his repressed rage and terror by beating with a cane the wooden railing of his house, playing the sadist teacher with his dumb pupils. "I have since realised," he philosophised later, "how much easier it is to acquire the manner than the matter. Without an effort I had assimilated all the impatience, the short temper, the partiality and the injustice displayed by my teachers to the exclusion of the rest of their teaching. My only consolation is that I had not the power of venting these barbarities on any sentient creature."

Soon after, while he was still in his seventh year, he was admitted to Normal School, supposed to be a model school fashioned on the British pattern. The only memories of this school which survived were the foul language of one of the teachers which shocked the child and the compulsory community singing of an English song before the lessons began—"evidently an attempt to introduce an element of cheerfulness into the daily routine." The Bengali boys could neither follow the words which were in English nor the tune which was unfamiliar. The only line which Tagore could recall in his later life sounded somewhat like this: *Kallokee pullokee singill mellaling mellaling mellaling.* After much thought he was able to reconstruct a part of what were perhaps the original words —*full of glee, singing merrily, merrily, merrily*! What the original of the word *Kallokee* was continued to baffle him.

He wrote his first verse in his eighth year. A young cousin, six years older, insisted on his writing a poem, explaining that nothing could be easier. All one had to do was to pour words into a fourteen–syllable mould and they would condense into verse. Thus the child scribbled his first verse in the popular Bengali metre, *Payar.* "The lotus of poetry blossomed in no time in this fourteen–syllabled form and even the bees found a foothold on it." The child was, however, disappointed. Was poetry no more than this amusing exercise? Nevertheless the experience was intoxicating. He got hold of a blue copy book in which he started scribbling his verses. "Like a young deer which butts here, there and everywhere with its newly sprouting horns, I made myself a nuisance with my budding poetry. "His companions tried to show off the infant prodigy and when he recited the verse in which he lamented that as one swims forward to pluck the lotus its floats further and further away on the waves raised by one's own arms and thus remains always out of reach, the elders smiled and said, "The boy has no doubt a gift for writing."

Though the child had less than enough of parents' company and of maternal care, his education was by no means neglected. The day's routing was well packed with lessons. He was wakened up while it was still dark and made to practise wrestling with a celebrated one-eyed professional wrestler. Hardly was the wrestling bout over and the dust removed for the body when a student from the Medical college turned up to teach him "the lore of bones". A human skeleton hung on the wall of the room and the child had to learn by jaw-breaking Latin names of the various bones. (The weird memory of the skeleton was later transfigured into a haunting short story.) At seven in the morning the mathematic tutor came and, slate in hand, the boy had to work out problems in arithmetic, algebra and geometry. Sometimes there would be a lesson in natural science illustrated with simple experiments, followed by lessons in Bengali and Sanskrit. At half past nine the servant brought the monotonous meal of rice, *dal* and fish curry which the child found unvaryingly insipid. At ten he was packed off to school.

Returning from school at 4.30 in the afternoon, he found the gymnastic master waiting for him to give him an hour's practice on the parallel bars. No sooner was he gone than the drawing master arrived. After the evening repast came the English teacher, and as the lesson proceeded by the light of an oil lamp. The child would nod, then jerk himself awake with a start, and then nod again, missing far more than he read. Recalling this ordeal the poet recorded in his reminiscences: "Books tell us that the discovery of fire was one of the biggest discoveries of man. I do not wish to dispute this–but I cannot help feeling how fortunate the little birds are that their parents cannot light lamps in the evening. They have their language lessons early in the morning and how gleefully they learn them!"

Brajeswar was the name of the servant who was in charge of looking after the child's meals. He had a way of appropriating part of the rations for himself. He would dangle each delicacy before the hungry boy and ask in a stern voice, "Do you want any more?" Knowing by the tone of his voice what answer he desired, the child invariably answered in the negative. The offer was never repeated. These short rations however suited Rabi's constitution, if not his appetite, well, "I was, if anything, stronger, certainly not weaker, than boys who had unlimited food. My constitution was so abominably sound that even when the most urgent need arose for avoiding school, I could never make myself ill by fair means or foul. I would get wet through, shoes, stockings and all, but I could not catch cold . . . If mothers want their children to be so healthy that they will be unable to escape from the school master, I recommend them to find a servant like Brajeswar. He would save not only food bills but doctor's bills also."

Meanwhile the blue exercise book was filling with verses. The reputation reached the ear of the teacher in the Normal School who one day sent for little Rabi and ordered him to write a poem on some moral precept which he set down. When the child complied and brought the verses the next day he was made to recite them before the whole class. "The only praiseworthy thing about this moral poem was that it soon got lost," recalled the author. "Its moral effect on the class was far from moral. It merely roused envy and unbelief. Stolen goods, they said."

In the winter of 1872-73 when Rabi was eleven years and nine months old, the Maharshi personally presided over the investiture with the sacred thread of his two young sons Somendra and Rabindra and his grandson Satya. The three boys, their heads shaved and gold rings dangling from their ears, were closeted in "a three-day retreat" on the third storey of the house, to meditate on the mystery of life and the universe. The budding twice-borns stared at each other's shaven head and giggled; they pulled at each other's ear-rings and scared the servants with their pranks. But the *gayatri* which they were made to recite left a deep impression on Rabi's mind. The splendid cadence and intonaton of this vedic verse appealed strongly to his feeling for rhythm and his sense of the mysterious sublime. The *gayatri* remained his lifelong companion and he continued to find in it a source of contemplative insight and strength long after he had discarded the sacred thread.

But the shaven head was for the time being a source of no little embarrassment, the more so as shortly before the ceremony he had been admitted to an English school called the Bengal Academy. The shaven head was sure to be a target of jeers of the irreverent Anglo-Indian classmates. While the ear-rings could be discarded the hair could not be made to grow to order. Rabi was worried and did not know what to do when providence came to his rescue. He was summoned by his father who asked him if he would like to accompany him to the Himalayas. Rabi was overjoyed and would have danced for joy if the Maharshi's presence had not restrained him. The next few days were spent in excitement. For the first time a full suit of clothes was ordered for him, including a gold embroidered velvet cap. And so one day, thus handsomely attired, the boy accompanied his father on the first great adventure of his life.

Their first halt was Santiniketan, now known internationally as a seat of learning, at that time its very name unknown. Little did the boy know that the spot he was visiting would be intimately linked with his life and would be known the world over as the scene of his biggest creative experiment. Its history is almost coeval with that of Rabindranath. Soon after Rabi's birth the Maharshi had happened to visit a friend whose country estate was situated about a hundred miles west of Calcutta. Getting down at Bolpur which was then, as it still is, the nearest railway station he proceeded in a palanquin and as the sun was about to set found himself in an open plain bereft of vegetation, stretching to the western horizon with nothing to break the view of the setting sun except a thin row of wild palms lining the horizon. The Maharshi was enchanted and sat down for his evening meditation under a pair of *chhatim* trees. When he rose from his meditation he had already made up his mind that the place would be his. He lost no time in negotiating for its purchase and later built a house and laid out a garden and named the place Santiniketan, which means an abode of peace.

There the father and son spent the first few days of their journey. This was Rabi's first experience of freedom of unrestricted physical movement in the midst of open nature which he loved; and he revelled in the luxury. The father, however, did not leave him entirely to his own resources. He read with him select pieces from Sanskrit, Bengali and English literatures, and in the evening made him sit by his side and sing his favourite hymns. At night when the Indian sky revealed the splendour of the stars, he gave him lessons in astronomy. In order to give him confidence and a sense of responsibility, he gave him money to keep and asked him to maintain accounts of the daily expenses; he entrusted him with the duty of winding his expensive gold watch. The watch was wound with such zeal that it had to be sent to the watchmakers in Calcutta for repair. But the Maharshi did not blame or chide the boy.

It was here that sprawling under a young coconut palm Rabi wrote his first verse-drama on a historical theme dealing with the defeat of the romantic warrior, the last great Hindu king of Delhi, Prithviraj. The drama was never published and the manuscript is lost. "In spite of the superabundance of its martial spirit," recalled the amused author later, "it could not escape an early death".

From Santiniketan the father and son left for western Himalayas, visiting several places on the way, their longest halt being Amritsar, a city sacred to the Sikhs. The Maharshi was an admirer of the Sikh faith and regularly visited the golden temple, accompanied by his son, and often joined in the community singing of the hymns. This early training in reverence for other religions helped to broaden the child's sympathies which were later to attain such wide dimensions.

By the time father and son reached the foot of the Himalayas it was April, the beginning of summer in the plains and of spring in the mountains. Their destination was Dalhousie, at that time a small cluster of bungalows over 7,000 ft. above the sea. The mountain-sides were covered with tall, graceful deodars and a riot of spring flowers which the boy had never seen before and of which the names were still unknown to him. High up were the snow peaks and beneath, as the road turned and wound upwards, he saw great gorges with thick clusters of giant trees, underneath whose shade a little rivulet trickled down, "like a little daughter of the hermitage playing at the feet of hoary sages wrapt in meditation." Already the spirit of Kalidasa was stirring in the eleven-year, wonder-eyed boy.

At last they reached their cottage at Bakrota, perched on the top of a mountain. The boy was now free to wander about and feast his eyes on the loveliness and grandeur of the Himalayas spread out before him. An iron-spiked stick in hand he roamed at will, wandering from peak to peak. The father kept no guard on him. "To the end of his life," testified the grateful son, "he never stood in the way of our independence. Many a time have I said or done things repugnant alike to his taste and his judgement; with a word he could have stopped me; but he preferred to wait till the prompting to refrain came from within. A passive acceptance by us of the correct and the proper did not satisfy him; he wanted us to love truth with our whole hearts; he knew that mere acquiescence without love is empty. He also knew that truth, if strayed from, can be found again, but a forced or blind acceptance of it from the outside effectually bars the way in."

But it was not all fun and spree. The Maharshi, for all the tribute his son has paid to his liberalism, was a stern disciplinarian and taskmaster. Early in the morning, long before the sun rose, he woke up the boy and practised with him Sanskrit declensions. "What an excruciatingly wintry awakening from the caressing warmth of my blankets !" Sanskrit lessons over, the father and son had their morning glass of milk. The Maharshi would then chant verses from the Upanishads, the boy listening, spell-bound by the sonorous rhythm. By the time the sun rose above the eastern peak they would be on their morning walk. Returning home the father gave him an hour's lesson in English, after which "came the bath in icy-cold water". There would be lessons in the afternoon and evening too.

The four months thus spent in his father's company, away from the dull routine of home and school, were not only the happiest days of Rabi's boyhood but became the richest experience and source of his early education. Their immediate effect was that when he returned to Calcutta he was no longer a child.

Poet in the Bud

I run as a musk-deer runs
mad with its own perfume.

THE home-coming was like the return of a little hero from a triumphant adventure. The Himalayas were not then what the automobiles and airplanes have made them. They were a faraway dream, a legendary abode of the gods, accessible only to heroes and sages of which one read in books. To have been in that fabled region and in the company of the fabulous Maharshi was an order of merit which immediately raised the boy's status in the family. The servants' regime was at an end. He was now welcome in the inner apartments where the proud mother was only too glad to show off her young prodigy to the other ladies who were all eager to listen to his adventures.

The inner apartments had become the more alluring ever since the new bride had entered its portals, "slender gold bracelets on her delicate brown hands" —his elder brother Jyotirindranath's wife, Kadambari. She was only a little older than Rabi who longed to be her playmate. "I circled round her at a safe distance, but I did not dare go near." She who came from outside to become one of them, who was unknown and yet their own, attracted him strangely and he yearned to make friends with her. But as soon as he drew near, the youngest sister would snap at him, "What d'you boys want here — off you go!" The humiliation made the disappointment more galling.

All this was now changed. The unwelcome intruder had suddenly become an interesting visitor. Every one wanted to listen to the story of his travels and the little romancer had no scruples to make it more colourful by a deft touch here and there. "I cannot say that my head was not turned." He was now the centre of interest at his mother's open-air gatherings on the roof-terrace in the evening. There he told his tales, recited poems and astounded the audience with the tit-bits of astronomical knowledge he had gleaned from his father. But the biggest feather in his cap was his recitation of *Ramayana* in the original Sanskrit of Valmiki. The ladies had known this epic in its Bengali version only; the original was a mystery to which none but the learned had access. "Do read us the *Ramayana,* Rabi dear," the proud mother would coax. No coaxing was needed. The prodigy was only too eager to astound the audience among whom was the youngest daughter-in-law of the family whose admiration he craved most.

But if he imagined that his new status would earn him an exemption from attendance at school, he was mistaken. The elders who directed his studies insisted on his going back to the Bengal Academy and also engaged two private tutors to coach him in Sanskrit and Bengali. The tutors soon found to their cost that while it was easy to take the horse to the water's edge, it was not easy to make it drink. So giving up all attempts to drag the pupil up the hard way of grammar, they began to read the classics with him, the Sanskrit tutor *Sakuntala,* the Bengali tutor *Macbeth* in English. The Bengali tutor soon discovered an effective way of dealing with the truant pupil. Having read a couple of scenes from *Macbeth* with him, he would lock him up in a room and set the prisoner free only after the latter had rendered in Bengali verse the scenes previously read with him. Thus the whole play was rendered into Bengali verse—the budding poet's first tribute to the great English dramatist. Unfortunately, the manuscript has not survived; only the first portion, the translation of the Witches Scene, published seven years later, in 1880, in the literary journal, *Bharati,* is extant. This specimen bears testimony to the young boy's amazing mastery of Bengali language and rhyme and, in particular, of the folk idiom.

But the Bengali Academy with its Anglo-Indian atmosphere, the foul slang of the boys, the lessons pelted at the dumb pupils, continued to be insufferable. It was probably during these dismal class hours that he wrote his first long poem, "Abhilash" (Desire or Yearning). This was published in the following year in the family journal *Tattvabodhini Patrika,* without the author's name; a foot–note described it as the composition of "a twelve year boy"

Soon after, he changed his school once again and was admitted into St. Xavier's—with no better result. While the teaching here was as dull and mechanical as in the previous schools, the atmosphere was rendered even more cheerless by the solemn observance of religious forms. Finally in 1875, at the age of fourteen, he gave up going to school altogether. No amount of family pressure could bully or coax him to suffer any longer "the eternal grind of the school mill" which he described as a "combination of hospital and gaol". His guardians gave up all hope of his career and even ceased to scold him.

But the truant from school did not idle away his time. He was a born devotee of Saraswati, the goddess of learning and the arts, though he refused to be led to her altar by any priest. He must woo her in his own fashion. The family atmosphere was congenial for such wayward pursuit of knowledge. Poets and scholars, musicians and philosophers, artists and social reformers, geniuses and cranks—they were all there in the family and more came in from outside. Dramas were written and acted inside the house and music was in the air. Bengal was in a ferment of renaissance and new books and literary journals carrying poems, serialised novels and translations from foreign literatures were achieving a popular response hitherto unknown. Young Rabi read voraciously whatever fell into his hands and listened eagerly to the compositions and conversations of his elders.

The newly awakened consciousness of the intelligentsia and its inevitable counterpart, the rising tide of nationalism, had found expression, a few years earlier in 1867, in the organisation of an annual cultural-cum-political festival known as the Hindu Mela, the Bengali precursor of the Indian National Congress founded eighteen years later. Like other progressive movements of Bengal of that period, this too had been sponsored by the Tagore family. In February 1876, young Rabi, aged fourteen, recited a patriotic poem at this annual festival. The poem was published in the *Amrita Bazar Patrika,* then an Anglo-Bengali weekly. This was not only Rabi's first public appearance but also the first occasion when his name appeared in print over his poem. Encouraged by the success he repeated the triumph by reciting another poem, "Prakritir Khed" (Nature's Lament), in public.

On 8th March of the same year his mother, Sarada Devi, passed away. He was then 13 years and 10 months of age.

Though this was his first introduction to death and the loss of this remarkable lady must have been deeply mourned by the family, the bereavement did not leave any marked impression on Rabi's mind. For one thing there had never been that clinging affection between the mother and son which would leave a void behind; secondly, his elder brother Jyotirindra and his charming wife Kadambari, "the new sister-in-law" referred to earlier, poured their affection on him and gave to this motherless boy a home in their little household such as he had never known before.

It was Rabi's good luck that at this critical period of adolescence he had in his brother a friend and guide who fostered and directed his budding, chaotic genius, and in his sister-in-law a playmate and guardian angel who not only replaced his mother but more than replaced her and chastened and sustained his wild adolescent yearnings. She was young enough to play at dolls' weddings and on such occasions invited her young brother-in-law to partake of the feast. She was an excellent cook and regaled him with dishes which were unknown in Brajeswar's cuisine.

She would make him assist her in household hobbies, in cutting betel-nuts or in laying out in the sun to dry finely cut mango slices which make a delicious preserve. She poured affection on him and yet constantly teased and snubbed him for failings, real or imaginary, so as not to make the precocious boy too conscious of his attainments. When he read to her his new compositions, she merely smiled and remarked, how much better other poets had written. She only praised his skill for cutting betel-nut finely and "would never admit that I had any other good quality, so much so that she even made me angry with God for giving me such a faulty appearance." Whenever he was inclined to compliment himself on his own performance she reminded him of a Sanskrit saying that "unworthy aspirant after poetic fame departs in jeers." Thus while she checked his conceit from growing, she sedulously encouraged the best in him, for at that time his most ardent ambition was to win her admiration.

She herself was a genuine lover of literature and music and had a keen and sharp sensibility. It was she who gave him a taste for the lyrics of Biharilal Chakravarty, a contemporary whom Rabi grew to admire. She also shared with him her keen appreciation of his eldest brother Dwijendranath's recently published poetic composition, *Svapnaprayan* (Dream Journey), a superb allegory and a masterpiece of metrical experiments whose "beauties had become intertwined with every fibre of my heart," to quote Rabindranath's own words. That was the time when the novels of Bankim Chatterji were being serialised in the literary journal *Bangadarsan,* "taking the Bengali heart by storm . . . When *Bangadarsan* came there was no midday nap for any one in the neighbourhood. It was my good fortune not to have to snatch for it, for I had the gift of being an acceptable reader. My sister-in-law would rather listen to my reading aloud than read for herself. There were no electric fans then, but as I read I shared the benefits of her hand fan." Thus there grew up between the motherless boy and this childless lady a warm affection and friendship which satisfied and sublimated the pent-up, chaotic yearnings of his adolescence and warmed his wayward genius into fruitfulness.

While she supplied the emotional stimulus and the caressing warmth and shade which he needed most at that age, it was her husband Jyotirindranath who gave the first necessary discipline and direction to his nebulous and uniformed talent. Himself at the peak of his creative powers, Jyotirindranath took young Rabi under his wing and made him an apprentice in the workshop of his genius. He sat at the piano and made Rabi sing; he composed new melodies and encouraged his young brother to improvise verses to fit the tune; he read to him first drafts of his dramas and gave him confidence by incorporating in them Rabi's suggestions and even compositions; he staged these dramas and made his brother act in them. He did not allow the difference between their age to stand in the way of the younger brother's full freedom of expression, either in intellectual discussion or in literary creation. This healthy and stimulating companionship enabled Rabi to shake off the diffidence which the repressed years of his infancy had given him.

"But for such snapping of my shackles," recalled the younger brother gratefully, "I might have become crippled for life. Those in authority are never tired of holding forth the possibility of the abuse of freedom as a reason for withholding it, but without that possibility freedom would not be really free. And the only way of learning how to use properly a thing is through its misuse. For myself at least I can truly say that what little mischief resulted from my freedom always led the way to the means of curing mischief. I have never been able to make my own anything which they tried to compel me to swallow by getting hold of me, physically or mentally, by the ears. Nothing but sorrow have I ever gained except when left freely to myself."

The apprenticeship was not confined to literary exercises only. Jyotirindranath took the young brother with him on his tour of the family estates at Shelidah in north east Bengal, and taught him to ride and took him on his tiger hunting expeditions. "The jungle was dense, and in its lights and shadows the tiger refused to show himself. A rough kind of ladder was made by cutting footholds in a stout bamboo, and Jyotidada climbed up with his gun ready to hand. As for me, I was not even wearing slippers, I had not even that poor instrument with which to beat and humiliate the tiger. Biswanath (the accompanying *shikari*) signed to us to be on the alert, but for some time Jyotidada could not even see the tiger. After long straining of his bespectacled eyes he at last caught a glimpse of one of its markings in the thicket. He fired. By a lucky fluke the shot pierced the animal's backbone, and it was unable to rise. It roared furiously, biting at all the sticks and twigs within reach, and lashing its tail. Thinking it over, I know that it is not in the nature of tigers to wait so long and patiently to be killed. I wonder if some one had had the forethought to mix a little opium with its feed on the previous night! Otherwise, why such sound sleep?"

Thus under the warmth of affection and encouragement, the fountain of Rabi's poetic exuberance was released. He was now fourteen and his first long narrative poem in eight cantos, running to over 1600 lines, was published in a literary magazine, *Gyanankur.* The poem was called *Banaphul* (The Wild Flower) and told the story of a young girl Kamala who was brought up by her father in a solitary retreat in the Himalayas. Like Sakuntala her playmates were the wild plants and denizens of the forest and like Miranda she had not set her eyes on any other human being save her father. The father dies and she is left an orphan, disconsolate. A young traveller passes by and struck by her loveliness and her plight takes her home with him and marries her. But Kamala unused to living among men finds it hard to adjust herself to the conventions of society and pines for her beloved forest in the mountains. She is, however, greatly attracted by her husband's friend Nirad, a young and handsome poet, and in her innocence confesses her love for him. Though Nirad is also secretly in love with her he is shocked by her frank avowal and spurning her in anger goes away, only to be killed by his friend, Kamala's husband, who suspects him of seducing his wife. Kamala is heart-broken at this murder and leaving her husband and home keeps vigil by the dead body of Nirad. After cremating him she returns to her mountain retreat to seek solace in nature, her first great love. But having known human love she is unable to find peace in solitude and finally jumps from a snowy peak into the river below. The waves like a mother's arms take back the child to its bosom. The wild flower plucked from its stem has withered.

The range of Rabi's interests was widening. He joined a Secret Society, called Sanjivani Sabha, founded by Rajnarayan Bose and his elder brother Jyotirindranath. Its aim was the political liberation of India and was modelled after Mazzini's Carbonari. Its sittings were held " in a tumbledown building in an obscure Calcutta lane" and its proceedings were shrouded in mystery. "This mystery was its only claim to be awe-inspiring, for as a matter of fact there was nothing in our deliberations or doings of which government or people need have been afraid."

Jyotirindranath was incorrigibly romantic and his fertile imagination lured him to incredible adventures, sometimes with Quixotic consequences. His own rendezvous with destiny petered out but it helped indeed to stimulate his brother's many-sided interests, not the least of which was his passionate concern in his nation's freedom.

On the first day of the year 1877 the new Viceroy of India, Lord Lytton, held a Durbar in Delhi to emulate the splendour of the Moghul emperors and to impress on Indians the newly acquired majesty of Queen Victoria as the Empress of India. At the same time a terrible famine raged over the land and numberless skeletons haunted the countryside. This ghastly contrast was the theme of a satirical poem written by Rabi and read on the occasion of the Hindu Mela of that year.

About this time Jyotirindranath started a literary monthly named *Bharati*, with his eldest brother Dwijendranath as editor. Like everything else he put his hand to, this magazine blazed a new trail in Bengali literature. Young Rabi had now a family forum at his disposal, though he needed little incentive to scribble. The fountain had been released and there was no holding back the gushing spray, with its bubble and froth, His first short story, *Bhikarini* (The Beggar Maid), an unfinished novel, *Karuna* (Pity), a historical drama in blank verse, *Rudrachanda*, a long narrative poem in blank verse, *Kavi Kahini* (A Poet's Story), a sheaf of songs in archaic style and many poems, articles, studies in western literature and translations poured from his pen, as fast as he could scribble. About these outpourings most of which he ruthlessly discarded from his Collected Works in mature years, he has said: "My mind had nothing in it but hot vapour, and vapour-filled bubbles frothed and eddied round a vortex of lazy fancy, aimless and unmeaning. No forms were evolved, there was only the distraction of movement, a bubbling up, a bursting back into froth."

He wrote this harsh self-appraisal at a time when he had already achieved the mastery of word and form, so that these early attempts must have made him blush for their crude effusions. And yet some of them are not devoid of intrinsic merit and are of considerable interest as illustrating the nebulous state, not only of his genius but of that literary period in Bengal when the old forms and values were dead or dying and the new ones had yet to take shape with this new star. The boy poet was feeling his way through a chaos and had to chase many shadows before he discovered his own form. The *Kavi Kahini* is in fact the story of this young poet's spiritual bewilderment and groping.

The poem begins with a highly idealised picture of a poet's childhood who is brought up in the lap of nature which is at once mother and companion to him. As he grows up he discovers that nature is more than a mere playground, it has its purpose and its laws which will yield their secrets only to objective, persistent study. And so the days pass happily, shared between love of nature and the study of its phenomena, until this adolescent Shelley feels a growing emptiness in his life and realises the need of human love and companionship: *Manusher mon chay manusheri mon*—a lovely line meaning, the human heart longs for human intimacy. He wanders disconsolate in the forest and chances upon a maiden with whom he falls in love. Her name is Nalini—a name that was to remain a favourite with Rabindranath. They live together. The poet is happy at first but soon wearies of dalliance in love and mere happiness. A restlessness seizes him, he leaves Nalini in search of what he himself does not know and wanders in the big world of men. When he returns, still disconsolate, he finds that Nalini, pining away in his absence, is on her death-bed. Then he realises that he had never ceased to love her and that it was this love that he was vainly seeking elsewhere. However, it is too late. Nalini dies and the poet is left to philosophise on universal love.

While this long narrative effusion bears an unmistakable impress of Rabi's reading of the English romantic poets, the other major attempt of this period, the sheaf of songs entitled *Bhanusimha Thakurer Padavali* (Songs of Bhanu Singh Thakur) has an altogether different impress. The three major literary influences on the poetic development of Rabindranath may be said to be the impact of Sanskrit literature, of medieval Vaishnav poetry and of Western literature. As the confluence of three rivers makes the spot sacred in India, so these three diverse streams met and mingled and made Rabindranath's poetry what it became. *Bhanusimha Thakurer Padavali* bears witness to the impact of Vaishnav religious poetry on this boy poet. When Rabi was about twelve or so these lyrics were being collected and published in Bengali and came into his hands. He was fascinated by their lyrical movement, their metrical boldness and the directness of their imagery. How much of its religious philosophy he understood it is difficult say; but despite the antipathy of his upbringing to its symbolism based on the worship of a human god, he had an intuitive appreciation of its underlying deep humanism. The poet understood the poet while the theologians wrangled.

This fascination grew until at the age of sixteen he was seized with a strong desire to pour his own vague yearnings in the same mould which would express the fervour of his feelings while screening their object. One day in the season of rains when thick clouds had gathered in the sky, he lay in his room alone and taking a slate in hand wrote the first of these lyrics in the archaic language of the medieval poets: *Gahana kusuma kunja majhe...*

The thick groves of flowers vibrate with
the melody of flute,
Casting off all fear and shame,
come, dear one, come.

In the manner of these poet she strung in the last line the name of the author which he transformed for the purpose into Bhanu Singh which like his own name Rabindranath is a synonym of the sun. And thus these poems came to be published in *Bharati* young Rabi explaining in an introductory note that while rummaging in the archives of the Brahma Samaj Library he had come across the manuscript of this 5th century poet.

Several readers were taken in by this hoax and Rabindranath has told us in his Reminiscences how a Bengali scholar, Dr. Nishikanta Chatterjee, who was in Germany when the issues of *Bharati* in which these lyrics appeared reached him, was so impressed by them that in his book on the lyrical poetry of India published in German he gave a very high place to this 15th century poet Bhanu Singh. Apart from this innocent literary fraud associated with these early lyrics, what is of chief significance is the fact that these were almost the only compositions of this period which the author in his mature years allowed to be included in his Collected Works.

The boy was growing fast and though he was by no means idling away his years, the Maharshi and the elders were worried about his future. A literary career by itself was no profession in those days and it was a matter of legitimate concern to the family how to harness the impetuous talents of this precocious boy to some useful and respectable occupation. His elder brother Satyendranath suggested to the Maharshi that he might take Rabindra to England with him (he himself was to proceed there shortly on leave, his wife and children having already preceded him) and give him a chance to become something, preferably a Civil Servant like himself, or, at any rate, a Barrister of one of the Inns of Court, a tribe held in high esteem in India in those days. The father agreed and Rabindra accompanied his brother to Ahmedabad where the latter was the District Judge—the idea being that a few months' stay with his England-educated brother would give him the necessary preliminary training and polish in the usage of English language and manners. Thus began Rabi's second sojourn outside Bengal, in western India.

The Judge's bungalow in Shahibag where he stayed with his brother was a 17th century palace originally built by Prince Khurram (later Shahjahan, the builder of Taj Mahal), its open terrace overlooking the river Sabarmati. Satyendranath's study was well equipped with books, both English and Sanskrit, and the lonely boy read voraciously of English literature and through English of European literature. The articles he contributed to *Bharati* during this period bear ample evidence of the wide range of his reading, some of the titles being, "The Saxons and Anglo-Saxon Literature", "The Normans and Anglo-Norman Literature", "Petrarch and Laura", "Dante and his Poetry", "Goethe",

"Chatterton", etc. He also freely translated from these European poets and included these translations in his articles on them as illustrative specimens. Besides these literary studies, he wrote a large number of light essays, playful and provocative, on a variety of themes. This early prose of his, unfortunately overshadowed by his reputation as poet, shows a firmer hold on form and a more concrete awareness of the world around him than his more famous and nebulous poetic compositions of the period. Here are a few lines from these essays translated at random:

"Very few persons are so rich as to afford to seem poor. For myself I am poor enough to flaunt gilded buttons. They day I can expose their brass, I shall have become truly rich."

"They say, love is blind. Does that mean that to see more is to be blind? For love sharpens the eye and enlarges the understanding."

"The difference between friendship and love is that while the former means two persons *and* the world, the latter means that the two persons *are* the world. In friendship one plus one are three, in love one plus one are one."

"Suffering is another word for obsession with self. That is why the sight of beauty brings joy by taking us away from ourselves."

"Some people say that woman is like the zero; when put on the right side of the numeral 1 (which is man) she gives him the strength of ten (10); but alas for the poor fellow who has her on the wrong side, she breaks him into a fragment of himself (.01). Needless to say, I do not agree with them who thus malign the fair sex."

"Our ancients said that modesty is woman's best ornament. But women put on so many ornaments that there is little room left form this one."

Though he stayed in Ahmedabad for about four months only, the period marks a stage in his mental development. It was here that he first composed his own music for his songs. This form of composition, at once literary and musical–sometimes the worlds came first and the tune followed, sometimes vice versa, sometimes both the words and tune came simultaneously—was to become a major creative delight which lasted till the end of his life. In all he composed over two thousand songs, words and music, which are sung in Bengal on almost every conceivable occasion and have a popular appeal which surpasses that of even his poetry.

It was in Ahmedabad too that he conceived the plot of one of his loveliest short stories, "Kshudita Pashan" (The Hungry Stones), which he wrote later. Staying in the house where the stones had been mute witnesses of scenes of revelry and intrigue redolent of the Arabian Nights, his fancy, free to wander, conjured up pictures of those days. "In Ahmedabad I felt for the first time that history had paused, and was standing with her face turned towards the aristocratic past . . . Today Shahibag stands silent, like a forgotten tale; all its colour has faded, and its varied sounds have died away; the splendours of the day are withered and the nights have lost their savour."

After a few months' stay in Ahmedabad, his elder brother felt that it would do Rabi more good and prepare him better for his visit to England if he stayed with a family where he would have more practice in conversational English and where he might learn to feel easy in the company of ladies used to the western way of living. So he sent Rabi to Bombay to stay with the family of a Marathi friend, Dr Atmaram Pandurang Turkhud, an eminent physician and a social reformer of advanced, progressive views. The burden of "educating" Rabi fell on the young daughter of the family, lovely to look at, who had lived in England and was highly sophisticated by the standards of those days. Anna (her full name was Annapurna) was only slightly older than Rabi. The teacher enjoyed her burden and the pupil was entranced with so lovely a teacher. How much he learnt during the two months he stayed there we do not know, but there grew up between the teacher and pupil a tender and innocent intimacy which left a permanent impress on his memory.

Recalling the episode at the age of eighty Rabindranath wrote: "My own attainments were only ordinary, and she could not have been blamed if she had ignored me. But she did not do so. Not having any store of book learning to offer her, I took the first opportunity to tell her that I could write poetry. This was the only capital I had with which to gain attention. When I told her of my poetical gift, she did not receive it in any carping or dubious spirit, but accepted it without question. She asked the poet to give her a special name, and I chose one for her which she thought very beautiful. I wanted that name to be entwined with the music of my verse, and I enshrined it in a poem which I made for her. She listened as I sang it in the Bhairavi mode of early dawn, and then said, 'Poet, I think that even if I were on my death-bed your songs would call me back to life.' There is an example of how well girls know how to show their appreciation by some pleasant exaggeration. They simply do it for the pleasure of pleasing. I remember that it was from her that I first heard praise of my personal appearance—praise that was often very delicately given. For example, she asked me once very particularly to remember one thing: 'You must never wear a beard. Don't let anything hide the outline of your face.' Every one knows that I have not followed that advice. But she herself did not live to see my disobedience proclaimed upon my face."

The name he gave her was Nalini, the name of the imaginary sweetheart in his long narrative poem *Kavi Kahini* published earlier. He used to read this poem to her and to translate it into English for her. She inspired not one but several poems of his in which he lingers lovingly on the name Nalini. Nothing more is known of their friendship, for it seems that shortly after she married a Scotsman and died not long after. But Rabindranath never forgot her memory and his references to her in his later life, whether in conversation or in writing, are instinct with tenderness and respect.

The Heart's Jungle

There is a vast jungle called the heart,
endless its maze on all sides,
here I lost my way.

IN September 1878, Rabindra sailed for England with his elder brother Satyendranath. His heart was heavy as the ship moved, for Bombay had been sweet in the company of his charming young teacher. Back at home in Calcutta was his sister-in-law whose thought was as much a stimulus as a nostalgia, interwoven with joy and pain. He was leaving behind all that had enriched his life so far. Ahead lay the prospect, not so much of fresh fields and pastures new as of being once again yoked to the mill of academic drudgery.

Fortunately the letters he wrote home have survived, a vivid record of the first impressions of his youthful mind, with all the swagger of immature sophistication characteristic of that age. He regretted later that he ever wrote them. Nevertheless, these letters, apart from their shrewd observations on English life and manners in the seventies of the last century, have considerable literary merit and are historically significant as early specimens of literary prose in Bengali written in the colloquial style. If they seemed "youthful bravado" to the author in his mature age, it was because he had outgrown the temper of youth which makes cheekiness so delightful and disarming. These letters first appeared in *Bharati* and were later published as *Yurop-Pravasir Patra* (Letters of a Visitor to Europe).

This was Rabindra's first voyage and he was not a good sailor—not then, at any rate; he regretted that he could not share the "rapture which the great poets of the world, from Valmiki to Byron, have felt at the sight of the sea." It was only when the ship reached Aden that he breathed a sigh of thanksgiving and could move about and mix with the other passengers, of some of whom he has given amusing portraits. "There was no dearth of ladies on board, but the gentlemen grumbled that not one was young or pretty." From Brindisi the brothers went by train to Paris which he found "too gorgeous" for his taste, though he enjoyed his first Turkish bath there. After the accumulation of dust and sand in Egypt, they needed a thorough scrubbing. "A Turkish bath is like having one's body laundered by a *dhobi*." At last they reached London. "Such a dismal city I had never seen before–smoky, foggy and wet, and every one jostling and in a hurry."

His brother's family were in Brighton and there he was happy and felt at home. Satyendranath's wife was kind and the two children, Suren and Indira, aged six and five respectively, doted on their young and handsome uncle. But he had not been brought to England to exchange a home in Brighton for the one in Calcutta. So he was soon put into a public school. "The first thing the Headmaster said after scanning my features was: "What a splendid head you have!"

In Brighton he had not only children to play with at home, but had interesting social life in the evenings, for his brother and his wife had many friends and received many invitations to dinners and balls. The boy had an eye for observation and described what he saw in his letters home:

"Here there is a pub in every street corner, but bookshops are rare."

"The girls play on the piano and sing, they sit by the fire and read novels, are expected to entertain visitors and enjoy flirting for its own sake."

"The people here imagine that I knew nothing of civilisation until my arrival here. The other day Dr—'s brother tried to explain to me at length what a camera was and at an evening party Miss– asked me if I had ever seen a piano before."

"I get up at six in the morning and have a cold shower, which seems to amuse all those who hear of it."

"Here the houses are well kept and very clean, the floor well scrubbed and the furniture shining, Their idea of cleanliness is, however, different from ours. While we would not mind having a spittoon in the room, here where people seem to suffer much more from cold and cough, they prefer to spit in their handkerchiefs which they put back in their pockets. Some men wear detachable cuffs and shirt-fronts which alone are regularly laundered. Ladies are very particular about their appearance but all they need wash regularly are the face, arms and hands. In many houses there are no bathrooms at all."

"Despite the many differences between the ways of women here and in our own country, there is one thing common between them. Society trains and equips them, each in its fashion, to win the highest bidder."

He could not, however, stay long in Brighton. His elder brother realised that if Rabindra was to derive any benefit from his education abroad, he should be made to live alone on his own. So he was brought to London and put in a lodging house facing the Regent's Park. It was winter and there was not a leaf on the trees in the Park. More than the cold, it was this dismal bleakness which chilled him to his bones. It seemed as if nature wore a perpetual frown, the sky was turbid and the light of day lacked lustre "like a dead man's eye".

In London he felt lonely. He knew no one. A tutor had been engaged to teach him Latin—a good soul but somewhat of a crank. He was obsessed with a theory that in each age one dominant idea is manifested in every human society all over the world, irrespective of there being any outward channel of communication between these different societies. He was so absorbed in this research that he had little time to spare for his pupil. This pretence of learning Latin lasted for some time until Rabindra changed his lodgings. When he offered to settle his dues, the honest tutor would not accept any payment, saying, "I have done nothing and only wasted your time." It was with some difficulty that he was persuaded to accept the fee.

From these dingy and lonely lodgings Rabindra shifted as a paying guest to the house of a professional coach, one Mr Barker, who was even more odd, though less pathetic, than the Latin tutor. The only other members of the household were "his mild little wife" and her pet dog. Whenever Barker wanted to punish his wife he tortured the poor dog. He was a very gloomy and morose man; the husband and wife hardly ever exchanged any conversation. They sat silent and glum through the dinner much to the discomfort of the embarrassed guest. If Barker wanted a second helping of potatoes, he would mumble, "Some potatoes" (the word "please" was inaudible). Mrs Barker would mumble back, "I wish you were a little more polite." "But I did say 'please'," Barker protested. "I did not hear it," said the wife. "It was no fault of mine," the husband remonstrated. There the conversation would end in a heavy silence. Mrs Barker was, however, kind and friendly to the young guest and often sat and chatted with him in the sitting room. But the guest found the atmosphere too heavy.

Providence came to Rabindra's rescue when he received a letter from Satyendranath's wife inviting him to stay with them in Torquay in Devon where the family had taken a cottage for the season. So off he fled to revel in the open country and in company of children, two sources of joy which never failed him. The landscape in Devonshire is attractive and he relished it to the full and yet he wondered why no fountain of poetry was released in him. He began to feel guilty of neglecting his muse and set out one day in earnest "to fulfil my poet's destiny". Selecting a lonely spot on a rock overhanging the sea, he wrote a poem which he entitled *Bhagnatari* (The Wrecked Boat). "I might have believed today that it was good, had I taken the precaution of sinking it then in the sea."

The pleasant interlude over, Rabindra returned to London and joined the London University where he attended Henry Morley's lectures on English literature. He read with him *Religio Medici* and some plays of Shakespeare and was much impressed with the professor's gift for teaching. The University education, however, did not last more than three months. During this period of his stay in London he visited the Houses of Parliament and heard Gladstone and John Bright speak on the Irish Home Rule.

Rabindra's days in London, after his return from Torquay, were pleasantly spent; he was lucky in finding a home with a friendly English family, that of one Dr Scott. When he first arrived at the house, only the white-haired doctor, his wife and eldest daughter were there. The two young daughters, alarmed at the prospect of their home being invaded by "a blackie", had gone off to stay with a relative. They returned only when they were assured that the stranger was harmless. In course of time he became everyone's favourite, including the dog Tabby's who would not eat until he had played with him. Mrs Scott treated him like a son and looked after him with more affection and solicitude than he had known from his own mother. Her devotion to her husband and family impressed him greatly. The daughters, too, grew very fond of him, particularly the third one who was more or less of his age and could sing and play on the piano. She taught him several English and Irish songs.

His earlier observations on English society and in particular the role and ways of its women, which had been mixed with not a little irony and caustic comment, now underwent a change and he began genuinely to admire the charm as well as the strength of character of women brought up in a free society. This admiration was freely expressed in his letters written home and caused a flutter among the elders who began to wonder if it was wise to let this impetuous boy loose in England after his elder brother returned home. So a peremptory order went from India that Rabindra was to cut short his studies and return with his brother.

Was the youth happy or heart-broken at this turn of events? He has himself stated in his Reminiscences that he was delighted at the prospect of returning home. "The light of my country, the sky of my country, had been silently calling me." This was no doubt true, for from the point of view of his creative expression, his stay abroad had been comparatively barren and he must at times have longed for the stimulus which had released and fed his powers at home. On the other hand, it must have been a painful wrench to break away from the new and sweet attachments he had formed abroad. "Mrs Scott took me by the hand and wept. 'Why did you come to us, she said, 'if you must go so soon?'" What the daughters said he has not told us, but a poem published in *Bharati* gives some idea of what he felt. Here is a rough and crude rendering of it in English prose, for what it is worth. The poem is entitled *Du Din* (Two Days).

Winter had set in, the trees were bare of leaves,
the earth covered under a white veil, when I,
a stranger from the east, arrived in this western land.
A two-day sojourn it was.
The winter is still there, the birds are silent,
the snow falls on the leafless trees. The passionate
kiss of spring has not yet awakened nature from
its death-like torpor. But my two days are over
and I must leave.
As I set my face homewards to the east, I ask myself:
Will I ever return to these shores, will I ever again
see the faces I have known? Years will pass and
perhaps one day when I am sitting alone by a river bank
in a far-away land and the sun is sinking to the
west, a storm of memory will of a sudden sweep
over my heart, a lightning flash will reveal
a face once familiar and the echo of an old song
will reverberate in the sky.
This face, made as if a million flowers had gone
into its making, and this hair loose and dishevelled
will haunt my sleep night after night and these eyes
wistful with longing will look into mine and a voice
broken with tears will whisper, "Must you leave? Must you?"

In February 1880 Rabindra returned home with his elder brother and his family, having spent some seventeen months abroad. He came back empty-handed, with no academic degree or distinction. The only thing he brought with himself was the unfinished manuscript of a long lyrical drama he had begun in London, with the significant title, *Bhagna Hriday* (The Broken Heart).

When he landed in Bombay, was Anna still there and did he see her or try to see her again? No one knows. His reticence will continue to baffle his biographer.

Although cast in the form of a drama, *Bhagna Hriday* is more a string of lyrics than anything else—a lengthy exercise in lyrical effusion, in 34 cantos or scenes, with over 4,000 lines. The plot is thin and almost reminiscent of the earlier narrative poems. There is the inevitable poet, young and dream-entranced, breaking others' hearts and not knowing what he himself wants. His friend and companion since boyhood is a girl called Murala who is deeply in love with him. The poet is too obsessed with his own chaotic ego to notice her love for him, though he values her friendship and shares his "sorrows" with her. "I've lost nothing, and yet I keep on looking—for what? I want nothing, and yet I keep on longing—for what? Why this despair when there never was a hope? Whence this wound when no one ever hurt me?" He sees a beautiful and wayward girl and thinks he is in love with her. She is Nalini—a name that never ceased to haunt young Rabi's imagination. But Nalini is a *belle dame sans merci,* who enjoys playing with others' hearts without giving her own. The disappointed poet wanders away. When he returns and finds Murala on her death-bed he realises that it is she he has always loved. But it is too late. There are several other characters in the drama and they all manage to break each other's heart. There is, as usual, some philosophising too, as when Murala discovers at the end that "one who owns nothing has everything; the homeless may make the whole world his own; to the friendless no one is a stranger." But neither the tragedy nor the philosophy is real, for the author was too young to have deeply experienced what he was trying to express. And yet the need to exercise his poetic gift was real and the poem has some lovely lyrical passages which show that the young author was steadily gaining mastery of the form.

Though the poem was not later included in his Collected Works, it did help to establish his reputation on its first appearance, for such lyrical ease and romantic abandon were something new in Bengali poetry. The Maharaja of Tripura sent his Chief Minister to Calcutta to wait on the young poet and to convey to him the Maharaja's felicitations on this literary achievement. What surprised the author in his mature years was not that he wrote this long drawn, overheated effusion at the age of eighteen and thought it good, but that others thought it good too. "The curious part of it is that not only was I eighteeen, but every one around me seemed to be eighteen likewise."

But however painful the pang at parting, this "broken heart" on his return home was more carefree and happy than ever. He poured himself out in a cascade of songs and wrote his first musical play, *Valmiki Pratibha* (The Genius of Valmiki). This is not a play to be read, as the author has himself warned us, but to be seen and heard on the stage. The theme is based on the legend of the first epic poet of India, Valmiki, the author of *Ramayana,* who was supposed to have been a robber chief. In Rabindranath's version it is not the plight of a bird that moves the robber chief but the piteous cry of a young girl caught hold of by his followers who propose to sacrifice her to the goddess Kali whom they wish to propitiate. Moved to pity, Valmiki rescues the girl, disbands the gang and wanders in search of his true vocation. The goddess Saraswati reveals herself to him and tells him that it was she who had assumed the form of the young girl to waken his humanity. She gives him the gift of song and says: "The music of pity which melted your stony heart shall become in your voice the music of humanity softening and chastening a million hearts. Your voice shall resound from land to land and many poets will echo your songs."

The chief significance of *Valmiki Pratibha* is neither its dramatic interest nor its poetic merit, but its musical innovation. With this play Rabindra led his revolt against the prevailing orthodox tradition in Indian music. What he was doing in literature he now tried to do in music. While caring for both the classical and folk traditions, he respected the inviolable sanctity of neither and freely took from each what suited his purpose. He was not even averse to borrowing from western melodies, although he did very little of that and made his own whatever he took from others. He did not, however, attempt the creation of new forms in abstract music. What he did was to break down the caste barrier between the classical and the folk idioms of musical expression. His own music is so inextricably blended with the poetry of words that it is almost impossible to separate the musical mode from the poetic mood. Each expresses and reinforces the other. Hence his songs cannot be fully enjoyed by those who miss the elusive music of the words.

He had heard serious European music, too, during his stay in England and had gradually learnt to appreciate its beauty. What he admired about European music was its romantic character, "its aspect of variety, of abundance, of the waves on the see of life, of the ever-changing light and shade on their ceaseless undulation." He had read in Herbert Spencer's *The Origin and Function of Music* that it is emotion that gives tuneful inflexion to speech. "Spencer's idea that through a development of these emotional modulations of voice man founds music appealed to me. Why should it not do, I thought to myself, to act a drama in a kind of recitative based on this idea? He tried it out in *Valmiki Pratibha* and was much encouraged by its stage success. He himself took the part of Valmiki and his young niece Pratibha that of the little girl whom the robber chief rescued. (There is thus a slight pun on the use of the world Pratibha in the title of the play.) Encouraged by the success of this play, he wrote another musical drama in the same mould, also based on an ancient legend of the Ramayana, and called it *Kal Mrigaya* (The Fateful Hunt). This too was successfully produced, Rabindra himself in the role of the blind hermit.

But a richer harvest lay ahead, waiting for the gathering heat of the sun to ripen it. Jyotirindranath and his wife left Calcutta on a long sojourn; Rabindra could not accompany them. He was lonely and unhappy; he missed the stimulus of his brother's company and the warmth of his sister-in-law's affection on which he had come to depend so much. His somewhat ignominous return from abroad, without any academic achievement to his credit, had not been well received by several members of the family who looked upon him as a gifted wastrel. Thus lonely, dejected and obsessed with morbid fancies, he sought release in self-expression and felt obliged to please nobody. The sheaf of poems that were thus born was later published as *Sandhya Sangeet* (Evening Songs), and is the first work of Rabindranath to bear the unmistakable stamp of his genius. He had discovered his form and could write as he pleased, unfettered by any examples of the past. "At last," said his heart, "what I write is my own." He poured himself out, and "as the stream does not flow straight on but winds about as it lists, so did my verse. Before, I would have held this to be a crime but now I felt no compunction. Freedom first breaks the law and then makes laws which bring it under true self-rule."

The public reception was gratifying. It was obvious that a new star had arisen. The author has himself told in his Reminiscences, how at a society wedding when the chief guest, the celebrated novelist Bankim Chandra took the garland off his neck and put it on young Rabindra who had just come in, saying to his host, "the garland to him, Ramesh; have you not read his *Evening Songs?"*

The poems are intensely subjective in mood, morbid and full of vapours of heated imagination. Some of the titles are expressive enough: "Suicide of a Star", "Hopelessness of Hope", "The Wail of Happiness", "Invitation to Sorrow", "Unbearable Love", etc. The young poet was in love with sorrow and revelled in the bitter-sweet despair. The name, *Evening Songs,* indicates the wistfulness of the mood as also the subconscious intimation that it was the sunset of the first phase of his creative development when "I was busy blowing up a raging flame with the bellows of my emotions." The sunrise was yet to follow.

The first poem is appropriately an ode to Evening, pictured as a lonely and mysterious woman, half visible in the shadows of gathering darkness, her dishevelled hair spread out, her face bent over the earth. "What is it you are softly humming to yourself? Day after day I have listened to it and have failed to catch either it meaning or its melody." He feels a strange kinship with her which he elaborates in the rest of the poem. In another poem he sympathises with the plight of a falling star driven to its suicide. In one poem he reproaches his sister-in-law for having left him behind. "She is gone—what more is there to say? They are gone—

what song is left to sing? Only the heart wails its monotonous chant: They are gone, they are gone, leaving behind a wrecked heart. They are gone and with them are gone the flower and the bird and the light that brightens the day. Like a torn and soiled garment I am cast away." (These are not translations but only summarised paraphrases in inadequate words, to indicate the drift of the idea or the mood.)

The dedicatory poem in this book is at the end and not at the beginning, as is the usual practice. The Spirit of Evening which he invoked in the first poem, vague and mysterious, has now assumed a concrete and familiar image. "Long ago, when I was a child, you wrapped me round with your affection as the evening envelopes the earth with its peace. Had the evening taught you its magic spell? For you looked into my heart and all the stars came out. You revealed my own hidden wealth to me, and without singing yourself, you taught me all the songs I know."

The melancholy expressed in this sheaf of poems is naive and adolescent but by no means insincere or affected. The author who in later years blushed at some of these poems and would have liked to exclude them from his published works stoutly defended them against the charge of affectation. "The fortunate possessor of good eyesight," he commented in his Reminiscences, "is apt to sneer at the youth with glasses, as if he wears them for ornament."

Dejected and oppressed with his self, Rabindra wrote to his father, who was as usual in the Himalayas, asking for permission to go back to England and resume his studies. The permission came and in April 1881 he sailed for the second time to England, accompanied by a nephew. On the evening before he sailed he delivered a public lecture in Calcutta on "Music and Feeling" illustrating his thesis with many songs. It was his first public lecture and he tried to prove, with vocal demonstrations, that the function of music was to express what the words fail to express. He was coming out of his shell into the public eye and had already published a strongly worded polemical article on "Death Traffic in China" in which he condemned Britain for her opium trade in that country. His sympathies were extending beyond the frontiers of his country and he was already beginning to voice the wrongs of humanity wherever perpetrated. This dualism in him, of intense subjectivity and a manly concern with the objective world, was a basic characteristic of his personality, from his childhood to death.

The second voyage to England proved abortive. The nephew who accompanied him had married recently, and began to get, as soon as the boat left Calcutta, as sick for wife as he felt sick of sea. By the time the ship reached Madras he had made up his mind to return home but lacked the courage to face the formidable Maharshi alone. So he persuaded his young uncle to give him the necessary moral courage by sharing the ignominy of faint-hearted retreat. The uncle seems to have readily complied—whether wholly out of altruism or because he too had left his heart behind, he has not told us. He was, however, aware of the serious consequences of this decision and went all the way to Mussoorie where his father was to report what he had done. "I went to him in fear and trembling. But he showed no sign of irritation, he rather seemed pleased. He must have seen in this return of mine the blessing of divine providence."

From Mussoorie he went to where his brother Jyotirindranath and his wife were staying in a villa on the Ganges at Chandernagore. There he spent some very happy days—"those ineffable days and nights, languid with joy, and with longing." The villa was known as "Moran's Garden". It was a big, rambling house with terraces and stone steps leading to the bank of the river. Often the three of them spent the afternoon in a boat, Rabindra singing and improvising music "in a veritable frenzy", and Jyotirindranath accompanying on his violin. It was here that Rabindranath first felt the spell of Bengal's river life which was later to grow into so potent an influence on his writings. His first full-fledged novel, *Bou-Thakuranir Hat* (The Young Queen's Market), was also written here.

Although in poetry and in literary essay the young author had found his individuality and created a form suited to his genius, in creative fiction he was yet to find his mettle. This first novel is a historical melodrama, cast in the mould which his predecessor Bankim Chandra Chatterji had made very popular. No wonder that when it was published the author received a letter from the famous veteran congratulating him on the achievement. The substance of the plot and the significance of the title may be summed up as follows: A brave and ruthless King persecutes his son for daring to show sympathy with his suffering subjects. The Prince is finally exiled. On his way to the holy city of Banaras he escorts his sister to her husband's kingdom. On arriving there they learn that the husband had in the meanwhile taken another wife. The disappointed sister accompanies her brother in the exile. The place where they had moored their boat is still known as the young queen's market.

As a work of fiction in itself, the novel has little to recommend it. Nevertheless its historical importance in the author's development is considerable. It is like a little nursery bed in a backyard where the seedlings were tried out which were later transplanted and made to flower elsewhere. Many situations and characters which the author later developed in his dramas are to be found here in their incipient form: a king indifferent to his people's welfare; a prince atoning for his father's wrongs; an old man, simple and jovial, seemingly naive but rich in intuitive wisdom and humanity who voices the author's philosophy of life, and young women, loving or hating, but always more dynamic and real than the male characters.

After this idyllic holiday in the villa on the Ganges, the two brothers and Kadambari Devi returned to Calcutta. They did not, however, go back to the ancestral house at Jorasanko but took up their residence in Sudder Street, not far from where the Museum now stands. It was in this modest house in the very heart of the bustling metropolis that the young poet had his first deeply felt spiritual experience which burst upon him as a vision so vivid and authentic that its impression lasted all his life. He has himself described it at length in his Reminiscences and later in *The Religion of Man.* One early morning as he was standing on the balcony of the house watching the sun rise behind the fringe of trees at the end of the lane, "all of a sudden a covering seemed to fall away from my eyes, and I found the world bathed in a wonderful radiance, with waves of beauty and joy swelling on every side." All the gloom and despondency which had weighed over and oppressed his spirit, forcing it to turn upon itself in a morbid relish of its own disease, fell from him like a garment cut from end to end. Nothing in the outside world seemed trivial any more. "The invisible screen of the commonplace was removed from all things and all men, and their ultimate significance was intensified in my mind."

It was a prolonged experience transporting him to a different plane of awareness where he saw and heard everything not only with his eyes and ears but with his entire being. And it seemed an endless wonder. The experience lasted four days during which he lived at a heightened level of spiritual exaltation when everything seemed more vivid, more real, more beautiful and more gladsome. At the end of the fourth day this state of extraordinary elation passed away and with it Rabindra had crossed over what he later described as the "borderland age" where the direct rays of truth hardly ever penetrate, where shadows chase one another. But though the border was crossed, it would take him long to arrive, and many a hurdle lay in the way.

Groping

Light, Oh where is the light?

On the very day of this remarkable experience Rabindranath wrote the famous poem *Nirjharer Svapnabhanga* (The Fountain Awakes) which maybe said to mark symbolically the beginning of his adult career as a poet. As he put it, the poem "gushed forth and coursed on like a veritable cascade." Like an ice-bound cave in the Himalayas his heart had been locked up in its own obscurity. Suddenly the sun's rays penetrated the frozen gloom, melting the snow. The freed water rushed forth, gurgling and cascading, leaping over the rocks and striking music from each obstacle. The poem itself leaps and dances with ecstasy of self abandon. In this mood of semi-exaltation, a rediscovery of the wonder of this world and the joy of living, he wrote a number of poems which were later published as *Prabhat Sangeet* (Morning Songs).

These lyrics mark a considerable advance over his previous work, not only in the healthiness of the poet's mood and outlook, but in the mastery of language and metre. In one of them which he later made the opening poem of the book, he chides himself for having shut himself up so long in a shadowy world of sick fancies, like a canker-worm that eats into the flower in which it is lodged. In another he reviews his own life, how as a child he had loved nature passionately, how later he lost his way in the wilderness of his heart and nature ceased to be a source of delight, and how he had now suddenly recovered his lost heritage, with widened dimensions. Thus he goes on, in poem after poem, celebrating his new faith with the zeal of a convert till one begins to wonder if this joy was not somewhat infected with a similar adolescent self-consciousness as was the melancholy which he had celebrated in the *Evening Songs*.

Nevertheless, these poems were an authentic herald of the majestic procession that was to follow and in language and metrical movement opened a new path in Bengali poetry untrodden before. Nor is every poem a mere effusion of the new-found joy. In some of them the backbone of thought is already forming which later was to make some of his poems perfect specimens of that blend of feeling, imagination, thought and music which is the mark of great poetry.

It was natural for the young man to assume that if the commonplace sights and sounds of a dingy street in Calcutta could bring him such joy, he would get more of it were he to visit the Himalayas. So he accompanied his brother and sister-in-law to Darjeeling which commands the view of the magnificent Kinchinjunga peak, the next highest to Mt. Everest. "But the victory was with that little house in Sudder Street. When, after ascending the mountains I looked around, I was at once aware I had lost my new vision . . . While I was admiring the gem the lid had suddenly closed, leaving me staring at the enclosing casket."

Where then was the beauty that had so recently ravished his heart? What was its secret? The poet fancied that what he saw as beauty or felt as music was merely the echo of the rhythm that beats in the heart of the Universe. This idea he expressed, vividly and poetically, in a poem written in Darjeeling which he entitled "The Echo". This poem, like several others he was to write later is tantalisingly abstruse and critics have not ceased to wrangle over its exact import. When it was first published two friends of the author laid a wager as to its real meaning. "My only consolation was that, as I was equally unable to explain the enigma to them when they came to me for a solution, neither of them had to lose any money over it."

Commenting on this academic itch to understand everything cerebrally, the author wrote in his Reminiscences: "But does one write poetry to explain any matter? What is felt within the heart tries to find outside shape as a poem. So when, after listening to a poem, any one says he has not understood, I feel nonplussed. If some one smells a flower and says he does not understand, the reply to him is: there is nothing to understand, it is only a scent . . . That words have meaning is just the difficulty. That is why the poet has to turn and twist them in metre and verse, so that the meaning may be held somewhat in check, and the feeling allowed a chance to express itself."

Two other poems included in this book also bear the germ of his favourite philosophy that Being is Becoming, that life is ever moving and renewing itself and that death is what helps it to renew itself. The poems are entitled "Endless Life" and "Endless Death". Life is replenished through death and death never dies. "Every year I have lived, I have died too." In another long poem, perhaps the most metaphysical and in some respects the most magnificent in the whole sheaf, Hindu mythology is linked to the speculations of modern physics in a cosmic allegory of the creation and dissolution of universe upon universe. In the midst of the Great Emptiness, limitless, timeless and lightless, sits Brahma the Creator, his eyes closed in the stony silence of meditation. Suddenly the eyes open and he utters the primeval hymn of creation. The emptiness is filled with burning nebulae and revolving globes of fire. Then Vishnu the Preserver blows his conch and order emerges out of chaos and the earth cools and is filled with life and beauty is born to fill the heart with delight. But the universes tire of revolving in the endless round of the Law and the Creation wearied of itself prays to Siva, the Lord of Destruction, for the peace of annihilation. Siva opens his third dread eye and the suns and the moons and the stars are shattered into bits and everything is reduced to nothingness in the cosmic funeral pyre. Once again the Great Emptiness rolls over and Brahma's eyes are closed in meditation.

One of Rabindranath's early ventures in Calcutta was to assist his brother Jyotirindranath to found the first Literary Academy in Bengal. Their idea in starting this Academy was to enlarge and equip the Bengali language as an adequate instrument of modern thought, particularly scientific thought. So the brothers set to work and founded the Saraswat Samaj, persuading many of the leading scholars and writers—the novelist Bankim Chandra Chatterji one of them—to join. When Rabindranath went to the great scholar, educationist and social reformer, Pandit Vidyasagar, to request him to join the Academy, the latter told him: "My advice to you is to leave us out—you will never accomplish anything with bigwigs; they can never be got to agree with one another." This sound warning, relevant then as now, proved true and the Academy after a good beginning petered out and ceased to exist.

In the summer of 1883 the two brothers and Kadambari Devi shifted to Karwar on the south-western sea-coast of India, the fragrant land of cardamom and sandal wood. The elder brother Satyendranath had been posted there as District Judge and here Rabindranath spent some very happy and carefree days, in the company of those he loved most, including the two children of Satyendranath, his playmates of Brighton days. Here he wrote his first important drama in verse, *Prakritir Pratishodh* (Nature's Revenge), later translated into English as *Sanyasi,* which portrays the eternal duel that goes on between spirit and life, between truth and beauty, between reason and love. A Sanyasi has shut himself up in a cave to attain mastery over his self and to transcend limitations of nature. The drama opens with the Ascetic standing outside his cave and announcing his liberation in a magnificent soliloquy of seventy-five lines, a fierce indictment of life and its seductions. "I have tasted the bliss which is Lord Siva's when he wipes away the unclean stain of creation from the void of eternity and sits entranced in his own invincibility." No more will the lightning flashes of pleasure lure him into the darkness of sorrow, for he has burnt all the senses in the funeral pyre of self-knowledge. He will now proudly walk the earth and pity mankind for their folly.

When he comes to the nearest town he sees a little untouchable girl who has lost her parents and whom the temple priest and every one else shun and drive away. She clings to the Sanyasi in her helpless despair; and pity and love which he has long despised stir within him. He is frightened at the thought of his becoming human and flees from her. When he returns, unable to keep away for long, he finds her dead. Death sets the seal on his realisation "that the great is to be found in the small, the infinite within the bounds of form, and the eternal freedom of the soul in love."

There are many other characters in the play but they can hardly be called characters proper. They are wayfarers and passersby, nameless and anonymous, who represent the daily panorama of life in a village or on the highway. As stated elsewhere, Tagore's dramas are full of such anonymous characters or types representing the various segments of society, which give him not a little scope for voicing his own comments or for merely reminding the audience that whatever drama goes on, the rest of the world continues to exist. These characters use the native dialect and, like some of Shakespeare's rough characters, indulge in crude humour, all of which provides a relief from the high flown thoughts and superb poetry of the main characters.

Having spent the summer and the rainy season in Karwar, the party returned to Calcutta in autumn where they now stayed in a villa on Lower Circular Road, near Chowringhee. This was not then a thickly built area as it is now, and in front of the villa where the brothers stayed was a *bustee,* improvised shacks of labourers and other lowly folk. From his window on the first floor Rabindranath would watch the daily drama of this crowded colony of humble folk, men and women at their various tasks and the children at play. "To me it was all like a living story". To the poet's delight was added the artist's eye. "A faculty of manysightedness possessed me at this time". He was curious to see with the mind what the eye sees, and with the eye what the mind imagines. "Appropriately, the poems he thus wrote were later published as *Chhabi O Gan* (Pictures and Songs) and are a remarkable document of his state of mind and at this period. He was watching and absorbing and growing, and all the time the craftsman was practising new strokes and improving his technique.

Not all the poems are pictures, however; nor do they come within a single kind. One of them for example, "Rahur Prem" (The Love of Rahu), is half-symbolic, half-metaphysical, an allegory of the turbulence in the dark depths of his own mind rather than a picture of what he could view from outside. It is perhaps the most powerful poem in the whole book, virile and intense. Rahu, the demon, who is in love with the moon and eternally chases her, is in Rabindranath's poem the sensual, greedy and devouring aspect of love which is ever present like a shadow. Whatever else the young poet had seen or not seen of life at first hand, he had known love. Innocent and sublime as he imagined this love to be, he could not have altogether escaped its agony and torture. This poem bears adequate testimony to it. A few lines are paraphrased below—shorn of the rhythm and sweep of the original verse. It is Freudian love taking to the Platonic.

> I understand and don't care for me. It matters
> little—for in any case you are and shall always
> remain my captive, your spirit chained to mine
> in the soul's unbreakable iron.
> Wherever you go, in whatever season, I follow you,
> Close at your heels, a visage of darkness, a vast agony,
> A desperate groan, the discord of a musical instrument
> Out of tune. I am your companion from the beginning
> Of time, for I am your own shadow. In your laughter,
> in your tears, you shall sense my dark self hovering near
> You, now in front, now behind. At dead of night
> When you are lonely and dejected, you'll be startled
> to find how near I am seated by you, gazing into your face.
> Wherever you turn I am there, my shadow sweeps over the
> Sky and covers the earth, my piteous cry and my cruel
> laughter echo everywhere, for I am hunger never
> appeased, thirst never quenched. I am always there,
> a dagger in you breast, a poison in your mind,
> a disease in your body.

His prose writings continued, polemical diatribes on social and political issues and thoughtful analyses of literary and philosophical problems. Those were happy days, carefree and unburdened with any responsibility, living with those he loved best and feeling daily his powers grow, seemingly idle but reaping a rich harvest. The earlier morbidity, the nameless hunger gnawing at his heart had given way to a robust and healthy outlook and he was beginning to enjoy the world and life with all the zest his nature was capable of.

But already the fates were laying a snare for him and the days of irresponsible and overflowing happiness were numbered. His brother Jyotirindranath was getting more and more involved in the meshes of his quixotic business enterprises and was no longer able to look after the family estates. The Maharshi, aloof and remote but alert and watchful like unseen Providence, decided that it was time his youngest son was properly yoked to the family chariot. If the Maharshi could himself attend to both God and the world, there was no reason why his son should not attend to both poetry and the family estates. But before he could do so the wild horse must be properly broken and harnessed. And so a silent edict was issued that the family must look for a suitable bride for the young man.

In accordance with the prevailing custom, the ladies of the family took upon themselves the responsibility of selecting a bride for the youngest son of the family. But they were not free to select whom they liked. The Maharshi, progressive in religious matters, was conservative in the observance of social forms. The girl must be of Brahmin parentage. The choice was necessarily limited to a few families belonging to the same Pirali sub-caste in the small provincial town of Jessore. The bride thus selected was the eleven-year old daughter of one Benimadhav Raichaudhury who happened to be an employee in the Tagore estate.

The family was humble compared to the Tagores, the girl was no beauty and was almost illiterate, having read the first Bengali primer only. History has its ironies and thus this unromantic marriage was arranged for one of the most romantic men of the age. Considering the social traditions that held sway in that period what happened was not very strange. Nor was it surprising that Rabindranath meekly submitted to the choice. For all his dashing romanticism and his dynamic individuality in the field of literary experiments, he was a docile and obedient son and was so much under the spell of his father's personality that not only was the latter's word law for him but he believed that the Maharshi could not be in the wrong.

Despite the obvious anti-climax, he was, however, in the long run none the worse for the Maharshi's arbitrary and seemingly unreasonable choice. The unglamorous bride proved to be an excellent wife, the kind he really needed. Himself incorrigibly romantic, what he needed from a wife was not further stimulus but an antidote. Had he married a mere beauty he might have tired of her, but he could not tire of the protective fence of care and comfort which his wife unobtrusively built around him, and never ceased to be grateful for the self-effacing devotion with which she helped his genius to fruition.

The bride's maiden name was Bhavatarini, a name so very old-fashioned as to have raised then, as it does now, a smile of amusement. After the marriage the name was changed into Mrinalini, a lovely name very likely given by the husband—perhaps his only initiative in this episode. Nalini was a name always dear to his heart and somehow Mrinalini seemed to incorporate it. As a matter of fact, he was at this time working on a prose drama of that name. The plot was familiar, a rehash of his earlier adolescent fancies centring round a lovely and true-hearted girl called Nalini. The drama was to be acted by the various members of the family and it was decided that each actor would be part-author and write his or her own part. The experiment was interesting and original—perhaps too original, for it did not work. In the end Rabindranath had to complete the drama by himself.

But before it could be produced a tragedy overtook the family. In April 1884, Kadambari Devi, Rabindranath's favourite sister-in-law, suddenly committed suicide. She was only twenty-five then. No one knows why she did so. If the secret was known to any members of the family it has passed away with them. In the absence of any authentic evidence, any surmise or guess would be profitless.

This tragedy left very deep scar on Rabindranath's mind. It was the first great sorrow of his life, his first experience of the terrible reality of death. He had known his mother's death earlier but he was then too young to feel its impact, and the loss was more than made up for by the affection his sister-in-law had poured on him. But her loss none could fill. During the most impressionable years of his life, she had been his comrade, his confidante, his refuge. After this he was to face death again and again and suffered many bereavements in his life, but no other loss ever had so profound an impact on his mind and his genius. It did not break him it made him. It was a churning of the soul out of which he emerged strong and mature. It was a love which left behind no despair, no embitterment, no howling against fate—only a deeper understanding of life and of the meaning of death.

"I had not realised till then," he recalled later, "that there could be gaps in life's familiar patchwork of smiles and tears, to which I had clung, unable to see anything beyond it. When death came and what had been there as part of life became suddenly a gaping void, I felt utterly lost. Everything else had remained the same, the trees, the soil, the sun, moon and the stars; only she who was as real as they, indeed far more real than they, for I had felt her touch on every aspect of my being—only she was not there, she had vanished like a dream. This terrible paradox baffled me. How was I to reconcile what remained with what had been?.. And yet in the midst of this suffocating darkness, there would suddenly blow over my heart, now and again, a breeze of gladness, taking me by surprise. The painful realisation that life was not everlasting was transformed into a source of comfort. That we were not prisoners for ever within the impregnable walls of life's solid actuality—this indeed was welcome tidings to gladden the heart... As this sense of detachment grew within me, nature's beauty assumed a deeper significance to my tear-washed eyes. Her death had given me the necessary distance and detachment to see life and world in their wholeness, in their true perspective, and as I looked at the picture of life painted on the vast canvas of death, it seemed to be truly beautiful."

The family was already running a literary monthly, *Bharati,* to which he regularly contributed. To this was now added another monthly magazine for juvenile readers called *Balak,* started by Satyendranath's wife. Unable to fill the journal otherwise, she put the responsibility of it on her young brother-in-law, who had to provide the monthly fare for its pages in the form of nursery rhymes, poems, stories, dramas and novels. He wrote a short historical novel for this journal called *Mukut* (the Crown), which many years later he dramatised for the school children of Santiniketan where it is still acted. But the appetite of a journal is inexhaustible. A demand came for another serial and he could not think of what to write. He was returning to Calcutta from Deoghar and as the railway compartment was crowded and he could not sleep, "I thought I might as well take this opportunity of thinking out a story for the *Balak.* In spite of my efforts to get hold of the story it eluded me, but sleep came to the rescue instead. I saw in a dream the stone steps of a temple stained with the blood of victims of the sacrifice—a little girl standing there with her father, asking him in piteous accents: 'Father, what is this, why all this blood?' and the father, inwardly moved, trying with a show of gruffness to quiet her questioning. As I awoke I felt I had got my story."

Thus he came to write the novel *Rajarshi* (The Royal Sage), weaving this dream episode into the story of a remarkable king of Tripura. The novel, though partly vitiated by historical melodrama, is a powerful indictment of the traditional Hindu ritual of offering animal sacrifice to please the dread goddess Kali. Five years later he used the same plot for a drama in blank verse, *Visarjan,* translated and published into English as *Sacrifice* in 1917. The play is a great improvement on the novel, both as a piece of literary art and as a passionate testament of Rabindranath's humanism and his courage in denouncing what seemed to him stupid or inhuman in the traditions of his own people.

The Maharshi, alert and watchful as ever, now made him Secretary of his Brahma Samaj to yoke this spirited horse more securely to the family wagon. The result was as anticipated by him. Rabindranath who had never before taken much interest in religion, much less in its institutional aspects, now began to take his new duties seriously. He composed hymns for congregational singing, wrote a paper on Raja Rammohun Roy and several articles propagating his father's religious faith; he even crossed swords with the redoubtable Bankim Chandra Chatterji who had lately taken to propagating the glories of traditional Hinduism. But the veteran had too genial an affection for the impetuous youngster and the latter too high a regard for the grand old man of Bengali letters for the misunderstanding to ripen, and since both the combatants were intrinsically noble, the duel was short-lived and did not persist as a feud.

Every generation has its illusion of progress and the intelligentsia is divided between those who wish to rush ahead and those who wish to hold back and keep what they have. But in India of the eighties of the last century this division was sharper, for western education and the knowledge of modern science were new and utterly different from the traditional forms of knowledge and ways of living. Those who had accepted the new way were intoxicated by it and found fault with everything that was old; those who feared the new clung passionately to the placid security of the old. Each side had its case and in a remarkable series of letters supposed to be exchanged between a conservative grandfather and a western-educated grandson, Rabindranath presented both points of view with such lucidity and convincingness that reading them one begins to agree with each case as it is presented. "However pure and beautiful the mountains from which the river Ganges takes its source," writes the young man to his grandfather, "it cannot reverse its current and flow back. It must follow its course through the dusty plains into the sea where lies the fulfilment of its destiny." The grandfather smiles and congratulates the youngster on his cleverness and reminds him: "Humanity is not flotsam and jetsam to drift along with the waters, following the path of least resistance. Humanity is like a rock in the midst of swirling waters holding aloft its great heritage over the flux." And so it goes on, argument and metaphor tossed back and forth, like the ball on a tennis court, to the delight of the spectator.

Although Tagore's own innate and persistent impulse all his life was to explore the new, his sensibility had been so deeply rooted and trained in the culture of his land that he could not ignore its heritage. Hence his reluctance to take sides in this battle which each generation renews for itself. His imaginative sympathy and understanding of human nature enabled him to appreciate the passionate partiality of both the outlooks and he himself entered the lists only when he felt that justice and humanity were at stake. He hated fanaticism of any kind and when he found that an extreme form of reaction was raising its head under the banner of Hindu patriotism and sentimental nationalism, running down everything Western and glorifying everything "Aryan", he wrote some biting satires which did not add to his popularity but which showed that the young man was a master of caustic irony and could wield a pen as vitriolic as Swift's. But he had an innate distaste for any kind of public exhibitionism and entered the arena only under extreme provocation.

His next book of poems, *Kari O Komạl* (Sharps and Flats), showed how much more worthwhile it was to attend to his muse than to engage in public controversies. He was essentially a lover, a lover of life, of this earth and all that lives and moves on it. Despite his abhorrence of cruelty, injustice and ugliness, few poets have loved this world such as it is and their fellowmen such as they are more tenderly and more consistently than this poet who seemed so aloof and remote. The very opening poem of his new book reaffirmed this faith;

I do not wish to die to this beautiful world,
I want to live as a man among men,
with the sun shining, the flowers in bloom,
and perchance some loving heart responding . . .

The poems in this volume are considerable in number and cover a large variety of themes and moods— poems for children, religious songs, patriotic admonitions, love poems and amatory poems which throb with sensuous delight, besides several translations from Shelley, Victor Hugo, Mrs Browning, Christina Rossetti, Swinburne and others, including a Japanese poet unnamed. Many of these poems are in sonnet form, not the orthodox Petrarchan or Elizabethan models but many variations on them; he made the sonnet his own and did what he liked with the form. Despite the variety of themes the main mood of these poems is of delight in life, an eagerness to savour its seductions, a delight and eagerness which at times became an intoxication, like a musk deer's drunk with its own perfume.

The poet has discovered the mystery of the woman's body and is entranced by its loveliness. There are poems on her arms, her feet, her breasts, her kisses, on the act of love—poems full of naive wonder and conceits; it is as though a child had found a wonderful toy from which he cannot keep his eyes off, looking at it, now from this side, now from that. For all that, the poems throb with adult blood. The poet fancies that the longing in a maiden's heart, fanned by the breeze of youth, blossoms into a pair of flowers on her breast. That is why their odour is so intoxicating. They up-surged at the call of love but paused, shamefaced, before the light of day and would fain be veiled under a robe. The kiss seems to him a rendezvous of the lips where two hearts drink each other. Wandering from their homes two loves have made a pilgrimage at the confluence of lips. Love unites the spirit and the body. "Every limb of mine cries to be linked to yours. Hearts in love long to mingle in the flesh." And yet the rapture of love brings its weariness. The embrace of soft arms cannot hold one for long and lips hungry for lips soon fall apart. In the end all the homage that memory pays to this wild wonder is a smile or, may be, a couple of tears. If all this is a transient game of the senses, a mere mockery of the spirit, then why such waste of emotions, why so much pain?—asks the young poet.

Not all this revelry of the senses can make him forget for long the image of her who had left him for the other shore. Often as he sits alone and looks at the sky, he is overwhelmed by a sense of a great void. "In this morning light dreaming in autumn's warmth, I know not what it is my heart desires. Some one is missing and that is enough to make this life a barren waste." Sometimes he is acutely aware of her presence. "Her glance is there—but where are the eyes? The kisses I feel—but where are the lips?" He understands that desire is the root of all sorrow, a vast snare in which men are enmeshed. "When I desire another, it is I who am caught in the coil. She does not become mine, I become hers. Trying to bind others, I get bound myself. I loot the earth's treasure to build a prison for myself and my life's boat, loaded with desires, is about to sink."

He also wrote about this time a light musical play or operetta called *Mayar Khela* (The Play of Illusion). It can hardly be called a drama, being no more than a series of songs or as the author himself described it, "a garland of songs with just a thread of dramatic plot running through." Some of the songs are very charming and are popular to this day. The theme, structure and mood of this play are so dominated by feeling rather than action or thought that as soon as one tries to analyse them they melt "into air, into thin air." Nevertheless, if the main idea in the play could be isolated it might be summed up as follows: Nature weaves a web of illusions in which we poor mortals are caught. We chase happiness in love and miss both love and happiness.

Is life then nothing more than "such stuff as dreams are made on?" Can one understand life merely by watching it from one's window and by an occasional sally outside it? Not until he jumped the fence of sheltered existence and lived life fully would the young poet understand its meaning, its beauty and its tragedy.

Coming of Age

Thus is it that thy joy in me is so full.

In the beginning of 1889 Rabindranath, now father of two children, daughter Madhurilata (or Bela) and son Rathi, took his family to Sholapur where his brother was then the District Judge. There he wrote a drama in blank verse, *Raja O Rani* (later translated in English as *The King and the Queen*), which maybe considered his nearest approach to a typical Shakespearian model, that is, plenty of action, much of it violent, contrast of characters and an inevitable sub-plot enlivened by intrigue.

King Vikram, ruler of a State in the Punjab, is married to a beautiful princess from Kashmir and is so passionately in love with her that he spends his time hovering round her, completely unmindful of the welfare of his State. Taking advantage of his infatuation for the Queen, her relatives from Kashmir manage to grab all important positions in the State and fatten on their spoils. Complaints reach the King but he has no ear for them, for he has no time to waste over "vulgar concerns" when life is short and love so sweet. The hungry crowds riot outside the palace crying for bread. "What is this noise?" inquires the Queen. "Nothing, your Majesty. Only hunger–vulgar hunger of the poor who were content with half rations and now find total starvation a little too much. The coarse, clamorous crowd who howl unashamedly for food and disturb the sweet peace of the palace!"

The Queen has a conscience, she pleads with her husband who turns a deaf ear and wishes instead to take her in his arms. Sick at this spectacle of love's shameless greed and egoist lust which have blinded her husband to all sense of duty and humanity she leaves him and goes to her brother Prince Kumarasen of Kashmir, to seek his help in ridding her husband's State of parasites who were sucking the people's blood. When King

Vikram learns of his wife's desertion he is livid with rage, his love for her turns into a passion for revenge, his wounded manliness into a voluptuous greed for violence and conquest. He leads his armies into Kashmir to teach Prince Kumarasen a lesson. None can withstand the fury of his onslaught, his armies are victorious everywhere and he occupies Kashmir. Prince Kumarasen and the Queen are forced to hide themselves in a forest. Prince Kumarasen is too proud to surrender and yet anxious to appease the tyrant's wrath and spare his people the hardships of occupation. He therefore sends his severed head to the King as his offering. The offering is brought to the Court by the proud and sorrowful Queen who falls down dead as she offers the tribute at the feet of the tyrant.

The conflict in this play is between love and duty, between a vain and infatuated man and a proud and humane woman. The woman triumphs by her suffering. In *Visarjan* (Sacrifice), also in blank verse and written soon after, the confrontation between the King and his Queen is placed in an entirely different setting. There the Queen is aligned with forces of reaction against her husband. The conflict in *Visarjan* is more dramatic in intensity, and is many-sided: between man and wife, between temporal power and priestly authority, between love and duty, between the dictate of humanity and the prescribed code of religion. There, too, the play ends in tragedy and the loss of an innocent life, but in the process the voice of love triumphs and the Deity dethroned in the temple finds its true place in the hearts of men.

All this while, whether he was writing new plays or indulging in his occasional sallies into political controversy or social reform, the poet was restless and unhappy. Now, as later in life, whenever he was in such a mood he wanted to travel. If he could not go far he must at least change his house. He shifted his residence from Jorasanko to Park Street, went to Darjeeling, then to Sholapur and Poona on the other side of India, back to Calcutta and then westwards to Ghazipur famed for its roses. Western India, with its rich historical associations, had always exercised a fascination over his mind, and in Ghazipur on the Ganges, with its acres of rose garden, he thought he had at last found a place fit for a poet to live in. He took his family intending his sojourn to be long. But he was soon disillusioned and discovered that "rose-gardens, when commercialised, were inspiring neither for the *bulbul* nor for the poet." After a few months' stay he returned to Calcutta, spent some time at Shelidah, then at Santiniketan and finally went back to Sholapur to stay with his brother Satyendranath. There he heard that Satyendranath and his young friend Loken Palit were planning a visit to England. Forthwith he made up his mind to accompany them.

In the course of all these wanderings and changes of abode, a small exercise book which was always with him was getting filled with poems. Whether he was gazing at the snow-capped Himalayas or sweltering in the heat and dust of the plains, the poems poured forth. The largest number were written in Ghazipur, whether because of or in spite of the roses, it is hard to say. The traditional *bulbul* might have been missing but the nightingale in Rabindranath sang full-throated in melodies unheard before. All this harvest garnered over a period of a little more than three years was published later as *Manasi* (Of the Mind) and immediately set the seal on his reputation. The poet had come of age. As this book was published after Rabindranath's return from England, its discussion would be more appropriate after a brief account of his second visit to Europe.

Though this time he sent no letters home to be published in *Bharati,* he kept a diary which was published after his return as *Yurop-Yatrir Dayari* (The Diary of a Visitor to Europe). The Diary is a charming and delightful piece of writing as all his prose writings in a lighter vein are, full of acute observations and genial humour. The first entry is dated 22 August 1890, the day the steamer sailed from Bombay. Musing on the deck and watching the shores of his land recede, the poet, who had probably not yet heard of dialectic materialism, wonders how far the character of poetry is affected by material means of communication available in any age. In the days of Kalidasa a lover separated from his mistress by a few hundred miles had to implore a cloud-messenger to carry his tidings to her and needed several cantos of verse for this purpose. In the steam age a sonnet or a lyric would suffice;

in the nuclear age even a couplet would perhaps be too much. But these musings evaporate as the ship heaves and tosses in the monsoon-troubled waters of the Arabian sea. As during his first voyage, Rabindranath took to his cabin and did not stir out—this time for four days.

Later in life he learnt to be a good sailor and did a fair amount of sea-travel, but he never grew to love the sea as he loved the rivers of his native Bengal. The ocean-liner seemed to him "a castle of indolence" where the passengers did not know what to do with their time. The Diary has some amusing descriptions of the passengers trying to kill time with merry-making. There was a beautiful lady on board who displayed her charms so generously that in the dining room all the eyes were rivetted on her—the jaws were mechanically chewing the food, the eyes were feasting on her limbs. His eyes too must have wandered, or else how could he have noticed? The next morning was a Sunday. While all other passengers were at their devotions in the chapel, the lady sat on the deck, receiving the devotion of a young and ardent Christian youth.

On arrival in London he took the first opportunity to visit the house where he had spent such happy days of youth with the Scott family. He was disappointed to learn that the family had left the house and no one knew where they had gone. But the youthful love was now a mere memory and London had many other compensations. English girls would be glad to read what he noted in his Diary about their grandmothers—or may be, great-grandmothers. "It is a pleasure to walk along the street here. One is sure to see a pretty face. Patriots at home will, I hope, forgive my admiration of these fair faces, their red lips and shapely noses and eyes that reflect the blue of the sky."

Once again he praises the European society where women, because they are accorded their due share of freedom, help to make the nation strong, and contrasts it with the Indian society where woman's sole function seemed to be to serve and pamper man and thereby emasculate him. But though he seemed to be enjoying his stay in London, his muse forsook him. This was to happen again and again in his life. A man of wide sympathies, a world citizen if ever there was one, he was so rooted in his native soil that outside India the fountain of his poetry and songs ceased to flow or flowed only in driblets. Suddenly he notes in his Diary on 5 October: "I am tired of this place, tired even of the beautiful faces. I have therefore decided to return."

A letter written to his niece Indira on the eve of his departure from London is significant. What provoked him to this outburst is not known. "Is man a mere machine made of metal," he wrote, "that he should function in strict accordance with rules? So vast and varied is the mind of man, so many its hungers and so diverse its claims that it must now and again swerve and reel and toss. This indeed is what makes man human, the proof that he lives, the refutation that he is not a mere bundle of matter. He who has never felt this weakness, who has never wavered on the brink, whose mind is narrow and strait, such a man is not truly alive. What we call instinct, what we always refer to disparagingly in our daily life—this it is that leads us out of the jungle of virtues and vices, elations and afflictions, into an awareness of the unlimited possibilities of our destiny. One who has never known the turbulence of life, in whom the petals of the mysterious flower within have not opened, such a one may seem happy, may seem a saint, his single-track mind may impress the multitude with its power—but he is ill-equipped for the life's true adventure into the infinite."

Soon after his return to India in November 1890 the poems of *Manasi* were published. Their wide range and sweep of imagination, their maturity of thought, their lyrical beauty and strength—like a rider at ease on a spirited horse, in firm control of his seat, using no whip, the horse obeying the slightest hint of his hand or heel—convinced even his detractors that here indeed was a poet. The poems cover five broad categories which were always to remain his major themes, though later the scope was to widen: love poems, poems of nature, poems dealing with social and national problems, religious and mystical poems and poems which use natural or legendary phenomena or historical anecdotes to embody the author's metaphysics or philosophy. Needless to say, these categories are not always clearly defined and merge into one another. The human and the divine, love of nature and of man, intuition and thought so mingle and interpenetrate in his consciousness that in his poetry, as in actual life, it is difficult to separate one from the other.

Recalling the legendary times when in the forest groves of Brindaban on the bank of the Jumna, Radha pined for Krishna and left her home in the stormy night to seek her love, he finds that Brindaban survives in the human heart, for even now on a stormy night of rain or a hushed evening of autumn, full-mooned, the longing for love overflows. The eternal Radha still pines. And so on a day when the sky is thick with the gathering clouds, a sharp wind is blowing, sand-laden, and in the distance flows the Ganges, not a sail on its waters, he sits alone and wonders, where is she? When she was with him for so many years he never told her the secret of his heart. She knew only the chattering, frivolous boy, small and half-grown. If only she were here now, how he would pour his heart at her feet! But she is gone and though the world goes on with its game all the same, he is for ever lonely in the darkness of infinite solitude.

But however fruitless the cry, however vain the burning fire of desire, can the human heart help loving and wanting? And when one loves and wants, is there a limit to the heart's desire? Can the appetite, whether of the heart or of the senses, be ever appeased? This dilemma which he posed in one of the finest poems of *Manasi,* he continued to face all his life. Since he was too human not to love and to want, he strove to sublimate his private longing into the perennial and universal longing of man for the ultimate source of all life and light and being.

In 1887, a ship carrying 800 pilgrims to Puri was wrecked in a storm and sank, all the lives lost. Rabindranath wrote a poem on this tragedy which is not only one of the best in this collection but is perhaps the best he ever wrote on a sea-storm. It is a magnificent poem whose rhythm heaves and swells like the demented waves of the sea lashed by wind, the imagery and diction conjure up the black terror of the elements, the accents resound with the thunder of doom. But Tagore would not be himself if he did not point out at the end that even in the midst of this fearful destruction, the little lamp of love and faith continues to burn in the human heart, which no storm has yet succeeded in blotting out for ever. An adequate rendering in English is beyond the capacity of the present writer who can only attempt a bare paraphrase, to indicate the tenor of the author's mood:

> Annihilation rolls and rocks on the breast of the shoreless sea, nature's festival of terror, the wild wind rages beating its hundred wings, the sky and the sea reel in a drunken embrace. The demons are let loose in an orgy of unrestraint, eyeless, heedless, homeless, pitiless—out of tune the mad music of nature, out of rhythm its meaningless dance ! There stand eight hundred men and women huddled on the deck of the reeling ship, numb with terror, while beneath the Ogress of the storm shrieks, Give ! Give ! Give ! The foaming sea, its million arms upraised, roars in chorus, Give ! Give ! Give !
>
> O God, thou art not. No pity is there, no life—only the mad revelry of the elements, merciless, unmindful of man's suffering, unaware of itself !
>
> And yet in the lap of this insentient, unfeeling matter, man nestles unafraid. Why has the demon of destruction failed to swallow his hopes and joys? Why does the mother leaping to destruction still hold her babe fast to her breast? Defying the challenge of elemental fury, stands the mother—who shall tear the babe from her arms? Whence this love, this strength in the pitiless flux of insentient elements?
>
> Pitying and pitiless—the two stand side by side in the same spot. A fearful riddle ! Great terror and great hope have built a common home. What then is true and what false? Day and night the question troubles the human heart, now elating, now depressing. The brute terror of the elements strikes, heedless of appeals. Then comes love and wrapping its arms around drives away all fear. Is this a duet of two Gods, this ceaseless breaking and making, this endless round of defeat and victory, of victory and defeat?

Another beautiful poem is entitled "Meghaduta" and was written on a rainy day in Santiniketan where Rabindranath had spent some days shortly before his departure for England in 1890. As he watched the clouds thicken in the sky, he was reminded of his predecessor Kalidasa who on such a day as this had written his great poem which has made immortal the love of all lovers throughout the ages whom distance has parted from their sweethearts. The poem is a new Meghaduta in honour of the old and shows that Rabindranath was now confident enough of his genius to claim kinship with the greatest classical poet of his country–like Dante paying homage to Virgil.

In Santiniketan too he wrote another magnificent poem addressed to Ahalya, the legendary victim of divine intrigue who had been turned into stone by her husband's curse. The poet imagines that during the long period of suspended human consciousness she must have shared the submerged consciousness of the mute, insentient things, for even they have a sensibility though it may differ from that of the humans. What did you feel, Ahalya, asks the poet, when you lay locked up in that hidden chamber where the mother-earth dwells beneath the painted, multi-coloured platform? Did you share the vast dumb love the earth feels for her children, the patience and pain of the silent nourisher of mankind? Did you share the sleepless vigil of the great mother, anguished at the noise and turbulence, the clamours and cries of her unruly children? So the poem goes on, hinting and guessing at the secret bonds that unite at some dim level of subterraneous consiciousness the worlds of nature and of man, until the earth's loving hand has wiped away from Ahalya all trace of man-made sin and she rises again from the womb of the great mother, a new-born virgin, bright and beautiful, like the dawn rising over the blue ocean of forgotten memories.

But however much he might enjoy nursing his private longings or brooding on the mysteries of nature, he could not remain indifferent to what happened in the society around him. This patriot and lover of his people was the severest critic of the follies of his countrymen. In a poem entitled "Duranta Asha" (Wild Hopes) he castigates them for being gutless and spineless and yet ever boastful of their past glory and Aryan heritage– "the goody-goody rice-fed, mother-cuddled Bengali" pulling at his hookah and shuffling his dirty cards with a smirk on his face while "wild hopes hiss like a serpent in the breast." Rather than this, "O that I were an Arab Bedouin! Beneath my feet the boundless desert stretching endlessly! The horse gallops, the sands fly, I pour myself into the sky, a fire raging in my breast day and night! Spear in hand, courage in heart, ever homeless, free as the desert wind!"

His gift for pungent humour and irony finds full scope in these satirical poems, in one of which he congratulates the "patriots" who are engaged in "building our country" by the easy way of cheering themselves and reviling those who do not cheer them, by filling reams of paper with petitions, always itching for battle, with pen and ink ready at hand. "Banga-Bir" (Heroes of Bengal) makes fun of the book-worm heroes who have read all about Cromwell and Mazzini and decided that we are as good as the best, for has not Max Müller told us that we are the Aryans?

In a very humorous poem he makes merciless fun of a newly married romantic youth trying to make love to his baby wife. The more poetic becomes his ardour the more scared is the poor child who starts crying for her nurse or for plums or for her doll to play with. In a more serious vein he discusses the tragedy of romantic love, which inevitably cools down after the first few years of married life, in two poems in one of which The Woman Speaks, full of controlled grief and subtle reproaches, the other where The Man Speaks, a plea masculine and reasonable but more likely to irritate the woman than to conciliate her. Rabindranath's understanding of the woman's heart was subtler and deeper than of the man's tangle of physical desire and male vanity.

Sometimes the ascetic in his Indian soul comes out and his zest for life weakens, "sicklied o'er with the pale cast of thought." It is as though Prospero's wand suddenly breaks and the wonderful panorama of life and this world seems insubstantial. Why all this pain and fever of wanting and striving? Everything must melt away like a shadow. Getting and not getting, they both end in sighs. Sometimes he feels that in all the loves he has ever known, in this life as in the many past ones, he has been seeking the one true love in many forms, the love of God, the spirit's ceaseless search, without its knowing, for its ultimate goal. The religious consciousness, the need of establishing a satisfactory relationship with the Absolute, which was to find its culmination in the *Gitanjali* period, is beginning to stir within him. But the love of life is strong and the mystic consciousness not yet overwhelming. So he wonders, in a poem entitled "Ashanka" (Doubt): Is it right to merge all the little loves into this one great love, to lose the light of a million stars and be dazzled by only one great light?

Whatever the young poet's achievement in the field of letters, the Maharshi was adamant that his son should also accept his responsibilities as a man and as a son of a land-owning family. Rabindranath could no longer evade his father's command that he should take full charge of the family estates which were at that time spread over a large area in north-east Bengal and Orissa. The young man had to obey. Much as he may have shied at first from this onerous responsibility, he was later grateful to his father for having yoked him to it. Not only he needed this discipline to make a man of him, but the years he thus spent in the heart of rural Bengal widened and strengthened his intimacy with nature and gave him glimpses into the varied landscape of his country which he would not otherwise have known. This was rich food for his poetry. But even richer was the intimacy he thus gained with the actual life of the common people, their daily drudgery and constant struggle against the indifference of nature and the worse indifference of a rigid social orthodoxy and of an alien political rule.

This proved an asset to his genius and provided the real backbone which made possible his success as a short story writer and helped him to arrive at a sound diagnosis of his country's social and economic malaise. The letters he wrote during this period, most of them to his favourite niece Indira, excerpts from which were later published as *Chhinna Patra* (translated into English *Glimpses of Bengal)*, are a remarkable testament of his widening sympathies as a man and his deepening sensibilities as a poet. As they were not intended for publication he wrote freely and without any self-consciousness. They provide not only glimpses of

Bengal but also glimpses into the author's own development.

The two aspects of nature he loved best, space and motion, the sky and the river, he had here to his heart's content. Few poets have loved space as he did, space above and space below, vastness that stretches beyond the reach of the senses. Again and again he talks of his "hunger for space" and once he wrote, "Goethe on his death-bed wanted 'more light'. If I have any desire left at all at such a time, it will be for 'more space' as well." In one of his letters he has described how one evening while reading an English book on aesthetics and plodding through its abstruse definitions and fine distinctions he suddenly felt wearied and dejected as though he had strayed into an empty mirage, filled with mocking voices. He threw the book on the table and as the night was far advanced blew out the lamp with the intention of retiring to bed. No sooner had he done so than the moonlight burst into the room through the open windows. Looking out at the sky flooded with light, he wondered how a little man-made lamp could have successfully shut out all this beauty.

He paid frequent visits to Calcutta to see his wife and children. The family had started a new literary monthly called *Sadhana* in place of the old one, *Bharati*. The pages of this journal during the four years of its life are an impressive record of the fecundity and versatility of Rabindranath's genius—poems, dramas, short stories, literary criticism, essays and polemics on many an aspect of national and social problems. From now on his work bears the impress of maturity and whatever flowed from his pen helped to illumine uncharted vistas of thought and expression in the literature of his language. If he continued to experiment—he never ceased to experiment—it was not because he had not found his form but because there is no end to this discovery.

The beautiful drama *Chitrangada* (English translation, *Chitra*) belongs to this period, written in 1891 and published a year later— the only one of his dramas written in spring. In winter, as he put it, "lyrical fervour is apt to grow cold, and one gets the leisure to write drama." And this is a lyrical drama *par excellence.* The breath of spring blows through every line of it, it throbs with the ecstasy of sensuous delight. Indeed, the theme is the enchantment of spring and the power of its spell on the senses. Spring is itself one of the characters in this play, which is one of Rabindranath's most beautiful plays, almost flawless as a work of art, and in a class by itself. Written in blank verse, it was his last great experiment in that form. The simple and bald episode, as recorded in the *Mahabharata,* was transformed by Rabindranath into a drama tense and vibrant with lyrical rapture and full of deep psychological insight.

Princess Chitra who had been brought up as a boy and trained in the rough art of the battle-field was plain and rugged to look at and knew "no feminine wiles for winning hearts." She could wield the bow with her hands but not with her eyes. One day while she was chasing a deer in the forest dressed in man's hunting costume, she came upon a man lying across her path. She asked him haughtily to move aside but he took no heed. Enraged, she pricked him with the sharp end of her bow. Instantly he leapt up like a tongue of flame but noticing a girl in hunting costume he merely smiled ironically. "Then for the first time in my life I felt myself a woman, and knew that a man was before me." She asked him who he was. "I am Arjuna of the great Kuru clan," he replied. The princess was stunned. Here before her was the fabulous warrior whom every damsel of the age worshipped in her dreams. In her confusion she was tongue-tied and failed even to greet the great warrior. Contemptuously he walked away.

The next morning she laid aside her man's garment and decked in feminine finery sought Arjuna out in the forest and tried to woo him. But Arjuna repulsed her advances and said that he was under an oath of celibacy and could not touch a woman. Humiliated and wounded in the core of her being, Chitra broke her bow into two and invoked by her penance Madana, the god of love. Madana appeared before her with his boon companion, Vasanta, god of spring and eternal youth. The Princess begged, "For a single day make me superbly beautiful, as beautiful as was the sudden awakening of love in my heart. Give me but one day of perfect beauty, and I will answer for the days that follow." The gods granted her the gift of perfect beauty—not for one day but for one whole year.

Chitra was transformed into a maiden of ravishing beauty. While she was washing her limbs and playing with water on the edge of a forest pool, Arjuna saw her and was swept off his feet. Forgetting his vow of celibacy he wooed her. For some months the lovers lived in the bliss of love's abandon. But Chitra was not fully happy. Ashamed that she had won her lover with borrowed beauty, she feared that she had created a rival in her own body. "I found that my body had become my own rival. It is my hateful task to deck her every day, to send her to my beloved and see her caressed by him. O god, take back thy boon!" The god assured her that in course of time the season of flowers would yield to that of fruit, and Arjuna wearied of the pleasures of the flesh, would himself seek the real woman in her. In the meanwhile, "O child, go back to thy mad festival."

And so it happened. The surfeit of pleasure brought about its inevitable reaction and the warrior in Arjuna began to long for a life of action and for a love "that can last longer than pleasure, that can endure even through suffering." His heart was restless "like a serpent reviving from its long winter's sleep." One day he met some foresters who talked of the warrior princess Chitra who was as valiant as she was noble, who had a man's valour and a mother's heart. Arjuna began to wonder who this other Chitra was. He asked his fair mistress who told him that the Princess was plain and uncouth, devoid of all feminine charm, her very virtues were like prison walls within which languished the woman in her. But Arjuna's curiosity had been aroused and he begged Chitra to let him meet the Princess.

Chitra, secretly pleased, promised to introduce the Princess to him. She begged the gods to take back her false beauty. The gods withdrew their gift and Chitra, restored to her old and true form, appeared before Arjuna and said, "I am Chitra, the Princess of Manipur—neither a goddess to be worshipped nor a mere female to be used or brushed aside as it pleases a man. If you care to have me as a comrade by your side in the path of danger and daring, if you let me share the great duties of your life, then only you will know my true self." The play comes to end with Arjuna's words, "Beloved, my life is full."

In the same year in which this lyrical drama was published, Rabindranath wrote and published his first social comedy in prose, *Goray Galad* (Error at the Outset), a comedy of errors interspersed with social satire, its polished and sophisticated wit matching Oscar Wilde's who also produced his comedies in London at about the same time. It deals with romantic effusions and matrimonial predicaments of three young intellectuals and their ladies. The plot is simple and straight, unencumbered with any sub-plots or irrelevant intrusions, and the farce runs merrily to its climax without undue strain on the reader's credulity. The dialogue scintillates with wit—its native idiom hard to render in another medium. There is a passing dig at the contemporary Victorian novel when one of the romantic youths complains of his dull, day-to-day "vegetarian existence" without a touch of the warmth of flesh and says, "I would much rather cease to be and live as a character in an English novel where I might make love to an Edith or an Ellen or a Leonara. The girl's father will forbid the match, the girl will threaten to commit suicide and finally in the last chapter everything will wind up in the everlasting bliss of matrimony. Thus, at 5 sh. a copy I'll run into several editions."

Call of the Soil

He is there where the tiller is tilling the hard ground and the pathmaker is breaking the stones.

HAVING wooed and won his Muse, the man in Rabindranath, like his Arjuna in *Chitrangada,* felt the need of a wider field of activity, of a fuller life as a man among men. The artist in him, too, looked for fresh pastures and newer modes of expression. The poet's imagination sought for firmer support in realistic observation, as a flowering creeper needs the firm base of a tree to wind upwards. Life in the country brought him in direct contact with the soil of his land, and the daily, prosaic, matter-of-fact business of looking after the estates enabled him to see at first hand how the vast majority of his people lived. He grew to love them and the love gave him an understanding of their helplessness, like a mother's of her crippled child.

"I feel a great tenderness for these peasant folk—our ryots—big, helpless children of Providence, who must have food brought to their very mouths, or they are undone. When the breasts of mother-earth dry up, all they can do is to cry. As soon as the hunger is somewhat appeased, they forget everything else. "In another letter he said: "If there be any undercurrent of the subconscious linking the minds of all men, then my heart's deep concern for their welfare will surely reach them and be of some good to them."

The "deep concern" was not merely verbal and poetic. He did whatever was possible under the circumstances to help these "big, helpless children of Providence" grow into self-reliant adults and thus initiated the first experiments in rural community development. The country was under foreign rule which rested on the support, tacit or active, of the vested interests, and it was no use expecting of the Administration any other interest save in maintaining "law and order". Besides, Tagore did not deem it a healthy state of society where the individual had lost his initiative and looked up to the State for help and guidance in matters where he could help and guide himself best. If the State did everything for the individual, people would continue to remain "big, helpless children," if not of Providence, of the State.

His programme of community development was therefore based on the twin principles of self-help and enlightenment. The latter was very important because if the people had lost their initiative it was not only because they had lost their political freedom or had become physically and morally lazy, but because their spirits had been crippled by all sorts of social inhibitions and religious superstitions. They were totally ignorant of the most elementary scientific knowledge and while they believed blindly and abjectly in every kind of religious hocus-pocus they were incredulous of the real miracles of science. Their misery and apathy were evidence enough that no misfortune was greater than ignorance, no sin greater than to revel in it.

It was this realisation, reinforced by painful memories of his own school days, of a mechanical system of teaching based on "cram and exam," which gradually obliged him to take upon himself the role of an educationist and social reformer and explains his lifelong passionate interest in the economic rehabilitation of the Indian village. His first practical experiments in this field were conducted for the benefit of the peasants on his family estates. Many years later when he was working out his educational experiments in Santiniketan, he founded a parallel institution adjacent to the educational colony and named it Sriniketan—a nucleus for experiments in rural community development. (*Sri* suggests well-being as well as beauty or grace.) He strove to build up, through social participation and service, a living communication between the students of his school, the budding intelligentsia who might become the active leaders of tomorrow, and the peasants rooted in the soil, the solid core of Indian economy and society. So long as the core remained unchanged India would remain static, whatever the seeming progress among the intelligentsia in a few big cities like Calcutta or Bombay.

Himself a leading intellectual among his people, his chief concern, as a man if not as a poet, for fifty years, from 1890 to the year of his death in 1941, was the Indian peasant. With his limited resources and in the limited field where he could function, he helped and made it possible for the peasants to build their own schools and hospitals, roads and water-tanks, set up cooperative enterprises and banks and a system of self-government, thus saving them from the extortions of usurious money-lenders and petty lawyers who fatten on litigation. The handsome amount which he received as Nobel Prize in 1913 was donated by him to his school in Santiniketan and invested in the agricultural cooperative bank he had earlier set up in one of the family estates at Potisar, so that two birds were killed with one stone. The peasants got loans at cheap interest and the school received a fixed annual income.

All this time while the benevolent land-owner was concerned with the welfare of his tenants, the artist in him was watching the life of the common people, their joys and sorrows, loves and enmities, their little deeds of patience and heroism, their capacity for sacrifice in the cause of family or religion and their cowardly acquiescence in injustice and oppression. Always seeking the great in the small, he found ample material in the lives of the common folk for his short stories. He had so far written poems, songs, dramas, novels and essays; in all these he had groped and fumbled till he discovered and achieved his form. But in the short story he showed himself a master almost from the beginning. He followed no known model or pattern—there was none in his own country and its literary tradition. He was the first Indian to give it form and though the short story is now very popular with Indian writers, no one can be said to have equalled him in his art, much less surpassed him.

Many of these stories were suggested by some scene or incident or character he observed while he lived in his house-boat on the river Padma (the house-boat too was named Padma). The genesis of some of them is referred to in the letters he wrote during this period. He sees a ghat (landing steps) on the river, its old stones covered with moss, and wonders how much the stones would tell if they could speak. And so the ghat speaks (the story called "Ghater Katha") and recalls how a charming little girl once used to come to the river—"so sweet she seemed that when her shadow fell on the water, I used to wish, if I could only catch that shadow and keep it clasped to my stones!" Kusum loved water as though she belonged there. Soon a time came when she ceased coming, and the ghat gathered from the talk of her playmates that the little Kusum had married and gone to her husband's home in another village.

Days passed. One day suddenly the stones felt the old familiar shiver of delight, which could only come from the tread of Kusum's feet. But there was no longer the same light music in her step. Kusum had returned to her village—a widow. She gradually grew into a young and lovely woman, "as the Ganges swells into beauty during the rains." One day a tall and handsome Sanyasi arrived in the village and took up his abode in the Siva temple near the ghat. Men and women of the village came to listen to his discourse, but Kusum was not one of them. On the day of the sun's eclipse many people had gathered from villages far and near to bathe in the holy Ganges, among them some women from the village where Kusum had spent the few months of her wedded life. The ghat heard one of the women say that the Sanyasi looked very much like Kusum's husband who had disappeared and was supposed to be dead.

One evening—it was full moon—Kusum came and sat on the steps. No one else was there. After a little while the Sanyasi came out of the temple and was coming down the ghat when he suddenly noticed a young woman seated on one of the steps. As he hesitated and was about to turn back, Kusum raised her head and the two looked at each other in the light of the full moon. Recovering herself she pulled the veil down on her face and did obeisance to the Sanyasi, who asked, "What is your name?" Kusum told her name. After this incident Kusum came every evening and brought flowers for worship and listened with rapt attention to whatever the Sanyasi said.

Then suddenly Kusum disappeared again and did not come

to the ghat or to the temple for a long time. One day the Sanyasi sent for her and she came and sat before him with downcast eyes. When he asked her for the reason of her long absence, she said that she had deliberately kept away because she was ashamed of her "wicked thoughts" and was unworthy to sit beside a holy man. When the Sanyasi cross-questioned her she confessed that she had a dream in which she found the Sanyasi making love to her. Since then the dream had obsessed her in her waking hours and she was unable to look upon the Sanyasi as other than her husband and lover. The Sanyasi was stunned. When he recovered. his poise he begged of Kusum to forget him and disappeared from the village. No one heard of him any more.

Kusum slowly came down the steps and stood looking at the water. "From her childhood she had loved this river and if now, in her crisis, the river did not take her in its arms, who would? I heard a splash—and then nothing more."

This is one of his earliest stories and a very characteristic one. In the world of Tagore's imagination nature is always an active participant, and here too nature and even the so-called inert matter are part of the story and help to create an atmosphere, a mood of half-pity and half-awe, which, rather than the plot, is the essence of the story. In a similar vein the Highway tells the story of what it has seen of secret longings and frustrated loves. In almost all these stories the author's tenderness and sympathies seem to be monopolised by women, generally young girls, and little children. His portraits of children and teenagers, whether girls or boys, are drawn with infinite tenderness and an almost uncanny understanding of their young, unformed minds. His adult male characters, on the other hand, are generally drawn with a touch of irony, even when they are tragic. However, in these early stories he was not primarily concerned with portraiture of personality or development of character but with depiction of a mood, creation of an atmosphere or sudden revelation of an unsuspected aspect of character or motive. This swift and intuitive grasp of the human potential of a scene or situation was akin to his lyrical genius which responded quickly to every impression from the outside. Once a suggestion was registered the imagination worked on it and soon wove a story round it.

And so when the village Postmaster—an educated young man freshly recruited from the city—called on him, he could see that the young man was bored in the quiet and sluggish atmosphere and wondered how he lived and spent his time. The famous short story, "The Postmaster", was born of this casual contact. The Postmaster of the story is also a city-bred young man stationed in a small malaria-ridden village of Bengal. An orphan girl of the village, Ratan by name, who had no one to call her own, worked as his maid. The Postmaster had very little work and to while away the tedium of the long summer evenings he would call the girl and engage her in conversation while he puffed at his hookah. He told her stories and "yarns" of the big city he missed so much and in course of time gave her lessons in reading and writing. The orphan girl who had never known any affection grew deeply attached to her young master and would wait eagerly for the evening hour.

One day the Postmaster took to bed with a severe bout of malaria. Day and night the little girl watched by his bedside and nursed him back to health. The Postmaster took all this devotion for granted and as soon as he was able to leave the bed, resigned his post and made preparations to leave for Calcutta. When Ratan begged him to take her with him, he laughed. What an idea ! When he was about to leave he offered Ratan some money which she refused. She broke down and cried, and begging him not to worry about her, ran away out of sight. The Postmaster sighed as he took his place in the boat, musing, Such is life—meetings and partings! But Ratan who knew no philosophy wandered about the Post Office, disconsolate, the tears streaming down her little face.

That this story had little correspondence with actual facts is obvious from a letter dated sixteen months later in which the author recalled that one evening as he was about to take up a book of Kalidasa's to read, "the Postmaster walked in. A live Postmaster cannot but take precedence over a dead poet . . . So I offered him a seat and gave old Kalidasa the go-by. There is a kind of bond between this Postmaster and me. When the post office was in a part of the estate building I used to meet him every day. I wrote my story. "The Postmaster", in this very room. And when the story was published in *Hitabadi* he came to me full of bashful smiles as he deprecatingly touched on the subject. "The fact that there was a city-bred Postmaster marooned in a village was all that was needed to set the author's imagination working on the problem of human relationship and the possible tragedy of a simple, guileless girl who might take for granted that her affection would be returned.

In the same way he must have often noticed in the streets of Calcutta big, hefty strangers from Kabul peddling dry fruits and nuts. These men known as Kabuliwallas were much dreaded by Bengalis who looked upon them as uncouth barbarians who lent money at usurious rates and were ready to kill at the slightest provocation, rough characters who might well steal children and carry them away in the big bags that hung on their shoulders. But surely, thought Rabindranath, they too were human and must love their children as parents do all over the world. And so the dreaded Kabuliwalla becomes in Tagore's story of that name one of the most lovable characters in Bengali fiction. The friendship between this big hulk of a man, unlettered and uncouth, from the rugged mountains of Afghanistan and the five-year old Mini with her ceaseless prattle and irrepressible mirth is a moving testament of human relationship overriding barriers of race, religion and social prejudice.

These stories are of various kinds and in varying techniques, mainly suggestive and impressionist, dealing with different aspects of Bengali life and depicting varied types of characters from many classes and walks of life. They are remarkable for their fine blend of keen observation and lively imagination, of pity and irony, of nature and life, and bear witness to the author's extraordinary gift for seizing on essentials, his wide humanity, his intolerance of social wrong and injustice and his matchless sense of form. Unlike many of his characters in dramas and novels who are either mere types or his own mouth pieces, the characters in his short stories are real and vivid, some of them unforgettable.

In several cases they first lived in his mind as his companions and he even gave them names before he wove stories round them.

He wrote in one of his letters: "If I do nothing else but write short stories I am happy and I make a few readers happy. The main cause of happiness is that my characters become my companions, they are with me when I am shut up in my room on a rainy day, and on a sunny day they walk about with me on the bright banks of the Padma. Today since early morning a petulant little girl named Giribala has entered my imaginary world." Giribala lives in Bengali literature as one of the most lovable specimens of Indian womanhood. Pity and irony pervade the mood of these stories, pity for wasted youth and frustrated ideals, for the bud that withers before it blossomed, and irony at man's egoism and at the inhumanity of a social and religious order which debase the living to exalt the dead.

There is the dumb girl Subha who receives more affection and understanding from animals than from her fellow beings; the devoted wife Kumo who loses her eyesight to pamper a conceited husband; the unfortunate Nirupma whose young life was crushed merely because her poor but doting father could not pay enough dowry; there is Kadambini who had the ill luck to revive on her funeral pyre, only to wander forlorn like a ghost, no one accepting the living for the dead until she died and "by dying proved that she had been alive;" the hapless Mahamaya who could not unveil her face before her lover; a whole gallery of tragic heroines crushed under the wheels of an unfeeling Juggernaut. Not all the women, however, are heroic or tragic. Some of them are, ironically, the protagonists of the very system which has thwarted their lives and warped their minds; some are nagging and cantankerous and drive husbands to despair; some prefer their jewellery to their husbands' love. Nor are all of them Hindu. One of his most romantic heroines is a Muslim princess who gives up everything for the sake of the Hindu general whom she admires and loves. True-hearted and brave, the final frustration of her hope (the title of the story, "Durasha", means Frustrated Hope) is depicted with masterly irony. Even more romantic is the story of the Moghul Princess Amina who is ready to avenge her father's death, only to discover that the Prince of Arakon in whose breast she was supposed to plunge her dagger is the very beloved vagabond Dalia in disguise with whom she had been in love.

Some stories deal with man's lust for gold, some with woman's relentless goading of husband or son to ambition, some with the tragedy of decrepit aristocracy clinging to the illusion of glory long faded, some depict uncommon types like a gifted vagabond whom no lure of riches or comfort or love can bind to a home, or an unruly tomboy who grows into a wonderfully mature and loving woman. Some are phantasies in which the natural and the supernatural are so skilfully blended that one wonders whether they are mere stories or subtle explorations of the subconscious. One of these relates the story of the skeleton which used to hang in the class-room of the child Rabi for lessons in elementary science. Some stories lay bare the political helplessness of the people and the callous cynicism of the alien rulers, like the beautiful story in which the charming Giribala, referred to above, figures. In a delightful story—a satirical phantasy—which he much later in 1933 developed into a play called *Tasher Desh* (The Kingdom of Cards), he relates the experiences of the traditional adventurers of Indian folklore, the Prince and his two boon companions, who are shipwrecked and stranded on a strange island whose inhabitants are all classified and labelled like a pack of cards. One is Five, another Six, another Jack or Queen; one is Diamonds, another Hearts, another Spades and so on. They sit, rise, fight and make love in strict accordance with a prescribed set of rules which no one understands but every one obeys. We laugh at the Fives and Sixes without realising that we are laughing at our own absurdities.

Strangely enough, during this period when his interest in the life of the common people of his country was most vivid and realistic, his poetry shows the sprouting of a mystic sensibility which was later to grow and suffuse much of his writing. This mysticism was not a creed or a philosophy which he consciously adopted; nor was it an escape from the bewilderment of reality which he found too much. He was not a philosopher, he found no bondage more irksome than that of a closed and formulated system of thought which has an explanation for everything. He had even less respect for fixed creeds. He loved this earth and this life far too passionately ever to turn away from them. The mystery of life never ceased to fascinate him, the pain he suffered, the cruelty and sordidness which he witnessed, instead of causing a revulsion, made him love his kind all the more. "How artificial and unreal are our notions of sin and virtue!" he wrote in 1894. "There is no higher religion than that of sympathy for all that lives. Love is the foundation of all religions."

The roots of mysticism in the sense of an intuitive awareness of kinship with all that lives and moves and what is seemingly inert were planted in his soul from childhood. Its "sprouting" at this period of his life simply means that this vague awareness became more conscious and explicit and became a quest for the guiding Muse of his genius and destiny, the Personality within and above his personality. In a letter of March 1894 he wrote: "I am overwhelmed by this awareness of the baffling mystery within which I can neither understand nor control . . . I am like a living pianoforte with a complicated network of wires hidden within it, but what makes it play and who comes suddenly to play on it and when and why, I do not know. I can only know what is being played at the moment, whether the keys are struck in joy or in sorrow, whether the notes are sharp or flat, high-pitched or low, whether the music is in tune or out of tune—but wait, do I really know even that?"

Fortunately he was not a philosopher and was content to be played upon without breaking his head over the why and how of it. In fact, he was disconsolate if no music came. Poetry was his oldest love and whatever his "dates" with other Muses, to this one he constantly came back. "The joy of writing one poem," he said in May 1892, "far exceeds that of writing sheaves and sheaves of prose . . . If I could only write one poem a day . . ." He almost did that. During the seven years from 1894 to 1900 he published as many major volumes of verse, besides several of drama, stories and other prose writing.

The first of these volumes of poetry is *Sonar Tari* (The Golden Boat), taking its name from the first poem in the book. On a rainy day, when the clouds thunder in the sky, the poet is sitting desolate on the edge of his field overlooking the river. The golden boat approaches and he dimly recognises the figure at the helm. The harvest of his field has been gathered and he fills the boat with it. The boat goes on its way, no one knows where, and the poet is left behind on the bank, forlorn. There was a time when a storm of controversy raged in the literary circles of Bengal as to the real meaning of this poem. What is the Golden Boat and who is at its helm? The author himself explained that the Boat symbolised for him Life which collects the harvest of our achievement and goes floating on the stream of time, leaving us behind. The Golden Boat reappears in the last poem of the book, but now the poet has been taken into the boat. His lost playmate, his Muse, the Beloved of his dreams, his guardian angel, half-known and half-unknown, is at the helm. He asks her again and again where she is taking him. She says nothing, but half smiling points to the distant horizon where the sun is sinking in the west.

> I boarded the boat and asked,
> "Shall we find new life there?
> Will hope yield at last its golden harvest?"
> You looked at my face and smiled
> And said not a word.

There are several very long and beautiful poems in the book, one on earth, the mother of all life, one on the sea, the first ancestor of this world out of whose lap the earth was born, one on Manas-Sundari, the Beauty behind all beauty, his childhood's playmate, his youth's dream, and now his very being. There is a lovely and moving poem entitled, "I will not let you go." The poet is about to leave on a journey, the household is in commotion, the servants busy packing, the wife adding this and that in anticipation of every contingency. Only the little daughter sits calmly on the threshold and says as he is about to leave, "I will not let you go." These simple words wrung out of the infant's heart sum up for the poet the perennial pathos of life. Everything goes and amid this unceasing flux of life and matter the eternal cry resounds, "I will not let you go."

Much as these poems glow with passion, it is passion suffused with thought and subdued by reflection. This reflective element will from now on be increasingly impressed on his poetry, the passion subdued will be the stronger, the thought subtler.

Sonar Tari was followed by a collection of poems published in 1896 under the title *Chitra*—not to be confused with the name of the English rendering of his drama, *Chitrangada.* Many Bengali readers would consider this volume as the finest fruition of Tagore's poetical genius. There is no doubt that some of the poems in this volume mark the highest reach of his achievement during this period, though his genius was like a mountain range that revealed different peaks in different weathers. The key to the title of the volume which also indicates the general spirit and tenor of the poems may be sought in the very first poem where the poet addresses the Universal Spirit or Nature as the Wondrous Lady whose beauty is manifest in a million forms. But though in the outside world her beauty overflows in many different sights, colours and sounds, within the mind she sits alone, unique—immanent and pervading.

Tagore's steadily growing apprehension of this Universal Spirit or Reality was intensely personal and he could only visualise it in terms of his own direct perception as well as his need of it. He was, above everything else, a lover who saw beauty in the commonest things, who felt its touch in the outside world and felt it in his inmost being and knew that at some level of the subconscious or superconscious the two were intimately linked. The same spirit that suffused and ruled this vast universe dwelt within him and guided his life and genius. He felt its immediacy and its intimacy and addressed it as the Lord of his life, his Jivan-devata. In his famous poem of that name he says, "O my Inmost Being, is your thirst quenched by coming into my heart? I have crushed my heart, like grapes in the press, and filled your cup with a thousand pourings of joy and sorrow. I have melted the gold of my desires and made of it ever new images for your transient sport." He goes on to confess his many limitations and begs the Lord to forgive them. "How can I, O Master-poet, sing adequately your music?"

One of the most beautiful poems in the book is an ode to Urvasi, the legendary Feminine of Hindu mythology who seduces saints and captivates the hearts of all men. Rabindranath pictures her as arising out of the foam of the primal ocean when it was churned by the gods—naked and flawless beauty, holding nectar in her right hand and poison in her left. Urvasi is the eternal woman, whom men have always desired but never possessed, for she is "not mother, not daughter, not bride."

Another poem, tender and exquisite, is entitled, "A Farewell to Heaven". It is in the form of a monologue by a soul who has had a long sojourn in paradise as a reward for its good deeds on earth. The term over and merit exhausted, the soul is about to return to earth and compares the chilly joy and unruffled peace of heaven with the woven web of joys and sorrows which is the life on earth. The poem is one long paean in praise of this lowly earth and its simple human attachments.

The struggle between the poet's heart enchanted with its own music and his conscience troubled by the plight of his countrymen finds passionate utterance in a long poem entitled "Turn me back now". It is a poem such as Mahatma Gandhi might have written had he been a poet. The poet reproaches himself for being content to play the flute—like a truant boy on a summer afternoon—when every one else is engaged in some useful task or the other and exhorts himself: Get up and see where the fires are raging and listen to the wail of your fellowmen crying for help, victims of a bloated pride of power that licks the blood of the helpless with its million tongues. He describes the condition of his people, hungry, naked and homeless in their own land, bereft of human rights and bereft of even the will to protest. Rise, O poet, and give voice to these dumb and stupefied faces, bring hope to these tired, emptied and broken hearts. Tell them to raise high their heads and stand united, and assure them: "They whom you fear are more scared than you—terrified of their sins."

But Rabindranath was not Gandhi. The heroic impulse vented itself in occasional spurts and though he anticipated the Mahatma not only in his ideals but in his programme of work, he could not be single-minded. He was not wedded to one ideal or mission, he had a harem of Muses to lure him away. For in the very next poem, written a few days later, he is haunted by memories of the old days, of the champaks and the jasmins that grew round the terrace of his sister-in-law's apartment. "How sweet it was when she gave those flowers with her hand!" In another he regrets that he could achieve nothing. "The *vina* was in my hand, the music was in my mind—who knew that half way through the music, the string would break!"

In between these two major volumes, *Sonar Tari* and *Chitra,* were published a long poem, *Nadi* (The River) and a lyrical drama in one act, *Viday-abhisap* (The Curse at Farewell). His earlier dramas were in blank verse which he now discarded in favour of run-on and enjambed rhymed couplets, which he found more to his taste. He naturalised this form in Bengali and achieved amazing results with it. As in the case of *Chitrangada,* Tagore takes a simple anecdote, in this instance a mythological one, from the *Mahabharata* and turns it into a conflict of high psychological significance—between devotion to knowledge (or duty) and the claim of love. The anecdote relates to the ancient feud between gods and titans. Sukra, the teacher of the titans, knew the secret of immortality and could restore the dead to life. The gods, anxious to learn the secret, send Kacha, the young son of their teacher, to Sukra to be his pupil. Seeing the handsome Brahmin, Sukra's daughter Devayani falls in love with him and persuades her fond father to accept Kacha as his pupil. Having completed his course of study and learnt the art of reviving the dead, Kacha comes to Devayani to bid her farewell. This is the starting point of this short drama which consists entirely the dialogue between the two.

"So you've at last attained," says Devayani, "what you had hardly hoped for. The knowledge coveted by the gods is now yours. But tell me, have you nothing more to ask for than leave to depart? Have all your desires been fulfilled—none left lingering in your heart to prick like a hidden thorn?"

"None," Kacha assures her.

"Then you must be the one happy being in creation," taunts

Devayani. "Go back to your Paradise and add to its splendour your own triumph. There they are waiting to welcome you back with music and conch shells and flowers. Ah, Brahmin, you have indeed spent hard and dreary days here, drudging in an alien land, with no one to comfort and delight you."

Kacha feels the sting and begs, "Not thus with a reproach, but with a smile bid me farewell."

"Smile ! This is no Paradise, my friend. Smiles are not so cheap in this world where longing like a worm in the flower gnaws at the heart's core, where desire like a baffled bee hovers round the closed petals of the heart's lotus. Here memory broods and pines in the deserted nook of departed joy. Go and waste no more of your time here."

Kacha tries to pacify and assure her that the happy memories of the days spent in the hermitage would always haunt him. The reminiscences are exchanged and she archly reminds him of how, but for her intervention, her father would never have consented to teach the son of a rival race. Kacha acknowledges the debt but she is not content with gratitude, and with subtle feminine suggestions forces him to admit that he loves her and recalls how he used to go out of his way, even neglecting his studies, to woo and win her.

"What made you fetch water for me while I tended the flower-beds and why need you have played truant from your studies to pet my little deer? And why did you have to sit on the grass beside me, singing songs learnt in paradise, while darkness hung over the hushed bank of the river, like eyelids drooping on languorous eyes? If knowledge it was you were after, why need you have ensnared in your coils this simple-hearted maiden? Or was it all a well-planned strategy to win access to my father's favour?"

Kacha, unnerved by her passionate utterance, protests that he truly and deeply loves her for her own sake. But duty calls and he must, even at the sacrifice of his happiness, go back to his people and put his knowledge at their service. He begs to be forgiven.

"Forgive! What forgiveness, O Brahmin, is left in the heart of a woman flamed to the fury of a thunderbolt? You will go back to the celestial realm where all regrets will be lost in the pride of your success. But what is left to me here—what ambition or mission can instil a meaning or pride in this thwarted and barren life of mine? In these woods must I drag on the humiliation of an aimless and forlorn existence, where memory with its thousand thorns will prick me at each turn and a secret shame gnaw at the very core of my being. Shame be yours, O heartless adventurer, who came and sat through the sunny hours in the shade of my life's garden and to while away time plucked all its flowers and wove them into a garland, only to snap the thread at the end and scatter all the glory of a woman's heart into dust ! Be this my curse at farewell—may the knowledge for whose sake you have spurned me never bear its full reward for you! You shall bear its burden and not enjoy its use, you will teach it but shall never be able to practise it."

This charming dramatic fragment was followed by a full drama, also in verse, *Malini,* a well-constructed play and much more dramatic, in spirit and in the development of the situation, than the lyric drama discussed above. It is both the vehicle of an idea and a study of conflicting loyalties—in which respect it may be said to belong to the same class as his earlier play, *Sacrifice.* Here, too, the forces of Brahminism, of Hindu orthodoxy, are ranged against the challenge of compassion, of universal love—in this case as specifically taught by the Buddha. Though by birth a Brahmin and the son of a Hindu reformer, Tagore's feeling for Hinduism was strictly eclectic and was more or less confined to his admiration of the philosophic wisdom of the Upanishads and the literary heritage of Sanskrit and medieval literatures. His admiration of Buddha, on the other hand, was boundless. In the Buddha, according to him, the Hindu race and thought had achieved its finest flowering.

He was to write many poems and plays drawing on Buddhist legends and motifs. Malini, the King's daughter in the play, is his first major Buddhist heroine. But the most live and convincing character in the play is not this lovely and saintly but somewhat shadowy maiden, but her chief enemy, the leader of the Hindu orthodoxy, in whose proud personality is symbolised the strength and obstinacy of his religion. The conflict is not only between obedience to "moth-eaten scriptures" and a religion of one's choice but between the poetry of pity and the prose of social necessity. "Pity is beautiful like the yonder moon that casts its spell in the sky, but is that the only enduring reality? Tomorrow the day will break and the hungry multitude will draw the sea of existence with their thousand nets and their clamour will fill the sky. Then this very moon will seem a pale shadow." But even a deeper conflict is that of personal loyalties. Should one, if faced with a relentless choice, betray one's conscience or one's religion, one's country or one's faith, the pledge of friendship or that of love? There is no answer to this dilemma and the choice must take its tragic course. All that Malini can do is to forgive and ask others to forgive.

The next major volume of verse, *Chaitali,* was published in 1896. Chaitali means a late harvest, the last gleanings of rice gathered in the month of *Chaitra* (March-April), before the fierce sun of May burns out the last drop of moisture from the earth. It was as though the poet was dimly aware that the period of his life's Spring was drawing to a close, the emotional exuberance and intellectual recklessness of early manhood would soon shed many of its leaves and petals in the hot blasts of an increasing spiritual austerity. Almost all the poems in the volume are short, most of them sonnets; the language is simple, no effort is made to invent new forms and modes; the themes are drawn from the lowly, everyday life he watched on the banks of the Padma or tinged with momentary regrets and memories of the past. A gentle, brooding sadness lurks in the mood these poems and a dim foreboding of the parting of these poems and a dim foreboding of the parting of ways. Before the sense of India's past overwhelms him in the next phase, he will glean a few immortal moments from the immediate present. A girl scrubbing her pots on the bank, her little brother hovering round, a day labourer returning from work, a decrepit old man hobbling along, a young man washing his mud-covered buffalo and calling it by endearing names—these and many other trivial and fleeting sights are painted in minute detail and with great tenderness.

Rich and varied as was Rabindranath's poetic output of this period, no less so was his contribution to prose. His short stories created a new form in literature and set a standard which has not been surpassed in Indian literary achievement—not even by his own later stories. His light humorous social comedies, particularly the two major ones, *Baikunther Khata* (The Manuscript of Baikuntha) and *Chira Kumar Sabha* (The Bachelors' Club), the former dealing with a kindly old bore who insists on reading out his manuscript to whoever comes his way, a simpleton whom every one avoids and imposes upon (who has not come across such a type?), the latter with the discomfiture of those who imagine they can do without women, are still popular on the Bengali stage and have not failed to delight and hold the audience. Apart from his creative prose, the range and quantity of his reflective prose of the period is astonishing. There was hardly a subject which he did not tackle, including philology and science, and in almost everything he said he opened out new lines of thinking.

Perhaps the most characteristic and in some respects the most brilliant achievement of his prose in this period is recorded in the pages of a book which is almost unknown outside Bengal, *Pancha Bhuter Dayari* (Diary of the Five Elements), which consists of dialogues and arguments on life and letters between five points of view humorously represented by the five elements, air, earth, water, fire and ether. The elements are dramatically characterised; fire and water are feminine—inquisitive and emotional, the other three masculine, earth stolid and opportunist, air an idealist, and ether vague. Wit and wisdom, logic and frivolity jostle each other in these pages. The author himself plays the part of a mediator, now provoking, now debunking and now clarifying the different points of view, an Indian Plato with a Shavian wink in his eye.

How much greater the author could be when he was truly himself than when he tried to be traditional, in the manner of oriental oracles dispensing wisdom, can be immediately felt by comparing this Diary with another little volume published at the end of this period in which too his wit and wisdom are recorded, not subtly and suggestively as in the dialogues of the elements but obviously and tritely in the form of aphorisms, epigrams and fables in verse. His countrymen love these clever and wise sayings and love to quote them—wisdom, like medicine, is more platable when dispensed in the form of tablets—but that the author himself did not attach much value to them might be guessed from the title he gave to the volume—*Kanika* (Trifles).

People's Bard

Let the promises and hopes, the deeds
and words of my country be true, my Lord.

EVEN while Rabindranath was writing that he wanted nothing more in life than to be allowed to watch its lovely panorama from his boat on the river, he was getting restless for a more active and crowded existence. Much as he dreaded the din and clamour of the market-place, he was drawn to it again and again and could not stay away from it for long.

Restlessness was in the air. The sleeping giant of nationalism was beginning to stir in his land and the British Government was getting nervous and apprehensive. Beneath its cloak of benevolence the sword rattled. In 1998 the Sedition Bill was passed to stifle nationalist agitation and the great scholar-patriot, Tilak, was arrested. The poet jumped into the fray and one the day before the Bill became an Act read his famous paper on "Kantharodh" (The Throttle) at a public meeting in Calcutta. He raised his powerful voice against the repressive policy of the Government and actively participated in raising funds for Tilak's defence. When, soon after, the plague broke out in Calcutta he assisted Sister Nivedita in organising relief and medical aid for the victims of this dead epidemic. The poet was turning into a healer of his people's wounds and a high priest of their national aspirations, not only raising his voice but leading an active hand in service at the front.

Parallel in mood and temper to his political activities were his literary offerings of the period— ballads, narrative poems, and dramatic episodes recreating his country's past. Plato would have warmly approved of him. "Hymns to the gods and the praises of worthy actions, "opined the Greek philosopher in his *Republic,* "are the only sort of poetry to be admitted to our state. For if you were to admit the pleasurable muse also, in songs or verses, we should have pleasure and pain reigning in our state instead of law." Did the philosopher overlook that pleasure and pain are the very pulse of life and without them the reign of law could only ensure the uniformity of lifelessness? Plato's approval of Rabindranath would have been short-lived in any case.

Two major volumes of this period, *Katha* (Ballads) and *Kahini* (Tales), are masterpieces of narrative verse and dramatic dialogue. They are a storehouse of legends and historical anecdotes culled from India's ancient past, from the Buddhist lore and the more recent deeds of heroism and sacrifice in the annals of the Rajputs, the Marathas and the Sikhs. The lyric poet, the dramatist and the story-teller have pooled their genius to make some of these pieces rank among Tagore's finest legacies to his people, cherished as much by the young as by the old. An idea of his power of seizing on the dramatic possibilities of a situation which is only baldly referred to in the pages of the *Mahabharata* can be had if one compared such pieces as "Karna and Kunti" or "Gandhari's Prayer" with the original narrative in the Indian epic.

The poet's increasing concern with basic moral and spiritual values is the chief characteristic of these poems, apart from their exquisite poetry, narrative skill and dramatic power. A rich disciple proud of his wealth came to the Sikh Guru and offered a pair of gold bangles inwrought with precious stones. The Guru let one bangle slip from his hand into the river below. The disciple jumped into the river to retrieve the costly gift. Failing to find it he begged the Guru to indicate the exact spot where it had fallen. The Guru threw the remaining bangle into the water and said, "There!"

Here is one about an ancient Hindu sage who taught the sacred sciences to young Brahmins. A little boy, poor but eager to learn, came and begged to be accepted as a pupil. The sage asked him if he was a Brahmin and who his father was. The child ran to his mother to inquire and came back and reported that his mother said she had had no husband and all the wealth that God had given her was in her little boy. The sage embraced the boy and said, "You are the best of Brahmins, for you have inherited the noblest heritage—truth."

There is the Buddhist tale of the monk Upagupta, a disciple of the Buddha. This handsome young monk was sleeping on the ground outside the city wall of Mathura when suddenly something struck against his chest and he woke up with a start. Vasavadatta, the beautiful courtesan of the city, had stumbled against him in the dark on her way to a tryst with a lover. She turned her lantern on the monk and seeing how handsome he was, invited him to go with her to her house, for "this hard and rough ground is no bed for you." The monk looked at her and said softly, "O bunch of loveliness, not yet. Go where you are going now. When the time comes I shall myself come to you." The days passed and one day as the monk was passing again by the city wall he noticed a woman lying sick and abandoned on the ground. The beautiful courtesan had caught the small-pox and the townsfolk, scared of the dread disease, had thrown her outside the city walls. The monk sat down beside the unconscious body and raising the woman's head rested it in his lap, poured water on her dry lips, smeared the body with cool and fragrant sandal paste and chanted prayers for her recovery. The woman opened her eyes and asked, "Who are you, O merciful one?" The monk answered, "Vasavadatta, I have come to keep my tryst."

In another poem called, "The Loss is Negligible," the poet tells the following story: On a winter morning the Queen of Kashi went with her companions to bathe in the Ganges. The wind was chilly and after the bath the Queen who was in a gay mood felt it would be gratefun if she could warm herself near a fire. Seeing an humble cottage nearby she ordered her companions to set fire to it. As the flames fanned by the wind shot up high the Queen was delighted and returned to the palace, pleased with a morning well spent. Meanwhile the scared villagers had run to the King's court and told their tale of woe. The King sent for the Queen and asked her how she could do a thing like that. The Queen smiled and said, "The loss is negligible". The King replied, "You shall judge that for yourself," and ordered that the Queen be divested of all her jewels and other valuables and asked to leave the palace. "Go and earn or beg your livelihood," he said to her. "Only then you will understand how great was the loss of the poor man whose cottage was burnt down for your moment's pleasure. After you have made enough to rebuild the cottage, I shall take you back as my Queen."

But "hymns to the gods and the praises of worthy actions" could not wholly satisfy a poet whose genius was primarily and intensely lyrical and individual. So, even as he was re-interpreting his nation's moral heritage to equate it with his own universal and humanist outlook, he was at the same time pouring out his personal agonies and playing with vagaries of thought and form in a series of exquisite lyrics and songs published consecutively in three volumes, each a landmark in his own development as well as in the literature of his country. Whatever Plato might have said of "the pleasurable Muse" she was Rabindranath's first and last love and whenever he strayed away from her for long, he went back to her with renewed ardour.

In the very first poem of the next volume, *Kalpana* (Dreams), he is aware of his immense need for space, even when bereft of light, and exhorts his spirit not to give up soaring, however vain the beating of its wings. "What if the dusk descends and the music is stilled, what if the companions have all flown back to their nests and a weariness creeps over the limbs and all around is wrapt in an ominous veil—even then, my bird, O my sightless bird, do not furl your wings, not yet!"

There are some beautiful poems on nature, particularly the magnificent ode to the "Year's End". The Bengali year ends in April when the hot winds blow and violent dust-storms sweep over the plains, followed by a merciful shower. On such a day the poem was in fact written and one can still hear in its passionate rhythm the convulsive fury of the time spirit as it destroys the old and brings in the new.

Not all the poems echo the poet's passionate longings, or bear witness to his reflective insights. Some are written in a lighter vein, with tripping measure and in a spirit of almost boyish gaiety, like the one which relates how the shoes came to be invented. But by and large the poet's instinctive and pagan love of nature, his voluptuous delight in its varying moods, is now weighed down with melancholy reflection. He sees a temple in ruins and pity for the deity, neglected and unworshipped, wells up in his heart Men have found other gods. A lovely poem—which might also have interested Freud—reproaches the god Siva for having burn to ashes, in a foolish fit of anger, the love-god Madana. For the ashes, carried away by the wind, are now scattered all over the earth and the anguish of sex repressed never ceases to trouble men. The poet's foreboding of the spiritual crisis and the cross that lay ahead of him is also reflected in several poems. His Lord of Life is increasingly claiming His dues. "I threw my heart into this world, you picked it up and have made it your own. I sought sorrow imagining it to be pleasure; you have turned that sorrow into joy."

But the pagan will not easily part from his Pan, the lover of life will not readily give up his many loves for the cheerless austerity of an exclusive devotion. For sheer delight in the creation of forms, light-heartedness of mood, playfulness of thought and liveliness of language, for the exquisite frivolity of genius, Tagore never wrote anything finer, whether before or after, than the book of poems with which he closed the fortieth year of his life. As though he had a premonition that half his life was over and before the second, more majestic but sombre, half began he indulged for a brief interlude in a full abandon to carefree enjoyment of life's fleeting moments. The book was appropriately named *Kshanika,* which means what is momentary and fleeting. Even more daring and significant than the treatment of theme and imagery, was his use of the language and style to suit his purpose. He took the liberty of using freely the colloquial language with its abbreviated sounds and drew such strength, vigour and music out of it that the experiment may be said to have revolutionised the future of Bengali poetry. In the language of the people he found at last his own true language and made it the language of literature. In a charming lyric he begs his "incomparable one" to forgive the frivolity of his mood and the liberties he cannot help taking with decorum, for in the season of rain when the sky pours itself out and the earth dances, how can the human heart repress its wild impulses? The "incomparable one" might well have been the Bengali reader, too, along with his Muse.

But this exquisite overflow of high spirits, of genial cynicism and unconcern, was itself a fleeting interlude—his parting gift to the dying century to which he owed so much. His offering to the new century was very different. No two books of his are in sharper contrast than the two which followed each other in quick succession : *Kshanika* which marked the end of 1900 and *Naivedya* (Offering) which marked the beginning of 1901. This latter bunch of one hundred poems and hymns, written in about as many days, can claim rank with the world's highest religious poetry. Several of them were included later in the English *Gitanjali.* The gay vagabond of *Kshanika* has become a chastened devotee, over-weighed with a sense of his responsibility to God and to man. The artist is subdued by the man of God and there is no room in these poems for high flights of imagination or dexterity of thought or emotional exuberance or metrical playfulness. The naked spirit is awed and humble in the presence of God and speaks in tones of utter simplicity. "Day after day I shall stand before Thee, O Lord, with folded hands." He has realised his own helplessness and will henceforth seek his light only from Him. All else is because He is. "Let Thy lamp burn in my home. Mine only heats the air and throws out foul smoke." He is not afraid of pain any longer. It is fear that distorts the truth. "Far as I gaze at the depth of Thy immensity, I find no trace there of sorrow or death or separation. Death assumes its mask of terror and sorrow its pain, only when, away from Thee, I turn my face towards my own dark self."

This volume of one hundred poems appropriately entitled "Offering" was dedicated by the author to his venerable eighty-three year old father—in grateful acknowledgement of his debt to him, for the spiritual and moral wealth enshrined in its pages was in a sense the Maharshi's gift to him. When he read out these poems in manuscript to his father, the latter was so pleased that he gave his son a purse to meet the expenses of publication of the volume.

Many years earlier when Rabindranath was in his youth, the Maharshi having heard that his youngest son composed religious songs, had sent for him and had them sung to him. One of them—now famous—opened with the lines:

The eye cannot see Thee, for Thou art the pupil in the eye,
the heart cannot know Thee, for Thou art its inmost secret.

The Maharshi was deeply moved and said, "If the rulers of this land had belonged to the people and understood their language, they would surely have rewarded the young poet." In the absence of such rulers the Maharshi himself gave him a handsome purse.

Despite their passionate sincerity and the mood of devotion that broods over them all, the poems cannot be called religious, as the word is conventionally understood. For even in his other-worldly and God-conscious moods, Rabindranath could not and would not avert his face from this life and earth. Deliverance was not for him in renunciation. "I feel the embrace of freedom in a thousand bonds of delight." Love of God and love of life went hand in hand in him and vindicated and fulfilled one another. Hymns to the divine were also prayers for his people, as in the well-known poem, "Where the mind is without fear and the head is held high . . ." His love for his country had no room in it for jingoism or xenophobia. He refused to hold the foreigner solely responsible for the ills of his land and said that they who inflict wrong and they who suffer it without resistance are both guilty in the eye of Heaven. When the poet wrote this, he had no idea that within a few years this truth would be proclaimed and vindicated by Gandhi.

In a very remarkable poem written on the last day of the dying century, entitled appropriately "Sunset of the Century," he denounced nationalism as the "Self-love of Nations" and saw in the brutality and terror of the Boer War an ominous warning of worse tragedies to follow. "The last sun of the century sets amidst the blood-red clouds of the west and the whirlwind of hatred."

Strangely enough, it was during this period of intense religious and moral idealism that Rabindranath wrote the two novels, *Nashta Nid* (The Broken Nest) and *Chokher Bali* (The Eyesore), which laid the foundation of the realistic and psychological novel in Indian literature. The novels written before these, whether by Bankim Chatterji or by Tagore himself, were historical romances or social melodramas or a mixture of both. The modern novel proper, whether realistic or psychological or concerned with a problem, begins with these two in Indian literature.

The Broken Nest is the domestic tragedy of the busy editor of a daily paper who has little time to spare for his very young and romantic wife. The bored wife seeks solace and stimulus in the company of her husband's young cousin, a lively and versatile youth. They inspire and instigate each other to write and both turn out to be budding writers. The inevitable complications arise and the happy nest is broken. The problem analysed in *Chokher Bali,* which is a fuller and a better constructed novel, is posed in a more complex setting. The story revolves round the dilemma of human relationship and describes what takes place behind the staid facade of a well-to-do, middle-class Bengali home of the period where a widowed mother lives with her only son on whom she dotes. One would imagine that nothing much ever happen in a home like that with its numerous inhibitions and restricted social contacts, and in fact nothing happens that may not happen in any Indian home. And yet passions, savage and violent, are unleashed within hearts seemingly placid, and battles rage until the home is nearly burnt down without flame or smoke being visible to the outside eye.

Altogether the first year of the present century is a very significant year in Tagore's life, fruitful in every respect, from the point of view of his literary achievement, his spiritual development, his public commitments and his struggles as a man. The year marks the end of his freedom as an individual owing no obligations save to his Muse and to his family. From now on his soul will be increasingly pledged to God. The lover will become a teacher and the poet will don the robes of a prophet.

He hardly knew what was coming. All he knew was that he could no longer continue looking exclusively after the family estates, that destiny was calling him to a larger field of activity. Life in Calcutta with its incessant clamour and distractions was too noisy and distasteful. He needed proximity to nature and earth, he needed quiet for his work and he needed activity to fill the leisure between writing. What better place than Santiniketan to suit all his requirements? His father had already built a house

Ancestral home of the Tagore family in Jorasanko

Prince Dwarkanath Tagore

Devendranath Tagore

Sarada Devi

Zamindar Rabindranath among his subjects

In Rothenstein's House in 1912

Rabindranath, 1913

Kadambari Devi

Rabindranath in Brighton

Rabindranath and Mrinalini Devi

With Bela and Rathi

Tree Plantation Ceremony

With Countess De Noai and Victoria Ocampo, at the Paris exhibition, 1930

Rabindranath, 1940

In Japan, 1916

Foundation Ceremony of Visva-Bharti

Rabindranath and L.K. Elmhirst

Einstein and Rabindranath

Inauguration of Hindi Bhavana

Gandhiji and Kasturba at Santiniketan (1940)

Conferring of Doctorate to Tagore at Santiniketan by Oxford University. With S. Radhakrishnan and Maurice Gwyer

The Last Journey

there, and had later added a temple, with no image or altar or other paraphernalia of any particular ritual or rites.

In 1898 Rabindranath had taken his wife and five children, three daughters and two sons, to his estate in Shelidah and had taken in his own hands their education. Although he had engaged an English tutor for his eldest son, he himself was the principal teacher of all his children. Having suffered from bad teaching in his childhood, he had thought much, and written also, on the fundamentals of teaching and now he gained a new insight by putting his principles into practice. But teaching one's children haphazardly is not enough; he needed a wider field for systematic experimentation and he thought, Why not shift to Santiniketan and start a small experimental school there? His imagination had already been caught by idealised pictures of *tapovana* or forest hermitages in ancient India where learned sages lived with their disciples and taught them the practice of simple living and high thinking. He would thus revive the ancient ideal and replace the soulless and mechanical system of education which the British rulers had imported from their Victorian slums by a new and creative one in which both teaching and learning would be pleasurable. He would combine the ancient spirit with the modern setting and recast the old in a new mould.

On 22 December 1901 he inaugurated his school at Santiniketan, with five pupils, among them his eldest son, and with as many teachers. He named it Brahmacharya Asrama, after the ancient forest hermitages. The orthodox Hindu must have squirmed at this sacrilege, for of the five teachers three were Christians, one an Englishman, his son's previous tutor. But that was always Tagore's way—to interpret tradition in his own fashion, to honour the dead on his own terms. The price was heavy, for he won the support neither of the orthodox who looked askance at him as an impertinent innovator nor of the radicals who were alienated by his harping on the past. He had to stand alone—a position ideal for a poet but inconvenient for a social reformer who needed money and men for his institution. Even his admirers and well-wishers were inclined to believe that the school was at best a poet's whim. He found it difficult to get enough funds or enough pupils for his school, and had to sell his house at Puri and part of his personal library to meet the expenses, while his wife magnificently parted with her jewellery to help him carry on.

The school, however, was not a poet's whim. It was his new sadhana, a medium of creative striving for the good of his people, his one epic which he continued to work on till the end of his life and which grew with his growth, remaining unfinished. A poet's dream it undoubtedly was, for who but a poet could "bring the earliest tidings of the unborn flower to a sceptic world?" How else explain the paradox that in the stormiest and most vital decade of his creative career, when he laid the foundation of an unrivalled position in the then metropolis of India and was beginning to win a grudging applause even from his detractors, he chose to adopt the vocation of a schoolmaster—the latest among the despised tribes of India—in an obscure corner of Bengal's wasteland! That he did so and preferred the hardships of a life of stark simplicity (Santiniketan then had little to offer by way of what are known as the amenities of civilised life) to the easy ways and glamorous society of Calcutta is evidence enough, if such were needed, that the new vocation was in the nature of a mission and not of play.

He had always been deeply interested in problems affecting the welfare of the people and of such problems none seemed more deserving of his attention than the prevailing system of education which, instead of developing, stunted the mind of the growing generation. He was one of the first to see through its limitations and its pretensions. It seemed to him wrong that the child, instead of being encouraged to express himself freely and happily in his mother tongue, should be forced from an early age to master the intricacies of a foreign idiom, thus expending all the resources of his tender and undeveloped mind in trying to balance himself of crutches, meanwhile forgetting the use of his limbs. He had not forgotten his own school days when "we had to sit inert, like dead specimens of some museum, whilst lessons were pelted at us from on high, like hailstones on flowers."

The child's mind is extraordinarily aware of his environments and receptive to sense-impressions. He imbibes with his limbs and with his senses long before he learns with his brain. He must therefore be provided with an environment which will stimulate and feed his curiosity and make his introduction to the world around him easy and joyful. He should be encouraged to do things for himself and should lean as little as possible on his teacher. The art of teaching so as to enable the child to love and understand his environment and to learn with his limbs and his senses before the brain is unduly taxed was first developed at Santiniketan long before Mahatma Gandhi adapted its basic principle to his system of what later came to be known in India as Basic Education.

The best teacher, according to Tagore, is nature. The classes in his school were therefore held in the open, under the trees, and the students were encouraged to study and love nature in its changing moods and phases. Education in the sciences, in which he greatly believed, must arise naturally from the study of nature and the training of the senses, which develop the child's curiosity and his aptitudes. No less important, said Tagore, is the influence of music and of the fine arts in training the child's emotions and his sensibility. Education to be real must be of the whole man, of the emotions and the senses as much as of the intellect. Man in his fullness, said Tagore, is not limited by the individual but overflows in his community. And so in his school, along with training in individual initiative and self-reliance, equal emphasis was laid on community service.

Nor is education a plant that can be made to grow as an exotic variety in the hothouse. If it does not strike roots in the soil and adapt itself to the natural environments, it has little value for the people as a whole. It was painful and humiliating fact that the intelligentsia of that generation—to some extent even of this—were borrowing their patterns of thought and behaviour, indeed even of their feelings and sensations, from the West, thereby justifying Tagore's charge that "educational institutions in our country are India's alms-bowl of knowledge; they lower our national self-respect; they encourage us to make a foolish display of decorations made of borrowed feathers." Life never imitates, it assimilates, and so he warned his people that "if the whole world grows at last into an exaggerated west, then such an illimitable parody of the modern age will die, crushed beneath its own absurdity."

These were the main principles of his educational ideal which he tried to implement with his very limited material resources and in a very humble beginning. It was not that having established the school, he left it to his assistants to run it, himself occupied with higher things. He was far from an arm-chair idealist, though not unoften he gave the impression of being one. What he believed in he did himself, pouring all his energy and his heart into it. He not only supervised the routine of school and asrama administration but participated in all its activities and himself taught the children. He loved children, loved being with them, and loved teaching them. It was his faith that every child carried a message from God that He had not yet despaired of man. Finding that there were no suitable primers and textbooks available in Bengali he wrote them himself and encouraged his colleagues to do the same. The poet could drudge as well as sing.

Lone Pilgrim

... make my life simple and straight,
like a flute of reed for Thee to fill with music.

As though to test the sincerity and strength of His new devotee, God sent him, as He had done to His servant Job of the *Old Testament,* a series of bereavements and afflictions. Within a few months of his finding a new home in Santiniketan, his wife Mrinalini fell seriously ill and was taken to Calcutta where she died on 23 November 1902. For twenty years this lady, self-effacing and gracious, had looked after him with unstinted devotion and had borne him five children. Though young and living in the midst of an aristocratic society, she dressed very simply and wore almost no jewellery and had cheerfully adapted herself to her husband's ideals. She grumbled only when he came in the way of her dressing her children in fine clothes. Nor did she remain unlettered for long. She soon acquired proficiency not only in her own language but in English and Sanskrit as well. At her husband's persuasion she translated into Bengali an abridged version of the *Ramayana* from the original Sanskrit. She also acted on the stage in his play *Raja O Rani* and gave an excellent interpretation of the role she was assigned. No wonder then that she won her husband's heart in the end, who gave ample proof of his devotion when she took to bed. For two months he nursed her day and night, refusing to engage a professional nurse. There were no electric fans in those days and contemporary witnesses have left on record their admiration of the husband who was always at the bedside, his hand-fan moving gently over her. When she died he spent the whole night on the terrace walking up and down, having given strict orders that no one was to disturb him.

As usual his feelings found expression in his poems. These were published in a small volume of twenty-seven poems remarkable for their depth of tenderness and for their simplicity of utterance. "My night has passed on the bed of sorrow, and my eyes are tired." She died before he could repay for the many gifts he had received from her and now all he could do is to offer to God what was meant for her. "Her night has found its morning and Thou hast taken her in Thy arms; and to Thee I bring my gratitude and my gifts that were for her." Absent-mindedly he looks for her everywhere in the house, only to realise that he will never again see her on this earth. "My house is small and what once has gone from it can never be regained. But infinite is Thy mansion, my Lord, and seeking her I have come to Thy door." He finds among her belongings a bunch of letters written by him to her, carefully preserved like a great treasure, and is deeply moved. He prays that her memory may bring order into his life as she had brought order into his home. The volume was published a year later as *Smaran* (Remembrance).

Grief disguised is more potent than grief expressed. Few readers would normally suspect that Tagore's poems on children so full of innocent delight were written during a period of great dejection and anxiety. Within a few months of his wife's death his second daughter Renuka fell seriously ill and the doctors advised a change of climate in the mountains. The father took her and the two young children, daughter Mira and son Samindra, now motherless, first to Hazaribagh and then to Almora in the Himalayas. He had not only to nurse the ailing daughter but to look after and entertain the two youngest ones who, in the absence of the mother, clung to him. For their sake he had to hide his own grief and anxiety and to share their little interests and listen to their prattle. Thus he wrote poems which were published in a volume entitled, *Sisu* (The Child), "a collection of poems about children, unique in the literature of the world," to quote the estimate of the Czech savant, Prof. Lesny. Many of these were later translated into English and included in *The Crescent Moon.*

Apart from their poetry, perhaps the most exquisite ever put in the mouth of children, they bear witness to Rabindranath's profound tenderness for children, his intuitive understanding of their wayward minds and his faith in the child's instinctive wisdom. What "Heaven lies about us in our infancy" is what they provide glimpses into. "Pearl-fishers dive for pearls, merchants sail in their ships, while the children gather pebbles and scatter them again . . . On the seashore of endless worlds is the great meeting of children."

In September 1903, nine months after her mother's death, Renuka died, at the age of thirteen. This precocious, moody and uncommon girl was very dear to the father who felt her loss deeply, though he gave no expression to his grief. He buried himself in his work and continued to fill the pages of his literary journal, *Bangadarshan.* Strangely enough, it was during this period that he contributed serially to the pages of this journal what may be described as perhaps the only novel he wrote merely for the sake of entertaining the reader with an ingeniously constructed story, unburdened with philosophy or any kind of sophistication, and not ending on a tragic note—*Nauka Dubi,* translated into English as *The Wreck.* It is a story based on the dilemma of mistaken identity resulting in an exchange of wives delightfully told, if somewhat naively, and interspersed with descriptions of nature of extraordinary loveliness.

Four months after the death of his daughter Renuka, the poet suffered another grievous bereavement. A young and promising poet, Satis Roy, whom Tagore loved as his own son and who, an idealist like himself, had joined his school staff at Santiniketan, and might in course of time have been his right hand, suddenly died of small–pox. The whole school had to be shifted to Shelidah for the time being, for fear of the epidemic. Soon after, his father, the Maharshi, passed away on 19 January 1905, aged eighty-eight. The death of this remarkable and towering personality marks the end of a very significant era in Indian history—the era of religious and cultural resurgence, of intellectual and moral stalwarts who paved the way of India's political awakening. Henceforth political ends and not moral or intellectual ideals will dominate the Indian scene, despite the great dreams of a Gandhi or a Tagore.

Lord Curzon, the strong–headed Viceroy of India, provided the necessary provocation and challenge in the last year of his office, 1905, by his proclamation of the partition of Bengal, thereby beginning the process of driving a wedge between the two major religious communities in the country which ultimately resulted in the partition of India forty-two years later amid a holocaust of violence and terror unprecedented in Indian history. Tagore had already warned his people of this danger and now he jumped into the fray, making fiery speeches, composing patriotic songs and heading huge processions in protest against the vivisection of the country. Students were being expelled from colleges for no other crime than the temerity to sing patriotic songs; to provide for their education he and some other educationists formulated and put into operation a scheme for national education and set up a Council of which the celebrated philosopher-yogi, Aurobindo Ghosh, became the first Principal. It was for this Council that Tagore delivered his well-known series of lectures on the principles of literature which were later published as *Sahitya*. He had hoped that by leading the popular discontent against foreign rule he would succeed in yoking the newly aroused passion for national freedom to a dynamic programme of national regeneration. He had planned and outlined such a programme in a series of remarkable lectures and essays in which he anticipated almost every basic principle of what later became a nation-wide mass movement of non-violent non-cooperation under the leadership of Mahatma Gandhi.

But Tagore was no Gandhi. He lacked the Mahatma's tireless patience and persistence, his calm judgement and unruffled will, his genius for strategy and his unrivalled gift of leadership. He rode the storm majestically for a time, but as soon as it raised in its inevitable howl of violence, he retired from the battle-field, a sadder and a wiser man. He was severely criticised for having abandoned the struggle which he had so heroically inspired, but be it recalled to Tagore's credit that he knew his limitations and wisely refrained from persisting in a course which he was unable to direct, that he was not deflected from what he thought was right by public abuse. That too was heroism. His patriotic songs, however, continued to inspire the national struggle, although they are remarkably free of any trace of jingoism or incitation of crude passions. In a sense it is very true what Ezra Pound said later: "Tagore has sung Bengal into a nation."

Whether his retirement from the battle-field was a loss to the political movement or not, it certainly was a gain to Santiniketan and to literature. Apart from a large number of articles on social and national problems, on education, literary criticism, folk literature and the philosophy of words and sounds, he wrote a number of humorous and satirical sketches and completed his next major volume of verse published in 1906 as *Kheya* (Crossing). The title is symbolic of the poet's mood of wistful expectancy, of waiting for the ferry to cross over to the other bank. The many bereavements and disappointments he had recently suffered had only served to steel his fortitude and to prepare him for the change that was coming. Most of the poems (some are songs) are dreamy and symbolic; eleven of them were later included in his English *Gitanjali,* and a few others in *The Gardener, Fruit Gathering* and *Lover's Gift and Crossing.*

"Prisoner, tell me who wrought this unbreakable chain?" "It was I," said the prisoner, "who forged this chain with great care. I thought my chain would bind the world leaving me free. And so I laboured at it, day and night, beating the iron in fire. When the chain was ready, I discovered that I had bound myself in its shackles."

The poet describes himself as a beggar girl who was on her begging round when the Prince stopped before her and stretching his hand, said, "Give me something." She blushed with shame. What could she give him? She took out a copper coin from her miserable bag and placed it in his hand. When she returned home and opened the bag, she found a gold coin in place of the one she had parted with. "Oh, why did I not give my all?" she wailed.

In another poem he is a woman waiting at night for her lover. "At dead of night came the King of the dark chamber." This symbolism he elaborated late in his famous drama *Raja,* known in English as *The King of the Dark Chamber.*

The year 1907 was packed with anguish and achievement.

Disappointment in public life was followed by a great personal sorrow. Whatever his engagements at Calcutta, Santiniketan or elsewhere, his pen was restless and was turning out some of his finest prose covering a large variety of topics. Apart from the major novel, *Gora,* which began to appear serially, he published four volumes of literary essays, each covering a separate category: *Sahitya* (literature and literary values in general), *Prachin Sahitya* (ancient literature), *Adhunik Sahitya* (modern literature), and *Lok Sahitya* (folk literature or literature of the people). The range was comprehensive, the analysis sober and lucid, and the style so charming that what he said was itself a fine specimen of literature. Rabindranath was one of the first Indian writers to include in his broad sweep of literary appreciation the entire range of Indian literature, from the classical to the contemporary, from the aristocratic to the plebeian, and to illumine and place each in the perspective of the whole. He was perhaps the first to appreciate sensitively, with enthusiasm and insight, the great treasure of India's folk literature long buried in the sands of neglect.

In November 1907 came the crowning tragedy of his family life. His youngest son, Samindra, a lovely and gifted boy who might have become something like his father, suddenly died of cholera at the age of thirteen, on the same day on which his mother had passed away five years earlier. In the course of five tempestuous years Tagore suffered an almost total break-up of his family life. He had lost his wife and two children; of the three surviving ones, the eldest daughter lived with her husband outside Bengal, the eldest son had been sent to the United States the previous year for training in agricultural science, and the third daughter Mira had been married a few months earlier. With the untimely death of his youngest son, he was reduced to utter loneliness. Loneliness in the midst of the crowd is even more oppressive and so for a time he retired into solitude on his estate at Shelidah. That was the only visible expression of the heavy hand of sorrow that lay on his heart. He had learnt not to muddy the waters of his Muse with his personal grief; his verse was becoming increasingly his offering to God, the medium of a higher love, shorn of all superfluous ornaments.

He had never been very popular with his people; he was far above their current prejudices and passions and too ahead of his time. Even his literary genius had won but a grudging and limited recognition and it is said that for long the pundits and purists used to set passages from his writings to school boys saying, "Rewrite in good Bengali." Indeed, odd and incredible as it may seem today, even as late as 1914 (after the award of the Nobel Prize) the Compulsory Bengali Composition Paper of the Matriculation Exam of the Calcutta University contained a passage from Tagore which the candidates were asked to "rewrite in chaste and correct Bengali." The only time he rode on the crest of popularity was when he led the agitation against the partition of Bengal, but that was for a brief while only and now he was blamed for having let down his people and was less popular than ever. He had alienated the ruling authorities who issued secret circulars asking the Government servants and loyalists not to send their children to his school or help it in any way. He was a political suspect and was under watch. He was thus forced, as much by outer circumstances as by an inner necessity, to stand alone, to rely entirely on his inner resources, to stand face to face with God. His religious poetry of this period which culminated in the passionate sincerity and utter simplicity of *Gitanjali* and *Gitimalya* was wrung out of his heart's blood. His religious insight, like that of all great saints and mystics, was born of deeply experienced sorrow and loneliness.

The most remarkable aspect of his deepening religious insight was that it enriched instead of eating into or warping his love of this earth and this life. He sought God not merely in the privacy of his soul but in every manifestation of His play in the outside world. The son he lost in his home he found again in all the boys of his Santiniketan; in their zest of living he recovered his own. How well he did so can be seen in the play he wrote for them in 1908—*Saradotsav* (Autumn Festival). The play is one long riot of innocent delight, a hymn to the joy of living. It is still a favourite with the boys of his school for whom it was composed and is acted in the open air, as many of Tagore's plays were intended to be, for in them nature is not merely a background but almost a participant. It might have been written, as Edward Thompson aptly observed, as a symbolic commentary with song and dance on Emerson's wise words, "Give me health and a day and I will make the pomp of emperors ridiculous."

This was followed by *Prayaschitta* (Atonement), very different in theme and mood from the previous play, though also in prose interspersed with songs. It is not a drama of feeling but of action, full of strife and intrigue and the clash of interests, although an idea and a moral run through it as they do in all Tagore's plays. It is a dramatisation of his first and very early novel, *Bou-Thakuranir Hat,* with the addition of a remarkable character who is the prototype of Mahatma Gandhi and anticipates the latter's campaign of non-violent civil resistance and non-payment of taxes as the people's answer to the tyranny of an unjust ruler, The play was Tagore's answer to his compatriots who had accused him of deserting the political battle-field. It was not desertion; it was renunciation, the spirit of which is most movingly portrayed in the last scene of the play.

The poet was in a full frenzy of the dramatic phase of his career and it was inevitable that he should dramatise the most intense experience of his life—his adventure with the Divine. He had sought God in beauty and had found Him in sorrow. Is Truth merely Beauty and Goodness or also the Ugly and the Terrible? What is the soul's relation to God? Must we approach Truth on our terms or on its own? These are the questions the poet has sought to answer in this his most symbolic and in a sense his most characteristic play, *Raja* (in English *The King of the Dark Chamber*). This philosophic allegory was followed by two other plays written in quick succession in 1911, and published a year later. They are very different from each other and from the previous dramas, although the central character in both of them is a young boy.

Dak Ghar, translated into English as *The Post Office,* is perhaps the most popular among his plays and was successfully staged in London by the Irish players in 1913. W.B. Yeats who was present at the performance testified, "On the stage the little play shows that it is very perfectly constructed, and conveys to the right audience and emotion of gentleness and peace." The German stage version of the play which the poet saw in Berlin in 1921 was suggestive of a fairy story. Writing of it to C.F. Andrews, he recalled: "I remember, at the time when I wrote it, my own feeling which inspired me to write it. Amal represents the man whose soul has received the call of the open road . . ." Or one who is athirst for the faraway, to quote a line from one of Tagore's earlier songs. Whatever its deeper symbolism, the play embodies the author's own reminiscent longing as a child for freedom from the confines of his regimented home.

The other play, *Achalayatan* (The Immovable), has not been published in English and is indeed hard to translate. The play is a rollicking satire on the self-complacent, self-righteous and unchanging obstinacies of Hindu society and is one long unsparing mockery of its absurd orthodoxies. The central character is a small boy by name Panchak who has been enrolled by his elder brother, a pillar of orthodoxy, as a novice in a monastic order which is Achalayatan, Castle of Conformity, surrounded by high walls and cut off from the rest of the world. The poor boy who suffers from irrepressible curiosity and mirth is looked down upon by the inmates as an incorrigible dunce and is constantly chided for his habit of singing. "What merit is there in singing? Even the birds can sing." He is ever playing the truant and keeps company with the neighbouring peasants, workers and other low-caste tribes and finds pleasure in their innocent games, their honest labour and in their lust for living. Finally the Great Teacher whom the monks and elders fear but have never seen arrives on the scene and himself leads the lowly and outcaste tribes against the Achalayatan whose walls are razed to the ground. The times have changed fast since then and what Tagore said six decades ago seems so commonplace and almost self-evident today that the present generation is hardly aware of their debt to the man who had the vision and the courage to say what he did, and at no little cost to his popularity.

But Tagore was no embittered Swift who enjoyed belittling

his fellowmen nor an impetuous revolutionary who in his impatience with old order would trample under foot the good along with the bad. He loved his country and its heritage too well to despise all traditional values. How fair he was in his defence of both the old and the new is evident in the novel which he wrote and published at this period and which many consider his best novel. *Gora* is more than a mere novel; it is an epic of India in transition at a crucial period of its modern history, when the social conscience and intellectual awareness of the new intelligentsia were in the throes of a great churning. No other book gives so masterly an analysis of the complex of Indian social life with its teeming contradictions, or of the character of Indian nationalism which draws its roots from renascent Hinduism and stretches out its arms towards universal humanism. Nor is it any the less interesting as a novel. The characters are well drawn and are clearly recognisable in their norms as in their oddities and remain memorable types. Their conflicts between themselves and within themselves as characters living and growing are delineated with great insight and sympathy and not a little irony. Despite the abundance of polemics in the book, inevitable in the nature of its theme, the author does not lose the thread of the main narrative whose interest is sustained to the end.

It is worth recalling how this novel came to be written. It is said that the main character, Gora, who gives the novel its title, was suggested by the personality of Sister Nivedita, the Irish lady, *nee* Margaret Noble, who became a disciple of Swami Vivekananda, the eloquent apostle of neo-Hinduism. Those who have read her books know what a passionate advocate she was of everything Hindu. Tagore who liked and admired her for her sincerity and courage must often have smiled when she preached Hinduism to him—more Hindu than the Hindu! Once when she was staying as his guest at his Shelidah estate, she would insist, when they sat out on the deck of the house-boat in the evening, that he tell her a story. So he began telling her the story of Gora and later wrote it down.

Gora is an Irish foundling whose parents were killed in the so-called Sepoy Mutiny of 1857. A kind Brahmin lady brings up the baby as her own. Gora, fair of skin and handsome, tall and well-built, proud and passionate, grows up to be a fervent believer in Hindu orthodoxy and a vehement champion of the caste system. In his crusade for what he believed was the only true and divinely ordained faith, he alienates his only true friend and spurns the girl who loves him and whom he in his heart loves. The anti-climax comes suddenly when he discovers that he is of foreign blood and therefore, in terms of his own faith, a *mlechha,* an outcaste. He has no place whatsoever in the orthodox Hindu society by which he had sworn. This realisation brings him to his senses and he understands the true significance of his nation's heritage. "Today I am really an Indian. In me there is no longer any opposition between Hindu, Mussulman and Christian. Today every caste in India is my caste, the food of all is my food."

The right understanding of his country's history and destiny which he made his hero realise at the end of this novel was also directly voiced by Tagore in a beautiful hymn to India which he wrote about the same time. It is too long to be quoted here, but a few lines may give some idea of it.

Awake my mind, gently awake
in this holy land of pilgrimage
on the shore of this vast sea of humanity
that is India.
Here I stand with arms outstretched
to hail man—divine in his own image—
and sing to his glory in notes glad and free.
No one knows whence and at whose call
came pouring endless inundations of men
rushing madly along—to lose themselves in the sea :
Aryans and non-Aryans, Dravidians and Chinese,
Scythians, Huns, Pathans and Moghuls—
all are mixed, merged and lost in one body.
Now the door has opened to the West
and gifts in hand they beckon and they come—
they will give and take, meet and bring together,
none shall be turned away

from the shore of this vast sea of humanity
that is India.

Two years later he elaborated the idea in a brilliant thesis which he first delivered as a public lecture in Calcutta and later published as *Bharatvarsher Itihaser Dhara* (The Course of Indian History). In the same year he echoed the sentiment in a famous song which is today the national anthem of India.

All the pain and suffering, the bereavements and rebuffs, the struggles and mortifications, both in the world outside and in his mind, which Rabindranath, who had begun his career as a carefree singer, went through in the first decade of this century were finally resolved and sublimated in the songs that poured forth from his full and chastened heart in 1909 and 1910 and published as *Gitanjali* in the latter year. Fifty-one of these 157 songs were later translated by him into English and published in the English book of that name which made him world-famous. They are too well-known to need any introduction or commentary here. Those who know the Bengali language is simple, the feeling sincere, the thought sublime. As the poet said in one of them, "My song has put off her adornments. She has no pride of dress and decoration. Ornaments would mar our union; they would come between Thee and me; their jingling would drown our whispers." Love of God and love of man, strength in sorrow and humility in joy, an innocent wonder that hides centuries of thought, invest these songs with an appeal that is both universal and perennial. The very first song (of the original Bengali volume) strikes the keynote of the poet's mood: "May I never celebrate myself in my achievement! Let only Thy will be fulfilled in my life!" Love is the keyword. He loves God because he loves the world and when the time comes for him to bid it farewell, his last words will be of thankfulness that what he saw on this earth was unsurpassable.

Fifty years of a rich and fruitful career closed in 1911. As though aware that a major phase of his development was at an end and an entirely new chapter was to begin, he wrote his reminiscences (*Jivansmriti*) of the earlier days upto the threshold of manhood. Why he did not make them up-to-date, why he left the most dramatic years of his life out of the picture it is difficult to say. Nor are these memoirs a chronicle of events as in a diary. As he himself put it while introducing them, "Life's memories are not life's history, but the original work of an artist." The artist is an impressionist and what he paints on the mind's canvas does not exactly reproduce what actually happened. "The two correspond but are not one."

Encounter with the West

Thou hast brought the distant near
and made a brother of the stranger.

TWELVE years of struggle without respite on many fronts had yielded a rich harvest, but the strain had been great, both on the body and on his mind. The high tension at which he had lived brought its inevitable reaction and the fiftieth birthday found Rabindranath sick in body and weary in spirit. Twice before a sojourn abroad had proved helpful and stimulating. Now again at the cross-roads, he looked wistfully towards the West. He had never been anti-West even in his most patriotic and introspective phase and had drawn inspiration and sustenance as freely from the values of Western civilisation as from the heritage of his own country. He took freely because he knew he could give back richly. And so in the beginning of 1912 he made preparations for his third voyage to Europe.

Meanwhile the intelligentsia of Bengal tried to make amends for their past neglect of their greatest poet by celebrating the fiftieth anniversary of his birth at a public reception on 28 January 1912, in the Town Hall of Calcutta, under the auspices of the Bangiya Sahitya Parishad, the leading literary society of Bengal. Tagore was due to sail from Calcutta on 19 March, but suddenly fell ill on the night before his departure and the doctors forbade an immediate voyage. His luggage, already on board, had to be sent back from Madras where the ship halted next. Disappointed at this unforeseen postponement of his voyage, he sought consolation and strength, as of old, by retiring to Shelidah on the bank of his beloved river Padma. It was here that he began to translate, for the first time, some of his *Gitanjali* songs into English. But let him tell the story in his own words, although his own words were in Bengali and the excerpt quoted below is an English rendering:

"You have alluded to the English translation of *Gitanjali*," he wrote to his niece Indira from London. "I cannot imagine to this day how people came to like it so much. That I cannot write English is such a patent fact that I never had even the vanity to feel ashamed of it. If anybody wrote an English note asking me to tea, I did not feel equal to answering it. Perhaps you think that by now I have got over that delusion. By no means. That I have written in English seems to be the delusion. On the day I was to broad the ship, I fainted due to my frantic efforts at leave-taking and the journey itself was postponed. Then I went to Shelidah to take rest. But unless the brain is fully active, one does not feel strong enough to relax completely; the only way to keep myself calm was to take up some light work . . .

"So I took up the poems of *Gitanjali* and set myself to translate them one by one. You may wonder why such a crazy ambition should possess one in such a weak state of health. But believe me, I did not undertake this task in a spirit of reckless bravado. I simply felt an urge to recapture through the medium of another language the feelings and sentiments which had created such a feast of joy within me in the days gone by. The pages of a small exercise-book came to be filled gradually, and with it in my pocket I boarded the ship."

During this enforced convalescence at Shelidah he composed many songs in which the devotional mood of *Gitanjali* continued to yield an equally rich flowering. In *Gitanjali* the poet had made an offering to his Beloved Deity of "a handful of songs." In *Gitimalya* he wove for Him "a garland of songs." Seventeen of these songs were translated by him and later included in the English *Gitanjali*.

In some of the songs, untranslated, the poet's disappointment at the abortive voyage and his restlessness find vivid expression. "I sit on the bank idling away the hours, waiting for the ferry which fails to turn up . . . Above the yonder mansion in the west the half moon is dreaming and within my mind I hear the call of a flute from far away." Again, "Now is the time to set the boat afloat on the waters. Ah me, the weariness of waiting on the bank is intolerable . . ." He chides himself for impatience. "It is only when I give up the helm that Thou wilt take it over. What is to be will be. Why this futile grabbing?" In the meanwhile he will sing songs to his Lord. "Now that all tumult is banned, let us whisper to each other, Thou and I. Let the heart murmur its secret in song." The very first poem of the English *Gitanjali* is from this collection: "Thou hast made me endless, such is thy pleasure. This frail vessel thou emptiest again and again, and fillest it ever with fresh life."

At last on 27 May 1912, Rabindranath sailed for London, accompanied by his son Rathindranath and daughter-in-law, Pratima. It was the English painter, Sir William Rothenstein, who served as midwife to the birth of Tagore's fame in Europe. Rothenstein had visited India in 1910 and had come to know the artist-brothers, Abanindranath and Gaganendranath, during his stay in Calcutta. "I was attracted each time I went to Jorasanko," writes Rothenstein, "by their uncle, a strikingly handsome figure, dressed in a white dhoti and chadur, who sat silently listening as we walked. I felt an immediate attraction, and asked whether I might draw him, for I discovered an inner charm as well as great physical beauty, which I tried to set down with my pencil. That this uncle was one of the remarkable men of his time no one gave me a hint."

When Tagore arrived in London where he hardly knew any one else, almost the first thing he did was to call up Rothenstein and, knowing his interest in his poems, gave him the notebook in which he had scribbled his translations. "That evening," writes Rothenstein, "I read the poems. Here was poetry of a new order which seemed to me on a level with that of the great mystics. Andrew Bradley, to whom I showed them, agreed: 'It looks as though we have at last a great poet among us again,' he wrote. I sent word to Yeats, who failed to reply; but when I wrote again he asked me to send him the poems, and when he read them his enthusiasm equalled mine. He came to London and went carefully through the poems, making here and there a suggestion, but leaving the original little changed."

What Yeats felt about these poems he has himself recorded in the Introduction he wrote for the first limited edition of *Gitanjali* published by the India Society of London. " I have carried the manuscript of these translations about with me for days, reading it in railway trains, or on the top of omnibuses and in restaurants, and I have often had to close it lest some stranger would see how much it moved me." Yeats' appreciation of the poems encouraged Rothenstein to call a few friends at his Hampstead house on the evening of 30 June when Yeats read out the poems to a choice gathering of distinguished writers. It was here that Tagore first met C.F. Andrews who became his lifelong friend and associate. Andrews who was at that time a missionary attached to the Cambridge Brotherhood has left his record of that memorable evening: "I walked back along the side of Hampstead Heath with H.W. Nevinson but spoke very little. I wanted to be alone and think in silence of the wonder and glory of it all. When I had left Nevinson I went across the Heath. The night was cloudless and there was something of the purple of the Indian atmosphere about the sky. There all alone I could think of the wonder of it:

"On the seashore of endless worlds children meet
On the seashore of endless worlds is the great
meeting of children."

Reviewing the poems after the publication of *Gitanjali,* Ezra Pound wrote: "It is a little over a month since I went to Mr Yeats' rooms and found him much excited over the advent of a great poet, someone 'greater than any of us.' It is hard to tell where to begin . . . We have found our new Greece, suddenly. As the sense of balance came back upon Europe in the days before the Renaissance, so it seems to me does this sense of a saner stillness come now to us in the midst of our clangour of mechanisms . . . I am not saying this hastily, nor in an emotional flurry, nor from a love of brandishing statement. I have had a month to think it over . . . There is in him the stillness of nature. The poems do not seem to have been produced by storm or by ignition, but seem to show the normal habit of his mind. He is at one with nature, and finds no contradictions. And this is in sharp contrast with the western mode, where man must be shown attempting to master nature if we are to have 'great drama'. It is in contrast to the Hellenic representation of man, the sport of the gods, and both in the grip of destiny . . . When I leave Mr Tagore I feel exactly as if I were a barbarian clothed in skins, and carrying a stone war-club.

"Briefly, I find in these poems a sort of ultimate common sense, a reminder of one thing and forty things which we are ever likely to lose sight of in the confusion of our Western life, in the racket of our cities, in the jabber of manufactured literature, in the vortex of advertisement. There is the same sort of common sense in the first part of the New Testament, the same happiness in some of the psalms, but these are so apt to be spoiled for us by association; there are so many fools engaged in mispreaching them, that it is pleasant to find their poetic quality in some work which does not bring into the spectrum of our thoughts John Calvin, the Bishop of London, and loathly images of cant.

"If these poems have a flaw—I do not admit that they have—but if they have quality that will put them at a disadvantage with the 'general reader,' it is that they are too pious. Yet I have nothing but pity for the reader who is unable to see that their piety is the poetic piety of Dante, and that it is very beautiful."

Tagore, however, was not in England when *Gitanjali* was published. Though his stay in England during this visit was not long— a little over four months—it was very hectic and fruitful, thanks to Rothenstein and the warm affection he received from his other British acquaintances and friends. It was almost as if in anticipation of this that he had written in *Gitanjali* ,"Thou hast made me known to friends whom I knew not. Thou hast given me seats in homes not my own." Among other celebrities, he met Bernard Shaw, H.G. Wells, Bertrand Russell, John Galsworthy, Robert Bridges, John Masefield, Sturge Moore, W.H. Hudson and Stopford Brooke. "Tagore's dignity and handsome presence," wrote Rothenstein, "the ease of his manners and his quiet wisdom made a marked impression on all who met him." He himself was much struck by "the breadth of view and the rapidity of thought that he found among his new friends," and said, "Those who know the English only in India do not know Englishmen."

Rothenstein proposed to the India Society that they should print for its members a selection of Tagore's poems for which Yeats agreed to write an Introduction. It was thus that *Gitanjali* was first published in English in a limited edition of 750 copies before Macmillans of London brought out a popular edition. There were many critics, both in Great Britain and India, who found it hard to believe that Tagore could write so well in English and attributed the success of *Gitanjali* to Yeats' having drastically revised or rewritten the poems. This impression is still current in some quarters which makes it desirable to quote what Rothenstein had to say about it, since he knew better than any one else, for he had not only read the original manuscript before sending it to Yeats but the final manuscripts as it emerged from Yeats' hands was with him and remained in his family. " I know that it was said in India that the success of *Gitanjali* was largely owing to Yeats' rewriting of Tagore's English. That this is false can easily be proved. The original manuscript of *Gitanjali* in English and in Bengali is in my possession. Yeats did here and there suggest slight changes, but the main text was printed as it came from Tagore's hands."

In October 1912, Rabindranath sailed for the United States, accompanied by his son and daughter-in-law. The son who had earlier graduated from the University of Illinois persuaded the father to spend some quiet months at Urbana where Tagore wrote his first original serious prose in English, later delivered as Lectures at the Harvard University and published as *Sadhana.* In these lectures he interpreted, in his own fashion, "the ancient spirit of India," as revealed in the utterance and example of her sages.

It was while Rabindranath was in Illinois that the India Society edition of *Gitanjali* was published in London in November 1912. The book was on the whole well received in the British press. The *Times Literary Supplement* wrote: "And in reading these poems one feels, not that they are the curiosities of an alien mind, but that they are prophetic of the poetry that might be written in England if our poets could attain to the same harmony of emotion and idea. That divorce of religion and philosophy which prevails among us is a sign of our failure in both . . . Some perhaps will refuse to fall under the spell of this Indian poet because this philosophy is not theirs. If it seems to us fantastic and alien, before we despise it we should ask ourselves the question: What is our philosophy? We are very restless in thought, but we have none that poets can express."

Indeed, critics were not wanting who refused "to fall under the spell of this Indian poet." One of them wrote in *New Age*, London, "any of us could write such stuff *ad libitum;* but nobody should be deceived into thinking it good English, good poetry, good sense, or good ethics." Some critics patted themselves on the back that so well had the British carried out their "civilizing mission" that the Indians could write such good stuff. "The chief significance of Mr Tagore's triumph," wrote a critic in the *Birmingham Post,*" is that it marks the culmination of the development of an offshoot of English literature, the importance of which has not been sufficiently recognised." The general reception of *Gitanjali* in the British press was, however, overwhelmingly favourable and the author was naturally pleased about it.

The reaction among Tagore's own countrymen was no less mixed. Basanta Kumar Roy, who was then living in the United States and who later published Tagore's biography in that country, tells us that several young Bengalis in the United States were furious when they read the following statement by an English missionary published in an English review : "For many centuries no such poet and musician has appeared in India." One of them "shouted in true American fashion, D—n it." Others cited many other Bengali poets, among them Nabin Sen and D.L. Roy, as much greater than Tagore. "His love lyrics," they went on to say, "are poor imitations of the poems of our Vaishnava poets of old, and his philosophy is the philosophy of the Upanishads. Let the Europeans and the Americans rave over Tagore. But there is nothing new for us in his writings."

At any rate Tagore's name was now sufficiently bandied about in the English papers for his reputation to have crossed the

Atlantic. While the ordinary American citizen was hardly aware of his obscure residence in Urbana, invitations from academic and other circles began to pour in, and Harriet Monroe published six poems of *Gitanjali* in the December issue of the Chicago magazine, *Poetry*. Perhaps the first journal in the West to publish his poems. This was followed by an invitation from the Chicago University for a lecture. It was while Tagore was still in Urbana that Basanta Kumar Roy came to visit him to persuade him to translate more of his work into English, for he felt certain that when his writings became known, "You will sooner or later win the Nobel Prize for Poetry. No other man in India or Asia has won that laurel." Naively Tagore inquired, "Are the Asiatics eligible for the Prize?"

Perhaps the doubt was not so naive after all, for when the Prize did come, there were rumblings of protest in many quarters of the West that an Asian had received it. "The awarding of the Nobel Prize for Literature," wrote an American paper, "to a Hindu has occasioned much chagrin and no little surprise among writers of the Caucasian race. They cannot understand why this distinction was bestowed upon one who is not white." The Globe of Toronto, Canada, wrote: "It is the first time that the Nobel Prize has gone to any one who is not what we call 'white'. It will take time, of course, for us to accommodate ourselves to the idea that any one called Rabindranath Tagore should receive a world prize for literature. (Have we not been told that the East and the West shall never meet?) The name has a curious sound. The first time we saw it in print it did not seem real." The *Times*, Los Angeles, complained that young modern writers in Europe and America had been discouraged by the award of the Prize "to a Hindu poet whose name few people can pronounce, with whose work fewer in America are familiar, and whose claim for that high distinction still fewer will recognise."

In January 1913 Rabindranath came to Chicago where he lectured on the "Ideals of the Ancient Civilisation of India" and on "The Problem of Evil". From Chicago he went to Rochester to attend the Congress of Religious Liberals where he spoke on "Race Conflict," and then to Boston where he delivered the series of lectures later published as *Sadhana.*

After visiting New York Tagore returned to London in April 1913 where also he delivered a course of lectures at the Caxton Hall. When he had arrived in London less than a year earlier, he was an unknown stranger. Now he had become a sensation and a curiosity. His play, *The Post Office,* was staged and three more volumes of translations were published before the year was over; *The Gardener, The Crescent Moon,* and the play *Chitra.* None of these books can be considered particularly pious or religious or philosophical and might have been expected to give the foreign reader a better perspective to his work. But the first impressions are always more vivid and lasting and Tagore would henceforth be regarded in the West as primarily a religious and philosophic poet. His own biblical personality and august mien and his insistent harping on the ideals of ancient forest sages helped to confirm the one-sided impression. Ezra Pound who saw him as one poet sees another tried to correct the distorted image but his was a lone voice. Reviewing *The Gardener* in the *Freewoman* he said: "Why the good people of this island are unable to honour a fine artist as such; why they are incapable, or apparently incapable, of devising for his honour any better device than that of wrapping his life in cotton wool and parading about with the effigy of a sanctimonious moralist, remains and will remain for me an unsolvable mystery."

In September Tagore sailed for India, having achieved both fame and health. It was while he was in Santiniketan that the news came on 13 November of the award of the Nobel Prize for his *Gitanjali.* The news was received with no small surprise and much rejoicing all over the country. In the little asrama at Santiniketan the children, who hardly knew what the Nobel Prize was but understood that their beloved Gurudev had been honoured by the world, went wild with joy. What did the poet himself feel? No doubt, he felt elated and proud and happy—and above all justified. He would not be human if he felt otherwise. The patriot in him felt happy, too, that his country's name had been put on the world's literary map and felt proud that he was the reason of it. But the poet in him was too sensitive not to feel a misgiving that his days of peace, of a quiet and uninterrupted pursuit of his vocation as a poet and as a teacher of little children, of intimate whisperings with his God, were over. Five days later he wrote to Rothenstein: "The perfect whirlwind of public excitement it has given rise to is frightful. It is almost as bad as trying a tin can at a dog's tail making it impossible for him to move without creating noise and collecting crowds all along. I am being smothered with telegrams and letters for the last few days and the people who never had any friendly feelings towards me nor ever read a line of my works are loudest in their protestations of joy. I cannot tell how tired I am of all this shouting, the stupendous amount of its unreality being something appalling. Really these people honour the honour in me and not myself."

The thought rankled in his mind and the patriot in him found it humiliating that the majority of his countrymen had needed the stimulus of foreign recognition to turn a grudging appreciation of his service to their language and literature into adulation. This sad and bitter thought found public expression on 23 November when a large deputation of 500 distinguished citizens of Calcutta representing divers professions and interests came by a special train to Santiniketan to offer him the nation's felicitations. In blunt but poetic words the poet told them that he could not accept a homage that was so unreal. Those among his audience who had always been his warm admirers understood for whom the snub was meant; the rest, thus deflated, never forgave him for what they considered his "inhospitable reply".

Though the Prize was awarded on the merit of an individual work whose poetic excellence and high idealism were almost universally acknowledged, the fact that it was given to an Asian invested the award with a significance which such awards do not normally have and made it look almost like a unique phenomenon. It was received everywhere with a shock of surprise and turned Rabindranath from an individual into a symbol—a symbol of the West's grudging recognition of Asia's submerged potential and its imminent resurgence. Tagore was the first to impress vividly on the intellectual consciousness of the West the fact—now amply demonstrated—that the "mind" of Asia was lying and would have to be reckoned with as a vital entity and not merely as an interesting specimen in a museum.

There were other reactions too, conditioned by varying biases. Devout and hopeful Christians saw in Tagore's poems the promise of a coming dawn. "We have been waiting anxiously," wrote the *Baptist Times,* "for some indication of the effect of Christian ideas on a truly representative Hindu mind. Here, surely, is the person we have been longing for—one sent before the chariot of the Lord to make His path straight. And when we remember that this poet's every word is eagerly caught up by waiting millions, may we not venture to assert that the new, the Christian India, is already at the door?" It needed the courage and clarity of mind of a Dean Inge to remind his co-religionists that "Tagore is not a Christian; but his attitude reminds us that there was a time when Christianity was an Asiatic creed—it was the time of the original Gospel. Again and again he seemed to be more Christian than the Christians." Then there were, as always, the usual clever people who believe they can see through everything. Some of them saw in the award the ingenious British hand trying to boost the glory of the Empire; others fancied that the Swedish literary circles, being pro-German, had deliberately tried to embarrass the British ruling classes. There is no end to human cleverness.

The actual facts, however, are simple enough. The first formal proposal was made by the English poet, Sturge Moore, in a letter brief and bald enough to be worth quoting. "Sir," wrote the English poet to the Secretary of the Nobel Committee of the Swedish Academy, "As a Fellow of the Royal Society of Literature of the United kingdom, I have the honour to propose the name of Rabindranath Tagore as a person qualified, in my opinion, to be awarded the Nobel Prize in literature—T.Sturge Moore." The records of the Selection Committee show that this proposal came as a surprise to the Swedish Academy. The two members whose eloquent and powerful support swayed the decision of the

Nobel Committee were Verner von Heidenstam, who was himself awarded the Nobel Prize three years later, and Per Hallstrom, member-Secretary of the Nobel Committee. In his official report to the Committee Per Hallstrom said:

"Undoubtedly it is a question here of something more remarkable than anything that European poetry has to offer at present, but its character is so different, and the whole world out of which it springs so unknown to us that we must hesitate before passing judgement without further evidence and research. In a way it goes against the grain to associate a monetary prize with this purely religious poetry. It is like paying for the Psalms (of David) or the songs of St. Francis."

"To make such comparisons would be ridiculous if it was a question of modern European poetry, however great its merits might be; it is not at all absurd when referring to *Gitanjali* . . . There is no mistaking the exceptional poetic beauty. The mode of expression is of classical simplicity, the image is only the spontaneous language of thought, and it does not need to be moulded into shape, it is even complete through the mere mention of the word. One thinks of the Brahmin lady in Goethe's poem, who scooped up water from a flowing stream with her hands, and the water became solid and malleable in her hands . . . All the English reviewers express the opinion that they are the witnesses of a truly epoch-making phenomenon, not only as regards the understanding of Oriental life, but also as far as its possible influence on European art is concerned . . . One must go to Goethe to find something comparable in modern poetry, but this does not mean that I wish to say that the personalities of the two poets have anything special in common . . . We are told that Tagore's compatriots consider that a new literary period, and the greatest in the history of their language, begins with his appearance. As far as an uninitiated person can guess from a translation, that does not seem to be an exaggeration. It is certain, however, that no poet in Europe since the death of Goethe in 1832 can rival Tagore in noble humanity, in unaffected greatness, in classical tranquillity."

No two regions could be more different from one another than the tropical lowlands of Bengal and the snow-capped highlands of Scandinavia, in physical climate and social environments. The fact that despite these vast differences, the poems written in the Gangetic delta found a response in the heart of a Scandinavian as sincere and deep as any in the hearts of Tagore's own countrymen is a vindication not only of the universal quality of the *Gitanjali* poems but of Tagore's almost fanatic faith that a single heart beats in the breast of mankind, despite the barriers built by patriots, politicians and priests.

No less profound was the impression made by these poems on a young and unknown lad of fifteen in the even more remote region of Iceland, who was to win much later a Nobel Prize for himself—the distinguished novelist, Halldor Laxness. Recalling this impression he writes, "This strange, distant and subtle voice at once found its way to the very depths of my youthful spiritual ear; and ever since, at given moments, I feel its presence in the innermost labyrinths of my mind . . . What an enviable god, this god of Tagore: the Great Friend, the Beloved, the Lotos flower, the unknown man playing a lute in the boat yonder on the river ! . . . Nowadays our god in the west is either the director of the Big All World Firm Inc., or the primitive imaginary playmate of the childish mind. He is the one we cry to in the hours of precipitate danger and in the hour of our death. This is why a spiritual reality like Tagore's probably shall remain only one more eastern wonder to the western mind yet for a long long time to come."

Home and the World

When one knows thee, then alien there is none, then no door is shut.

THIS long sojourn in the West helped to broaden Tagore's sympathies which were already broad enough, and deepened his understanding of the intellectual and spiritual urges that have spurred the western mind to great achievement. From now on he belonged to the world as much as he belonged to India. Or so he believed—not because he became world-famous but because he felt with the world. There have been many men world-famous who were world-scourges, and many who have failed to see beyond their noses. But Tagore made the world's destiny his own and felt deeply the agony if there was suffering or injustice in any part of the world. This world-consciousness which was very real in him exposed him to not a little misunderstanding in his own country.

Of his many foreign friends the two who came to be most closely associated with him and his work in Santiniketan at this time were the two remarkable Englishmen, C.F. Andrews and W. W. Pearson. Being more Christian than missionary both of them broke away from their organisations in order to be free to serve the people in the spirit of Christ as they understood it, and became Tagore's associates and lifelong friends.

Gandhi, not then a Mahatma and, in fact, hardly much known even in his own country, was at that time engaged in his lone and heroic struggle against racial discrimination in South Africa. Tagore who had anticipated, with the true insight of a poet-seer, the advent of the Mahatma in his dramas and verse, was already with him in spirit, so that when Andrews and Pearson left him in November 1913, for South Africa to study the Passive Resistance movement on the spot, they carried with them his goodwill and best wishes for the success of Gandhi's mission. "Let me dwell for a moment longer," recalled Andrews later, "on these early days when Willie Pearson and I had just left Santiniketan, and had landed in South Africa. During that period of new spiritual vision and illumination thoughts of the poet and his asrama would come clear before us in all our conversations. It was the first full flush of our common enthusiasm and love for him and it coloured all our existence with its own bright hues. The very sky itself seemed more glorious as we spoke about him and shared our thoughts together. This was also for us both the happy moment of discovery of a new friendship with Mahatma Gandhi. These two affections were blended into one in a very intimate manner. Often under the stars at night we would sit in the silence and then speak to one another in quiet accents of the wonderful evenings we had spent with our Gurudev on the terrace outside his little room at Santiniketan. Those were golden moments and Mahatma realised with deep sympathy our own hearts' devotion to the poet. He often spoke to us of his own great longing to meet him. Thus we were all drawn together into a single circle of affection."

The end of the year 1913 was marked by Calcutta University conferring a doctorate on Tagore at a special convocation held on 26 December. It had been an eventful and exciting year, rich in rewards and honours, but poor in creative achievement, the only year in the decade which closed with it in which not a single new book of his was published in Bengali, the language of his creative expression. The three books published in London, *The Gardener, The Crescent Moon* and *Chitra,* were all translations. Several songs were, however, written by him during this year, some during his sojourn abroad and some in India. The only one written in the United States in the beginning of the year is significant for its employment of the metaphor of buying and selling. The poet imagines himself carrying his burden of wares and hawking them from place to place. The King threatens to take his wares by force, the aged millionaire offers to buy them with gold, a lovely maiden tempts him with a smile, but the burden remains—until a child playing with a sea-shell pulls him by the sleeve and says, all this is mine. He is relieved of his burden only when he hands over his wares, without any payment, to the child to play with.

These songs which he continued to write, both words and music, and which were published in 1914 in two volumes, *Gitimalya and Gitali,* are some of the finest he ever wrote and continued the religious strain of *Gitanjali,* though the mood was changing. His faith had gained firmness, his confidence in man's destiny was now more robust and his acceptance of life and its responsibilities more gladsome. As he says in one of them, the thorns in his life would find their meaning when the rose blossoms. In a sense Tagore's songs are his greatest gift to his people. Their joy is equally shared by the literate and the illiterate, by the young and the old, and through them is expressed an endless variety of moods and feelings in all their modulations and nuances. The words, rhythms and symbols used are so simple as to seem spontaneous, as if they could not but be what they are. They are his "offerings" in the true sense of the word and because they are the intimate outpourings of his soul, welling forth from the subsoil of racial consciousness, their appeal is universal, He often said in his old age that while all his other achievements might be forgotten, his songs would continue to be sung by his people.

Once a young teacher, a new comer at Santiniketan, asked him bluntly, "You talk so much of God, how much of it is from direct knowledge?" After a moment's silence, Tagore gently replied, "All I can truthfully say is that at times I have felt His presence—more deeply and intimately when I am seized by a new song than in any other mood." He said the same thing in one of these songs: "My song touches Thy feet where Thou standest on the other shore—but me Thou eludest ever."

Many of these songs bear witness to the current crisis of his spirit and the fluctuating moods he was passing through, now of elation, now of a vague foreboding. He is assured that his God wants him to love this world. "If the heart were not meant to love, then why hast Thou filled the morning sky with songs, why this wonder of the stars in the sky, why this profusion of flowers on this earth, why these whispers in the wind?" He knows that he is going to be caught more and more in the turmoil of work and asks reproachfully, "If Thou needs must bind me with work, why then must Thou distract me with so much beauty?"

He is uneasy and not sure what the future has in store for him. "I was going along my lonely path when the light in my hand went out. This sudden storm which is driving me into the dark is now my only companion. I have lost my known path and I stumble, not knowing when and where this night will find its morning." He must calmly face the struggle and not be scared of suffering. "How will you conquer sorrow if you flee from it? The poison must burn itself out in its own fire. Be not afraid of the fire; once it burns itself to ashes, there will be no more burning then."

The nostalgia for the past which had temporarily overwhelmed him in the early years of the century had now faded and his old and manly faith in the forward march of life, in the free commerce of minds which enrich themselves by giving and taking had been fully restored. This is evident from a letter he wrote to Sturge Moore on I May 1914: "Literature of a country is not chiefly for home consumption. Its value lies in the fact that it is imperatively necessary for the lands where it is foreign. I think it has been the good fortune of the west to have the opportunity of absorbing the spirit of the east through the medium of Bible. It has added to the richness of your life because it is alien to your temperament. In course of time you may discard some of its doctrines and teachings but it has done its work—it has created a bifurcation in your mental system which is so needful for all life growth. The western literature is doing the same with us, bringing into our life elements some of which supplement and some contradict our tendencies. This is what we need. It is not enough to charm or to surprise us—we must receive shocks and be hurt. Therefore we seek in your writings not simply what is artistic but what is vivid and forceful. That is why Byron had such immense influence over our youths of the last generation. Shelley, in spite of his vague idealism, roused our minds because of his fanatic impetuosity which is born of a faith in life. What I say here is from the point of view of a foreigner. We cannot but miss a great deal of the purely artistic element of your literature but whatever is broadly human and deeply true can be safely shipped for distant times and remote countries. We look for your literature to bring, us the thundering life flood of the west, even though it carries with it all the debris of the passing moments."

About this time Tagore's young friend, Pramatha Choudhury, who had married his niece Indira, started a literary magazine, *Sabuj Patra* (Green Leaves), which, as its name shows, represented a movement for new experiments in literary writing. Though Choudhury (whose pen-name was Birbal, after the witty courtier of Emperor Akbar) was a brilliant writer himself, the main burden of maintaining the prestige and popularity of the journal fell upon Tagore's shoulders. As though he needed this incentive, he responded to the pressure with an abundance of literary output as remarkable for its quality as for its variety—poems, short stories, essays and novels. The stories he wrote at this period do not have the freshness and charm which mark the stories he wrote in the nineties when he lived in his boat on the Padma and watched the changing landscape of nature and life on its banks with gentle and detached affection and ironic sympathy. These later stories dealt with middle-class life and its problems, in particular the tragedy of woman in a Hindu household, and if they lack the sweet aroma of fresh fruit, they have the appetising smell of well-processed cheese.

The author's irony in exposing the cowardice and selfishness of the smug Hindu husband is as subtle and sharp as his courage is admirable in denouncing injustice perpetrated in the name of holy scriptures and tradition. Haimanti, the brave daughter of a helpless father in the story of that name, finds deliverance in death; the clever, beautiful and strong-willed Mrinal who had a mind of her own redeems her futile existence by her courage in renouncing her husband and home. The story which is entitled "A Wife's Letter" is in the form of a letter which a wife writes to her husband when she leaves him after fifteen years of suppressed agony. She is Tagore's Nora flinging her manifesto of independence in her husband's face. Needless to say, the author was reviled in the Bengali press for his indictment of social injustice—abused by the very leaders who were clamouring against political injustice. In a third story, "Aparichita" (The Unknown Girl) he shows how an educated and spirited Bengali girl is more than a match for the namby-pamby youth who imagined he was doing her favour by condescending to marry her. All these stories are in the first person singular and the central character in each is made to reveal his or her own inmost feelings. Another very beautiful story is "Boshtami", the story of a woman who had renounced her home to become a devotee of God. Tagore had actually known such a woman in a Bengali village and he later described her, with much respect and feeling, in his *Creative Unity*.

The summer holidays were spent in Ramgarh in the Himalayas. At first he was happy and felt as though he had till then been "living on half-rations". He wrote to Andrews, "My life is full". But soon an uneasiness crept over him, followed by a vague but intense agony, a premonition that a great disaster was about to overtake the world he loved so much. There were no menacing clouds in the political horizon and the great war when it came, came suddenly in August. How and why he should have sensed its advent, is difficult to explain. That he felt it and felt it agonisingly is obvious from the letters he wrote and from the testimony of those who were with him and around him at that time. "God knows it is the death pang that is tearing open my heart," he wrote to Andrews. He also expressed the mood in a poem. "Look, there comes the all-destroying. The flood of agony spreads out in a sea of pain, the thunder roars in the dark and the lightning flashes amid the blood-shot clouds—a lunatic shaking with laughter in his sport of death!"

The poet was restless and, as usual when he was so, kept on the move from place to place, now Santiniketan, now Shelidah, now Darjeeling, Agra or Allahabad. When at last the Great War broke out, he did not look upon it as a European misfortune in which Asia was not concerned, much less gloat that England's difficulty was India's opportunity. Nor did he take sides. To him the war was as a wound in the breast of humanity, its pain and horror to be shared by all its limbs, however seemingly far removed. In an address to his students at Santiniketan he emphasised that as the sins of fathers are visited on children, so all humanity must share the guilt and its punishment for whatever crimes are committed by man anywhere. In a moving poem he said: "All the sorrows of the earth, its sins and crimes, its heart-breaks and its lust for violence, have swelled like a tidal wave overleaping the banks, blaspheming the skies. Nevertheless, O ye brave and afflicted ones, hold on to your oars and steer your boat over the howling, demented waves, with hope undying in the breast. Whom do you condemn, my brother? Bow down your head—the sin is yours and mine. It is the ulcer in the heart of Time that has burst at last. The poisoned fumes of the faint heart's funk, the bully's insolence, the vulture's greed, the rancour of the disinherited, the accumulated insults to the divine in man—these have at long last burst through the flesh of Time, scouring earth and sea with their foul breath of destruction."

This and many other poems (including a sonnet on Shakespeare) he wrote during these uneasy months when he moved restlessly from place to place, alternating between anguish and elation, nostalgia and expectation, vaguely apprehensive that he stood on the brink of a new phase of himself. What in him will recede or die and what will emerge, he did not know. All he knew was that he must move on, renew and, if need be, outgrow himself. They were all published in 1916 in a slender volume called *Balaka* (A Flight of Geese). This volume, dedicated to his young English friend Pearson, marks one of the great peaks which Tagore periodically scaled in his Himalayan pilgrimage. The book takes its name from the poem written in Kashmir where the author, watching in the evening " the curving stream of Jhelum glimmering in the dusk like a scimitar," is suddenly roused from his reverie by "the lightning streak of a sound hurtling across the void" and looks up to see a flock of geese winging their way to somewhere far away. This migratory flight of birds symbolises for him the perennial motion in all things, moving or seemingly motionless, the passage of the time spirit, the unending quest of life and of the soul, the eternal cry in the heart of the universe: "Not here, not here, but somewhere else!"

The echo of this cry reverberates through all the poems in the volume which, whatever their theme and form, are all hymns to the endless wonder of the motion that keeps all things in a flux, renewing and surpassing themselves—be the object addressed

Shahjahan, the royal builder of the fabulous Taj Mahal, or the lost angel of the poet's life, the deceased sister-in-law, Kadambari. He must have chanced upon an old photograph of hers, for the poem is addressed to it. The memory is painful, no doubt, but instead of luxuriating in the sorrow as he would have done in his youth, the poet finds comfort in the thought that in a sense she is even more real in his life now than before. "If you are not before my eyes, it is because you are the very light that shines in them–you are the green in the earth's green, the blue in the heaven's blue, the inmost rhythm in the harmony of my universe. No one knows—not even I—that you are the music in my songs, the poet within the poet."

The same idea, of life perpetually renewing itself, of Winter throwing off its mask to reveal itself as Spring, is embodied in a delightful phantasy which he wrote for his boys at Santiniketan–*Phalguni* (The cycle of Spring). The play was staged both at Santiniketan and in Calcutta, Tagore playing the double role of the Poet and the blind Baul or wandering minstrel. The plot is very thin, in fact there is hardly a plot at all, just enough to provide an excuse for a riot of song, dance and gaiety to express the author's mood in spring. A group of young urchins pursue the old man Winter and disrobe him, only to discover that he is none other than Spring. Edward Thompson who was present at the first performance felt that "it was wild-wood music, such as the spirit of the bamboo, the spirit of the south wind, the spirit of the flowers might sing, if they took human voice." When the play was staged in Germany during the author's visit in 1921, one student from the audience stood up and said in broken English (as Rabindranath recalled later) that they had been told that an old man from the east would speak to them, but what he had heard was the youth of the east speaking.

Soon after writing *Phalguni,* Tagore had his first meeting with Gandhi in March 1915. Having done his work and won his fight in South Africa, Gandhi had returned to his country but had not yet made up his mind what he was going to do or where he was going to stay. He had earlier disbanded his Phoenix colony and school in South Africa and had sent the boys, about twenty, to

India. Andrews who was the link between the two great men had suggested that the boys might be accommodated in Santiniketan until Gandhi came and made his own arrangements for an asrama of his own. Tagore readily agreed and the boys had been in Santiniketan some months when Gandhi came to see them. It must have been interesting to watch these two sets of boys living side by side, Tagore's little Ariels, singing and dancing and romping about, and Gandhi's little saints, too wise and sober for their age. But they got on splendidly and Tagore grew to love Gandhi's boys as his own. He found them "very nice" and "very lovable", but as he wrote in a letter to Andrews, he wished they were not so "completely nice".

Although Gandhi stayed for hardly a week in Santiniketan and had not yet become the Mahatma whose mere name was to cast a spell in later years, he left a permanent impress of his personality on the inmates of Santiniketan. This was his second visit to the asrama; he had come a month earlier when Tagore was not there. The six days that Gandhi spent in Santiniketan during this visit laid the foundation of a lifelong friendship between him and Tagore, two makers of modern India, and brought into relief the obvious contrasts as well as the veiled kinship between their personalities and the dynamics of their idealism. So glaring and seemingly irreconcilable looked the contrast that many of their respective admirers were misled by it. Beneath the mask of what seemed contrary was a kinship so deep and subtle that only they themeselves were aware of it, barring a few common friends and admirers of exceptional sensibility, like an Andrews or a Jawaharlal Nehru. The so-called disciples or "devout followers" of both saw mostly the grimace in the mask and not eh smile concealed behind it.

In his characteristic, matter-of-fact and practical manner, Gandhi looked around, made friends with all, put his finger on the weak spots and taught the inmates of the asrma how to implement their own ideals better. He told them that they must do wholly without hired labour and take upon themselves the responsibility of keeping the asrama clean, as they kept their own bodies, clean, and of running all its services including the cooking of food, washing dishes, etc. The young are always drawn to new adventures and both the pupils and the teachers warmly welcomed Gandhi's advice. When Tagore was told of it, he smiled and said that the experiment contained the key to Swaraj. And so on 10 March 1915 the experiment was launched. On the following day Gandhi left for Rangoon. That the experiment did not last very long surprised neither Gandhi nor Tagore. Their idealism was not without a hard core of realism and a sense of humour. The memory of the experiment survives in the observance of 10 March every year as Gandhi Day (Gandhi Punyaha) when all the paid servants are given a holiday and the teachers and pupils do all the cooking themselves and give an annual spring-cleaning to the asrama. A typical example of recurrent symbolism in Indian tradition.

Gandhi's reformist zeal did not spare the poet's personal diet either. Watching him eat *luchis* one evening at dinner, Gandhi remarked that white-flour pancake fried in ghee which the poet was eating with obvious relish was poison. Rabindranath smiled and said softly, "It must be a very slow poison, for I've been eating it for about half a century now."

Gandhi and Tagore—the saint who strove to make politics holy and the poet who made holiness seem beautiful. Gandhi's practice was always in advance of his ideology; Tagore had wings to his thoughts and feet to his practice. However firm and unfaltering the feet, they could not keep pace with the wings. Gandhi, the stern ascetic, was more humane than the humanist; a kill-joy in theory he brought comfort to millions of human hearts. Tagore, the pagan-lover, saw heaven where Gandhi failed to see it. These two faces of modern India, one rugged, one chiselled, both equally luminous, represent two aspects of Indian *sadhana* or realisation of life's truth. Few felt their join impact more sensitively or understood their inner kinship better than the saintly Englishman, C.F. Andrews. Let him estimate them whom he loved so well: "Personally, I have never in my whole life met anyone so completely satisfying the needs of friendship and intellectual understanding and spiritual sympathy as Tagore. His very presence always act as an inspiration. To be with him, to be at unison with him in some creative work, is a privilege which it is very difficult to state in words. Indeed, it has been by far the greatest privilege of my life. No one has been more fortunate than I have been in personal friendships. Side by side with the friendship with the poet, I have had the supreme happiness of a second personal friendship with Mahatma Gandhi. His marvellous spiritual genius has appealed to me in a very different way. For his character, in his own way, is as great and as creative as that of Tagore himself. It is, however, of more ascetic order. It has about it rather an air of religious faith of the Middle Ages than that of modern times. Tagore is essentially a modern; Mahatma Gandhi is the St. Francis of Assissi of our own days."

The Governor of Bengal, Lord Carmichael, who at the beginning of 1914 had formally handed over to the poet the Nobel Prize Diploma and Medal on behalf of the Swedish Academy, visited Santiniketan on 20 March, nine days after Gandhi had left. Having won recognition abroad, Tagore had become respectable in the eyes of the British Government of India. Gone were the days when the Government servants were warned not to send their children to his school. Now the highest British dignitary in Bengal came to pay his respects. Tagore gave the honoured guest a cordial reception and elaborate arrangements were made in the asrama to welcome him. "Patriots" were not wanting who criticised Tagore for honouring the representative of foreign rulers. Tagore knew that whatever he did would seem wrong in the eyes of some of his countrymen, that he would never cease to be maligned for his radicalism and reviled for his conservatism. He knew it and yet was hurt by public criticism. He would not learn the politician's art of wooing the public and yet felt sorry that he could not win the hearts of his people who never forgave him for not sharing their superstitions, the biggest of which was the patriotic delusion that they were God's chosen people.

However brave the reflections in his writings on the vanity of fame or popular goodwill, Tagore was in fact vulnerable to unjust criticism, and often the criticism was unjust, if not malicious. In a letter to Andrews dated 1 February 1915, he tried to analyse this susceptibility: "You are right. I had been suffering for a time from deep depression and weariness. But I am sane and sound again, and willing, to live another hundred years, if critics would spare me. At that time I was physically tired; therefore the least hurt assumed a proportion that was perfectly absurd. However, I am glad that there is still that child in me who has its weakness for the sweets of human approbation. I must not feel myself too far above my critics. I don't want my seat on the dais; let me sit on the same bench with my audience and try to listen as they do. I am quite willing to know the healthy feeling of disappointment when they don't approve of my things; and when I say, 'I don't care', let nobody believe me." Ten years earlier he had said in a song: "They call you mad. Wait for tomorrow and keep silent. They will bring their wreath." The tomorrow took a long time to come.

That he was "sane and sound again," whatever the cause of the previous fit of depression, is evident enough in the famous "Four Chapters" he was writing at that time for the journal, *Sabuj Patra,* which were later published as the novel, *Chaturanga,* a magnificent testament of the sanest and soundest common sense. Compact, well-knit and tense, with an undercurrent of sympathy and irony of which blend Tagore could be a master when he was detached and not overcome by sentiment or bias, this short novel is one of Tagore's best and has been described by a competent critic as "a work of art without blemish". There are only four chapters and four characters in the book one of whom tells the story. The central character is Sachish, a young and ardent idealist whose quest for truth and inner fulfilment is traced through different phases. He has grown under the influence of his uncle Jagmohan whose aggressive rationalism and innate nobility of mind had turned him early in life into an atheist and a positive humanist. Jagmohan's God-denying humanism is contrasted in the first chapter with his brother's God-believing meanness and cupidity.

Sachish, revolted by his father's sickening orthodoxy, is a follower of his uncle's way of life. He comes across a young girl, an orphan, who had been seduced by his own elder brother and thrown on the streets. He takes the girl, now pregnant, to his uncle's house who gives her shelter and treats her as his daughter.

To safeguard her future Sachish offers to marry her. But the girl, though she is grateful to her benefactors, is really in love with her seducer and prefers to commit suicide to the shame of marrying anyone else. This incident comes as a shock to Sachish's cultivated belief in human rationalism. Soon after, the city of Calcutta is scourged by plague and as there were not enough hospitals in the city, the humanitarian uncle turns his own house into a hospital for the poor, himself nursing the victims. He catches the dread disease and dies. "He deserved it," comments his orthodox brother.

Sachish is disconsolate after his uncle's death and wanders about in search of a faith to fill the void in his life. He falls into the company of a typical Vaishnav saint and becomes his disciple. He is happy in his "escape" until a young and lively widow, an unwilling and rebellious disciple of the Guru, distracts his attention. This girl, Damini, like Binodini of the earlier *Chokher Bali,* is one of Tagore's few characters so full-blooded and real that no reader having known them ever forget them. Damini loves Sachish but cares little for the Guru the facade of whose piety does not deceive her. Sachish who believes that human love is a snare tries to avoid her but cannot help being conscious of her. Once when the party has camped for the night in a cave, Sachish cannot sleep, haunted by a vague dread of some primeval beast hidden in the cave about to creep over him with its clammy paws. Just then he feels a touch on his feet. In panic he kicks hard. It is Damini who receives the kick in her breast.

Unable to escape from thoughts of Damini, Sachish finally begs her to release him from her spell by voluntarily renouncing her desire for him. She understands with her woman's insight the hell he is passing through and understands also that in his frame of mind, having known love only as the beast of desire that stands between him and his quest, he is incapable of accepting her love in its true meaning. She gives up her chase of him and marries the fourth character in the novel, Sribilash, the narrator, who is deeply in love with her. She fills his days with happiness, but not for long, for she dies soon after—the kick she had received in the cave has caused an injury from which she never recovers. Her renunciation of him releases Sachish not only from her spell but from his obsession with a religious pursuit that was little better than an escape. He returns to his humanitarian mission in Calcutta, a sadder and wiser man.

In the same year as *Chaturanga,* was published Tagore's major novel of this period, *Ghare Baire* (The Home and the World), in which each of the three major characters reveals his or her own thoughts in a dairy. The setting is the political excitement in the stormy years of the first decade of the century when Tagore himself had been drawn into its vortex for a time. This novel is his answer to the critics who had accused him of desertion. The answer went home, for the novel only provoked worse abuse. The portrayal of the revolutionary patriot who has no scruples to deceive his friend and seduce his trustful wife was so vividly drawn that the author was accused of being immoral and unpatriotic. For three years after its publication the critics continued to tear the novel to pieces—a tribute to its impact on their minds.

The atmosphere of the novel is tense, reflecting the tensions of the period it depicts. It was a stormy period of national upsurge, of an upheaval of violent passions long submerged, of a clash of ideals and interests. The sombre narrative scintillates with brilliant sparks of thought as the flints of opposing arguments strike against one another. It is a clash all along, of the old with the new, of real politik with idealism, of the means with the end, of love claimed as of right and love given of free will, of home-bred virtue with the wild wind from the outside. Although a poet's manifesto, the novel is equally a testament of Gandhi's philosophy of non-violence, of love and truth, of his insistent warning that evil means must vitiate the end, however nobly conceived. As one reads it one begins to understand, better than any expositions can demonstrate, how akin Tagore was to Gandhi in spirit, whatever the seeming difference in their ways.

The plot, like all Tagore's plots, is very simple—the usual, age-old triangle, two men and a woman. Nikhil, the titled nobleman, owning vast estates in the country, is an unusual representative of his class, almost too good to be true, although Tolstoy had already made the type familiar, both in his life and in his novels, and

Tagore himself had tried to live up to it when he was managing his family estates. Nevertheless, the character, as it emerges in the novel, is more shadowy than real. His friend and protege, Sandip, the patriotic firebrand, splendid wind-bag and shameless seducer, on the other hand, is far more real and convincing—except that he speaks a language which only a Tagore could put in his mouth.

Bimala is Nikhil's wife, an ordinary, domesticated type who becomes extraordinary when her passion and her vanity are aroused—a real and convincing character. She comes under the spell of Sandip's fiery eloquence; the admiration soon warms into attraction under the hot breath of Sandip's sensual vitality. "So long I had been," writes Bimala in her diary, "like a small river at the border of a village. But the tide came up from the sea, and my breast heaved; my banks gave way and the great drum-beats of the sea waves echoed in my mad current. I could not understand the meaning of that sound in my blood." Nikhil knows what is going on between his wife and his friend and could easily put a stop to it, but he values love only when given out of free will and in open competition with the outside world and not as an obligation or under duress. What happens between the three, let the reader find out for himself, for the book is available in English translation—*The Home and the World.*

A significant title in more senses than the one employed for the novel. Tagore himself was tossing between his love of his home and the lure of the world. Having experienced the stimulus of a triumphant sojourn abroad, the comparatively monotonous and dull routine of life at home seemed insipid and enervating. He was restless once again. "I have the call of the open road, though most of the roads are closed," he wrote to Andrews in June 1915. "I am in a nomadic mood, but it is becoming painful to me for want of freedom. I am carrying, as it were, my tents on my back, instead of living in them." The brave music of the distant drum was calling him. There were new worlds to explore, fresh minds to meet. He felt he had something to say and his voice must reach the world's conscience. Europe was demented in an orgy of mutual slaughter, but Japan and America were detached and sane (so he imagined). They would lend their ear to his message of human brotherhood and the desperate urgency of the peoples of East and West learning to understand that the two hemispheres formed one single whole.

All through the year 1915 he had played with the idea of visiting Japan and wrote in a letter to Rothenstein on 4 April, "I give up Japan—at least for the present. Not for any sudden failure of courage or enthusiasm but for the same blessed reason that brings a modern war to its halt. My finance is hopeless, mainly owing to the European complication." But he did not have to give it up for long. In may 1916, while the War was still on, he sailed for Japan, accompanied by Andrews and Pearson. He travelled by a Japanese ship and was much impressed with the discipline, efficiency and friendliness of the captain and the crew. As he put it, his taste of Japan began with a Japanese ship, as the taste of Indian food begins at the finger-tips.

In Rangoon where the party halted for two days, he was charmed with the gay-coloured Burmese women who work harder than their men. In Hong Kong he was even more impressed with the grace and strength which physical labour, well regulated, can impart to the human body. Watching the Chinese labourers at work on the quay, their half-bare bodies glistening in the light, he wrote: "Their bodies were spare and perfectly moulded, not the slightest superfluity anywhere . . . Work seemed to vibrate from their bodies like music from lutes." What he then noted about the future of China is worth recalling: "Seeing such strength, skill and joy of work thus concentrated in one place, I realised what an amount of power is being stored throughout the land in this great nation. When such an immense power gets its own modern vehicle, i.e. when science comes under its control, what power on earth will be able to offer it resistance? Then to its genius for work will be added the materials to work with. All the nations that are now enjoying the fruits of the earth dread that awakening of China, and want to put off that day unwelcome for them."

Tagore stayed in Japan for a little over three months, visiting several places. Many aspects of Japanese life and landscape attracted him; in particular, the people's sense of discipline, their fortitude of body and mind, their self-restraint in expression, their love of beauty and the charm of their women. Commenting on the fact that he "never heard anyone singing in the streets since I have been here," he noted in his Diary: "The hearts of these people are not resonant like a waterfall, but silent like a lake. All the poems of theirs that I have hitherto heard are picture-poems, not song-poems."

The influence of these poems remarkable for their brevity may have worked on his mind when he yielded to the requests of young ladies to inscribe something on their fans or autograph books. These stray epigrams or verses were later collected and published as *Stray Birds* and are some of them translations of his Bengali verses and some written directly in English. They are by no means literature of any high.quality, though many of them are interesting in themselves. Some of them are quoted below as specimens:" I cannot choose the best. The best chooses me." "Every child comes with the message that God is not yet discouraged of man." "He who is busy doing good finds no time to be good." One was prophetic of Japan's future: "Your idol is shattered in the dust to prove that God's dust is greater than your idol."

Though the Japanese welcomed Tagore with enthusiasm—the poet-seer from the land of the Buddha—the enthusiasm cooled off as soon as he warned them in his lectures against imitating, not the humane values of the western civilisation but its lust for power and its blind worship of collective egoism in the name of the Nation. "Europe is supremely good in her beneficence where her face is turned to all humanity; and Europe is supremely evil in her maleficent aspect where her face is turned upon her own interest, using all her power of greatness for ends which are against the infinite and the eternal in Man." He admired the Japanese for being modern but reminded them that "True modernism is freedom of mind, not slavery of taste. It is independence of thought and action, not tutelage under European schoolmasters. It is science but not its wrong application in life." But his words fell on deaf ears, for was he not the poet of a nation defeated and enslaved?

In September 1916 Tagore sailed for Seattle. The lectures

delivered during this second visit to the United States were published in two volumes, *Nationalism* and *Personality*. While the lectures in the latter volume were much appreciated, embodying as they do some of Tagore's profound reflections on art, education, philosophy and the divine potential in the human personality, his forthright denunciation of nationalism as a cult of evil provoked violent attacks in the American press. The *Detroit Journal* warned the people against "such sickly sachharine mental poison with which Tagore would corrupt the minds of the youth of our great United States."

The relentless schedule of an organised lecture tour and the tempestuous tempo of American life to which he was not used and which jarred on his sensibilities proved a strain on Tagore's health, aggravated by an ugly incident instigated by his own countrymen during his stay in San Francisco. Some excitable young Indians, more patriotic than intelligent, belonging to a revolutionary organisation known as the "Gadar" Party, had misconstrued his denunciation of nationalism as betrayal of Indian nationalist aspirations. Tagore had been Knighted by the British Government the previous year and these impetuous patriots, putting the two together, assumed that this Indian Knight was a British agent who had been sent to the United States to blacken his own nation. The British authorities, on the other hand, uneasy and resentful of Tagore's uncompromising denunciation of war, were apprehensive of the possible effect of his speeches on the American mind. They were therefore not averse to encouraging rumours that the Indian poet was being used as a tool of German propaganda to alienate American sympathy from the British and Allied war effort. Thus made the innocent target of mud-slinging from both camps, Tagore was deeply hurt and mortified, and became more homesick than ever. He terminated his contract for the lecture–tour prematurely and sailed for Japan in January 1917.

After a month's stay in Japan on his way back, Tagore returned to India in March 1917. There he saw the face, not of aggressive nationalism, but of repressed nationalism being trampled under foot by the very country whose youth were dying elsewhere in defence of their own nation. And yet it was a brave British lady whose voice was at that time most eloquently raised on behalf of India. Annie Besant who had advocated Home Rule for India was interned by an order of the Madras Government and Tagore who admired her for her many great qualities made a public protest against her internment. He was once again being drawn into the political arena of which the stormy centre was no longer confined to Bengal. He was now too important to be left alone by his people and, as ever, too impatient to keep quiet when he saw his people suffer. At a public meeting in Calcutta he captured the hearts of his audience by singing a patriotic song freshly composed. At the end of the year when the Indian National Congress met for its annual session in Calcutta he recited on the opening day a long poem which has come to be known as "India's Prayer". He received a great ovation from all the political leaders gathered on the occasion.

Tagore's health was breaking down; the mental strain had proved too great, not only the strain of work and engagements but deeper strain of the dilemma within him, the perpetual struggle between the poet and the patriot, or between the poet and the prophet. When the poet had the upper hand, he wanted nothing but to sing, to be able to watch the panorama of nature and life," to be glad and good-for-nothing," as he put it. When the patriot or the prophet was roused, he would notice that God's trumpet lay in the dust and it became his duty to pick it up and give a call to battle. He was aware of this conflict and this vacillation and knew also that his own primary duty or dharma was as a singer, as God's minstrel and not his soldier. "Preaching I must give up," he had written earlier in a letter to Andrews, "and also trying to take up the role of beneficent angel to others. I am praying to be lighted from within, and not simply to hold a light in my hand."

But he could hardly help hold a light in hand also. The doctors enjoined complete rest. That the doctors' orders were observed more in the breach than otherwise is obvious from the number of letters, written in his own hand, day after day. One of them, in reply to Gandhi's query, is of particular interest in view of the language controversy in India which has persisted to this day. While agreeing with Gandhi that "Hindi is the only possible national language for interprovincial intercourse in India," he went on to add that it was "truly a foreign language to the Madras people," and that for this and various other reasons "Hindi will have to remain optional in our national proceedings until a new generation of politicians, fully alive to its importance, pave the way towards its general use by constant practice as a voluntary acceptance of a national obligation."

The political situation in the country was getting increasingly out of hand. Tagore's warning to his people was coming sadly true. For lack of adequate constructive channels, the impetuosity of the Bengali youth driven underground was exploding in terrorist activities. The British Government, now confident of victory in Europe, retaliated brutally. Violence must be put down with greater violence, hatred met with greater hatred. This age–old philosophy of power was working its havoc. Tagore who had never believed in terrorism, even for legitimate patriotic ends, and had courted unpopularity by raising his voice against it, could not remain indifferent to the suffering of these brave young men under the heavy hand of British repression, How much he strove on their behalf privately—apart from his impassioned public protests—is indicated by the following letter addressed to Mr Gourlay (Private Secretary to the Governor of Bengal) on 18 February 1918, when he was still under doctors' orders not to exert himself in any way: "When I wrote to you last I thought it would be of no loss to anybody in the world if I gave up my attempt at rectifying wrongs and stick to literature. But occasions come when to remain in the shelter of one's own special vocation becomes a crying shame. And a particularly harrowing account of the helpless condition of a state prisoner having come to my notice from a trustworthy source, I am compelled to write to you again." This was only one of many such cases he espoused and each caused him considerable emotional stress.

Added to this strain was the anxiety caused by the serious illness of his eldest and most dearly loved daughter Bela who died in May the same year. On 28 February he had written to Pearson who was then in China: "I have come once again to Calcutta from Santiniketan, for Bela's condition has grown worse. Death is the obverse side of life, it is one with it, and I do not look upon it with any particular fear. But disease is evil, and when we do not know how to fight it, it makes one's heart rebellious."

How rebellious his heart was growing is evident from the stories and incidents he was narrating in verse which were published in the same year as *Palataka* (The Fugitive). In the poems of *Balaka* published two years earlier his imagination had taken wings and soaring heavenwards had watched with serene confidence the changeless beauty of the changing universe, in which everything is in perpetual motion, moving towards something beyond, no one knows what or where, but the motion itself was joy, an end in itself. In *Palataka* the poet has come down to earth and broods on life's pathos and irony, its fugitive joys and fragile claims.

The stories are told very simply, the verse is free and flexible, the metre keeps pace effortlessly with the tempo of the narrative, the language is colloquial and racy. The stories are little sad episodes from everyday life, mostly dealing with the circumscribed life of woman in a Hindu household, her frustrations and her nobility and strength of suffering. They are told with great delicacy and tenderness of feeling free from sloppy sentimentalism. Written in the same year in which he saw his eldest daughter suffer and die, they bear unmistakable traces of his personal sorrow—a sorrow which, because he bore it with fortitude and humility, has only deepened his sympathy with all that lives and suffers.

No indictment of the Hindu joint family could be more devastating, the more so because wholly devoid of rancour, than the monologue uttered on her death-bed by the daughter-in-law who has drudged patiently for twenty-two years in the service of husband and his family. Now as she lies dying she refuses all medicine, for living itself has become a disease which only death could heal. She wants the windows of the room to be thrown open to let the air blow in, precursor of the greater freedom that lies ahead, The death-bed is her bridal bed, for by it waits Death the bridegroom in whose arms she will find the joy she missed in life.

There is the little Manjuli married off to a man "five times her age" by her self-righteous father, always smoking the hookah and quoting scriptures. Soon she returns home a widow and grows into an attractive woman. When her mother, heart-broken at her daughter's wasted youth, dies Manjuli drudges day and night to serve her father. But the old rheumatic widower cannot do with out a wife and goes off to marry a young bride, having found adequate sanction in his scripture. When he returns, the house is empty, for Manjuli disillusioned and wiser has eloped with the neighbour, a doctor who had always loved her and whom she had always loved in her heart. The angry father is horrified at her wickedness and curses her. Both these tales, named "Mukti" and "Nishkriti" respectively, show the way to "deliverance".

Another touching episode contrasting a woman's humanity with male egoism is called "Phanki" which may be translated as " Deceiving" or "Evading". It is narrated by the husband whose 23-year old wife Binu has fallen seriously ill and is advised change of air by the doctor. For the first time in her married life Binu gets a respite from her cramped and inhibited existence in her in-laws' joint household where all she could get of her husband was in furtive snatches "like a patchwork of broken sentences." The big eyes in her wasted face shine with delight as they now travel together by train westwards. At a wayside station where the train is to be changed, Binu is moved by the tale told her by the porter's wife Rukmini and asks her husband to give Rukmini twentyfive rupees for her daughter's wedding. The husband humours the sick wife by telling her that he has done so when in fact he gave Rukmini only two rupees, along with a scowl and a threat that he would report her to the station master for harassing the passengers if she did not disappear from his wife's sight. Two months later Binu dies, full of gratitude to her husband for filling the last days of her life with perfect happiness. The disconsolate husband cannot forget the deception he had practised on his trusting and loving wife who because she was happy wanted to share her happiness with all and sundry. On his way back he halts at the same station and looks frantically for Rukmini to make amends. But Rukmini is nowhere to be found.

The ghastly massacre of Jallianwala Bagh at Amritsar on 13 April 1919 was followed by a reign of terror under Martial Law. So strict was the censorship on press, so heavy the iron curtain that no news of the tragedy and the subsequent horrors was made public for several weeks. When the news trickled through at last and reached Tagore he was deeply perturbed, and cancelling an important engagement in Santiniketan, hurried to Calcutta where he invited the political leaders to organise a public meeting of protest over which he offered to preside, but even the leaders were so confused and unnerved that his offer came to nothing. He then did what his own conscience dictated. He lived up to his own song written years ago: "If they are afraid and cower mutely facing the wall, then O thou of evil luck, open thy mind and speak out alone." Without telling any one and without taking even his own son into confidence, he wrote a letter to the Viceroy, Lord Chelmsford, on the night of 29 May, returning his Knighthood and had the letter published the following morning. After reminding the Viceroy that the brutality of the measures taken was "without parallel in the history of civilised government," he went on: "The very least I can do for my country is to take all consequences upon myself in giving voice to the protest of the millions of my countrymen, surprised into a dumb anguish of terror. The time has come when badges of honour make our shame glaring in the incongruous context of humiliation, and I for my part wish to stand, shorn of all special distinction, by the side of those of my countrymen who their so-called insignificance are liable to suffer a degradation not fit for human beings."

It was not the renunciation of Knighthood, which in any case added little to his stature, but the courage with which he voiced his people's anguish which fear had hushed in every other breast that gives its historic importance to the letter. It was a gesture which restored the self-respect of the nation and gave his people courage and faith at a time when they were sorely needed. The British ruling authorities never forgave what they deemed an unheard-of impertinence.

The Eagle-Sized Lark

Thou art the sky and
thou art the nest as well.

The sweet singer who had been content with his lone pilgrimage between his nest and the sky had now been caught in the world's mesh. The messenger of freedom will himself no longer be free. To *be* god would no more suffice; he must *do* good. He had won the world and the world in turn had won him. He would now seek his home everywhere in the world and would bring the world to his home. And so the little school for children at Santiniketan became a world-university, Visva-Bharati, a centre of Indian culture, a seminary for eastern studies and a meeting place of the east and the west. The poet selected for its motto a Sanskrit verse: *Yatra visvam bhavati eka-nidom*–where the whole world meets in one nest.

The idea had germinated in his mind since his last tour of Japan and the United States and he made his first public announcement of it at a special gathering in Santiniketan on 22 December 1918. On almost the same day three years later the University was formally inaugurated. During this interval the nuclei of several branches of learning and the arts were laid; in course of time they grew and several more were added. The University, like its predecessor the School, was no doubt the product of a poet's dream but like many dreams when it materialised it turned out to be a pointer to the future. Tagore had always believed that "on each race is laid the duty to keep alight its own lamp of mind as its part in the illumination of the world. To break the lamp of any people is to deprive it of its rightful place in the world festival." Once India had such a mind which was lit by its own flame, fed with its own oil. Today the University graduates had become little better than "rag-pickers at other people's dustbins."

"The mischief is," as he put it, "that as soon as the idea of a

University enters our mind, the idea of a Cambridge University, Oxford University, and a host of other European Universities, rushes in at the same time and fills the whole space. We then imagine that our salvation lies in a selection of the best points of each, patched together in an eclectic perfection. We forget that the European Universities are living, organic parts of the life of Europe, where each found its natural birth. Patching up noses and other small missing fractions of our features with skins from foreign limbs is allowed in modern surgery; but to build up a whole man by piecing together foreign fragments is beyond the resources of science, not only for the present time, but let us fervently hope for all time to come."

Tagore now had an additional incentive to travel. He needed it. He was restless. The world's adulation was like an intoxicant; he wanted more of it. It is true that it was necessary for him to travel to secure for his project both publicity and material resources, but the necessity was welcome because of an inner and personal need. In a letter of 15 April 1918, he was frank about it. "You may have read in books that some birds leave their nests at certain times and fly away over the sea. I am such a bird. From time to time something calls me from beyond the ocean and my wings flutter. So I have arranged to board a ship at the beginning of May and cross the Pacific Ocean." But for some reason the foreign tour did not materialise. He had therefore to content himself with travelling in his own country. He made an extensive tour of south India visiting several towns where he lectured on his educational ideals. This was followed by a tour of western India during which he presided over the Gujarati Literary Conference in Ahmedabad and spent some time with Mahatma Gandhi at his newly founded asrama on the bank of Sabarmati.

This period, 1917-19, hectic with political and educational activities, was comparatively less crowded with new literary creations. The only two important and original works in Bengali written during these years were *Palataka* (Fugitive), published in 1918, and *Lipika* (Sketches), published much later in 1922. His publications of 1917 are either translations of Bengali works or lectures written directly in English: *My Reminiscences, Sacrifice and*

Other Plays, The Cycle of spring, Personality and *Nationalism.* But though comparatively meagre in volume, the character of his Bengali compositions of the period reveals a very high quality of thought, imagination and feeling and marks a new departure in technique and a fresh field for experimentation.

Palataka has been referred to above. The other volume, *Lipika,* written in 1919, is of an altogether different kind. It consists of short pieces or sketches, some descriptive, some allegorical, some reflective, some satirical and some reminiscent. They are written in prose, but a prose which has all the rhythm and music and elusive beauty of poetry. It is possible that the author wanted consciously to capture in Bengali prose the artless beauty of rhythm and expression he had unconsciously achieved in his English translations of *Gitanjali.* On the other hand, these pieces are strangely reminiscent of the prose-poems he had written thirty-five years earlier as dedicatory offerings to the memory of his sister-in-law after her sudden and tragic death in 1884 and which were published as *Pushpanjali* (Flower Offering). Her thought is certainly present in some of these pieces with their tender and wistful brooding as he looks back on the long road he has left behind, strewn with memories like lost melodies. There is no self-pity, no undercurrent of grievance in these recollections which are instinct with wisdom which comes of "sorrow that has now turned into peace."

The general and dominant mood, however, is one of reflection rather than of feeling, of calm intellectual detachment, of a playful subtlety of thought which occasionally drifts into conceits. The satirical pieces are full of irony and wisdom without bitterness. One of them called *Tota Kahini* (The Parrot's Training) exposes the folly of mechanical textbook education against which he had protested all his life. A poor bird had to be educated, for it was disgraceful that in a civilised society it should go about merely hopping and chirping and being happy. So a golden cage had to be built for it and learned pundits engaged to devise suitable system of teaching. The paraphernalia devised was so stupendous that every one remotely connected with the cage prospered. But the poor bird died. "The Raja poked its body with his finger. Only the inner stuffing of book leaves rustled."

Two other little satires may be referred to in passing—"Trial of the Horse" and "Old Man's Ghost". The former is really the trial of Man whose cupidity and craftiness ignore nature's design, harnessing all things, living and non-living, to his own use. When the gods wake up from their periodic fit of slumber and discover what man has made of creatures who were designed for other purposes, they frown in anger. Brahma, the chief of the gods, who is in charge of this special portfolio, warns man: "Unless you set free my horse I shall take care that he grows the teeth and claws of the tiger." "That would be ungodly," protests man, "thus to encourage ferocity." Summoning logic and scientific evidence, man explains to Brahma that the horse is not fit for freedom and that it is precisely in the interest of equestrian well-being that man had to invent the harness. The Old Man's Ghost is obsession with Past which rides on the shoulders of Present, subjecting the welfare of the living to a vain glorification of national culture and an unreasoning dread of change.

Unknown to Tagore, a kindred spirit in the west had felt and said the same things about war and nationalism—with even more courage, for Romain Rolland was in the midst of the conflagration in which his own country was deeply involved. "Truth is the same to all nations," he had said, "but each nation has its lies which it speaks of as its idealism." Rolland had been impressed by Tagore's lectures on Nationalism delivered in Japan in 1916 and had immediately recognised in him a spirit akin to his own, one who was like him "above the battle" where hatred and violence drive nations to mutual slaughter and yet not above the battle where the spirit of man defends its banner against unreason and passion. He had translated portions of these lectures into French and had used them in his articles during the war. The war over, he now wrote to Tagore in June 1919 asking him to add his signature to the Declaration of Independence of the Spirit which Romain Rolland had drafted on behalf of the European artists and intellectuals.

Tagore signed the Declaration on 26 June and in a letter

dated exactly two months later Rolland wrote to him: "The reading of Nationalism has been a great joy for me; for I entirely agree with you thoughts, and I love them even more now that I have heard them expressed by you with this noble and harmonious wisdom which, being you own, is so dear to us... After the disaster of this shameful World War which marked Europe's failure, it has become evident that Europe alone cannot save herself. Her thought is in need of Asia's thought, just as the latter has profited from contact with Europe's thought. These are the two hemispheres of the brain of mankind. If one is paralysed the whole body degenerates."

On 15 May 1920 Tagore sailed for Europe, accompanied by his son and daughter-in-law. In England he was happy to meet old acquaintances and to make new ones. He could, however, sense that the atmosphere was not as cordial as one his earlier visit before the war. Much had happened since then. Tagore's condemnation of war, his outspoken comments on the British rule in India and, above all, his renunciation of the Knighthood had resulted in a cooling off of the earlier warmth. Even before the ship had reached the English shores he had sensed the chilly aloofness and arrogance of the Britishers on board and wrote in a letter: "The people here want us to fight their battle and supply them with our raw materials, but they keep us standing outside their doors over which is written on the notice-board: "Trespassers from Asia will be prosecuted." When I think of all this, my thoughts shiver with cold and I feel homesick for the sunny corner in my Santiniketan... He went on to say that he was "already counting the days of my return journey." And yet this foreign sojourn of his was prolonged for more than a year.

A co-passenger on board was the Agha khan who would recite to him Hafiz and other Persian poets. This might explain his writing later from London in a facetious vein: "The poet Hafiz was willing to exchange the wealth of Samarkand and Bokhara for a mole on the cheek of his beloved. I am willing to give the whole of London away for corner in Santiniketan. But London is not mine to dispose of; neither was the wealth of Samarkand and Bokhara and Persian poet's."

The debate in British Parliament on the Jallianwala Bagh tragedy and the public exoneration of General Dyer's heinous conduct in ordering a general massacre of the innocents pained him deeply and undermined his earlier faith in the British sense of justice and humanity. "The unashamed condonation of brutality expressed in their speeches and echoed in their newspapers is ugly in its frightfulness," he commented, and reiterated his faith which he fully shared with Gandhi that "our true slavation lies in our own hands." But as soon as he met the right type of Englishman—and there was no dearth of such—his mood changed to one of faith and elation. A few days earlier he had written to Andrews: "When I am in the west, I feel more strongly than ever that I am received in living world of mind. I miss here my sky and light and leisure, but I am in touch with those who feel and express their need of me and to whom I can offer myself."

A doubt must have gnawed at him at this self-complacent sentiment, for he immediately added: "It is not unlikely that some time hence my thoughts will no longer be necessary to them and my personality will lose its flavour; but does it matter?" However much he was carried away on the waves of self-elation—and it was not unoften—he was too wise not to know in his heart of hearts the vanity of human glory and that in the long run nothings really mattered.

Among the new acquaintances he made in London was the romantic soldier, Lawrence of Arabia, who told him that he was ashamed to go back to that country because the British Government had failed to keep the promise he had made to the Arabs on its behalf. While discussing India's problem Lawrence told Tagore that the only way to win the respect of an Englishman was to hit back harder than he hits, for then he would come to his senses and recognise the other as a brother. Tagore's letters to C.F. Andrews written during this visit show how swift could be the change in his mood from elation to disappointment, and how sharply divergent were the pulls within him of the poet, the patriot and the prophet of international understanding

In Paris Tagore was given a reception at Musée Guimet and made the acquaintance of the distinguished philosopher, Bergson, and the orientalist Sylvain Levi who later visited Santiniketan as the first foreign visiting professor of Visva-Bharati. From Paris Tagore went to Holland where he visited several places, his lectures attracting big audience. After visiting Belgium where he was received in audience by the King, he returned to London where he suddenly decided that he must visit the United States, "for they must ltsten to the appeal of the east."

He landed in New York and addressed several gatherings, both there and in other places. A New York journal reported about his lecture on "A Poet's Religion" at the Brooklyn Civic Forum: "Never has the Forum had as large an audience as that which turned out to hear the famous writer from the east. Hundreds were turned away." But in so far as he had any hopes of raising large funds for his University he was disappointed.

In the beginning he was optimistic, imagining that this young and new world which had just rescued the old world from the suicidal clash of warring nationalisms would respond to his appeal for help to establish an international university, an active centre for promoting human understanding, at Santiniketan. "Our loyalty," he said, "must not be for any land of a limited geography. It should be for the nationality of the common idea, to which are born individuals belonging to various nations, who are carrying their gifts of sacrifice to the one great shrine of Humanity. "He himself believe fervently that though "the past has been for men, the future is for Man," His faith was sincere and robust and no setbacks, now or later, could ever shake it. His disappointment and dejection in America were the result of the failure of his own expectation of material resources, aggravated, no doubt, by the bustle and noise of American life which jarred on his nerves.

That there was something inherently wrong in the commonplace assumption (unfortunately encouraged by some who were near and dear) that his ideal needed American dollars for its realisation, he now and again understood with a sharp stab of pain and shame. In a letter to Andrews of 13 December he confessed: "I am trying to console myself with the thought that something very big and great is going to be the outcome of the effort I am making.

But deep in my heart I know that simplicity of life and endeavour makes for real happiness. When we realise in some measure our ideal of perfection in our work, it matters very little what its dimensions are. Our trust in bigness very often betrays our want of faith in truth."

Four days later, he wrote again: "When all my thoughts were furiously revolving, like dead leaves, in a whirlwind of desire for raising funds, a picture came to my hand; it was that of Sujata offering a cup of milk to Buddha. Its message went deep into my heart. It said to me: 'The cup of milk comes to you unasked when you have gone through your *tapasya'* ... Every morning I sit by my window and say to myself, 'I must not bow my head to this ugly idol worshipped by the west with daily human sacrifice.' I remember that morning at Shelidah when the Vaishnava woman came to me and said, 'When are you coming down from your three-storied building to meet your love under the shade of the trees?' Just now I am on the top storey of the skyscraper to which the tallest of trees dare not send its whisper; but love silently comes to me saying, 'When are you coming down to meet me on the green grass under the rustling leaves, where you have the freedom of the sky and of sunlight and the tender touch of life's simplicity?' I try to say something about money, but it sounds so ludicrous and yet so tragic that my words grow ashamed of themselves and they stop."

This third visit to the States was, however, fruitful in many personal and human contacts which were after all of far greater value than the million dollars he failed to raise. He renewed old acquaintances and made new ones, among them the two remarkable ladies, Helen Keller and Jane Addams. Even more valuable was the foundation laid of a lifelong friendship with Dorothy Straight and Leonard K. Elmhirst whom she later married and who was at that time a student of agriculture at Cornell. Tagore had heard of this young English idealist from a common friend and sent him a telegram to see him in New York. The friendship thus begun grew with the years and Elmhirst later became his chief associate in the planning of a remarkable centre for experiments in regional development of rural education and economy at Sriniketan, a fitting counterpart of the neighbouring cultural and international centre at Santiniketan. Both he and his wife continued to help the Institute with generous financial assistance even after Elmhirst's return to his country.

In March 1921 Tagore returned to London from where he flew to Paris, his first experience of air flight. There he met Romain Rolland whom he had long wished to see. From Paris he went to Strasbourg to address the newly established French University on the "Message of the Forest". Proceeding to Geneva he spoke at the Rousseau Institute on "Education". While he was holidaying at Lucerne, he received the news that a committee formed in Germany, consisting of eminent writers and scholars, had celebrated his sixtieth birth anniversary with a gift of a large collection of German classics to the Visva-Bharati Library.

After brief visits, with lecture engagements, at Hamburg and Copenhagen, Tagore went to Sweden in response to a longstanding invitation from the Swedish Academy. After his address to the Academy the Archbishop of Upsala said, "The Nobel Prize for literature is intended for the writer who combines in himself the artist and the prophet. None has fulfilled these conditions better than Rabindranath Tagore." From Stockholm he came to Berlin where he addressed the University on 2 June. "Scenes of frenzied hero-worship," reported a local paper, "marked a public lecture given by Rabindranath Tagore. In the rush for seats many girls fainted." So large was the number of persons turned away that the lecture had to be repeated the following day. In Munich Tagore met Thomas Mann and several other men of letters and learning. Moved by the physical privations which the people of Germany had to face in the wake of the Armistice, the poet donated the proceeds of his lecture for the benefit of "famished children" of Munich.

The strain, physical and emotional, of the German tour affected his health and he longed to return to India to the quite of Santiniketan. But though he resisted the pressure of several other invitations he could not decline the one received from the Grand Duke of Hesse to be his guest at Darmstadt where he also wanted to see the German philosopher Count Herman Keyserling whom he had met in India during the latter's visit in 1911. Keyserling was perhaps the first foreigner to recognise and appreciate Tagore's genius. The recognition was almost intuitive, for at that time he had merely met Tagore and had not read any of his works. Later, as the acquaintance ripened, his admiration of Tagore knew no bounds. "Rabindranath Tagore is the greatest man I have had the privilege to know," he wrote in 1930. "He is very much greater than his world reputation and his position in India imply. There has been no one like him anywhere on our globe for many and many centuries . . . he is the universal, the most encompassing, the most complete human being I have known."

Tagore stayed in Darmstadt for nearly a week during which there were no official programmes, no receptions and no formal lectures. But crowds used to gather in the grounds attached to the palace and every morning and evening Tagore would come out and meet them and invite questions which he would answer, Count Keyserling acting as his interpreter. He was deeply impressed, not only with the warm affection with which the common citizens welcomed him but with their genuine interest in philosophical and metaphysical problems.

From Germany Tagore went to Vienna to give two lectures and then to Prague where his visit led to a warm personal friendship with the eminent indolgists, M.Winternitz and V. Lesny, both of whom were later invited by him as Visiting Professors at Visva-Bharati. Prof. Lesny was the first foreign scholar to translate Tagore's writings from the original Bengali. He also wrote a biography of the poet which was later translated and published in English. Because of these contacts and friendships Tagore retained a very warm affection for Czechoslovakia. But though the visit was stimulating, he was tired and homesick and returned to India in July 1921, after an absence of nearly fourteen months.

If he imagined that he was returning to peace and quiet, he was soon to be disillusioned. India was seething with unrest, the somnolent masses were being roused by the magic wand of the Mahatma, who had given a call for a nation-wide movement of non-cooperation with the British regime which he described as "satanic". Tagore had himself invoked for years, in his poems, songs and plays, the image of such a deliverer who would give voice to the dumb and strength to the unarmed; and he fully endorsed Gandhi's insistence on non-violence. But actuality hardly ever corresponds with the idea, and however much one may welcome a storm, it is nonetheless distressing when the dust and the grit get into the eye.

The Mahatma, though a more incorrigible idealist than Tagore, was also a revolutionary leader of men and was obliged on occasion to over-dramatise a situation and exaggerate certain aspects of it to rouse adequate mass fervour. Like Nelson he often held the telescope to his blind eye and truthfully declared that he saw nothing. But Tagore who merely watched, and that too with an eagle eye, saw everything. And there was much to make him uneasy. Sudden upsurge of patriotic zeal in a people who had not felt it for a long time and had hardly any historical memories of such phenomena was bound to result in an exaggerated sense of self-righteousness and a contempt for everything foreign. Tagore who had been denouncing this very aspect of nationalism in other countries found the sight extremely painful in his own. Only a few months earlier he had written to Andrews from New York: "The complete man must never be sacrificed to the patriotic man, or even to the merely moral man. To me humanity is rich and large and many-sided."

Not that the Mahatma believed otherwise. He too said, "For me patriotism is the same as humanity. I am patriotic because I am human and humane. My patriotism is not exclusive. I will not hurt England or Germany to serve India . . . A patriot is so much less a patriot if he is a lukewarm humanitarian." But it was not in this light that the vast majority of his followers took their patriotism. Disciples take from the Master not what he wishes to give but what they wish to take.

There were certain other aspects, too , of the non-cooperation campaign which jarred on Tagore's sensibility. He hated the sight of excited crowds gloating over bonfires of foreign-made cloth. he pitied the students being made to give up schools and colleges to become pawns in the hands of politicians. He refused to believe that spinning was the sole panacea for India's economic ills, though he had always pleaded for the revival of cottage industries, including spinning. He could spin yarns, he once said jokingly, more easily than yarn, and looked upon the Congress propaganda for spinning as itself a big political yarn.

Without directly referring to the Mahatma or criticising his leadership, Tagore gave eloquent expression to his faith in the necessity of intellectual and moral cooperation between India and the west in a public lecture in Calcutta entitled *Sikshar Milan* (Meeting of Cultures). So isolated was he even among his own people in Bengal that his speech provoked a rejoinder from the popular Bengali novelist, Sarat Chandra Chatterji, in an article entitled *Sikshar Virodh* (Conflict of Cultures). Soon after, the Mahatma visited Calcutta and on 6 September 1921 the two had a long conference behind closed doors in the poet's house at Jorasanko, the only other person present at the interview being Andrews. No authorised report exists of what transpired, but it was understood that Gandhi had come to persuade Tagore to give open and active support to his political programme. It was equally well understood later that the two had parted as friends, agreeing to disagree.

While Gandhi and Tagore were in conference, a large crowd had gathered outside the house and eager to show its sympathy with what the Mahatma stood for and to teach the world-obsessed poet a lesson, had collected large bundles of foreign cloth from nearby shops and set up a bonfire right in the midst of the open courtyard in Tagore's house. Leonard Elmhirst has related that Tagore himself some time later gave him a gist of his conversation with the Mahatma on that memorable day. It seems that when Gandhi asserted that his movement was based on the principle of non-violence, Tagore said, "Come and look over the edge of my verandah, Gandhiji. Look down there and see what your non-violent followers are up to. They have stolen cloth from the shops in the Chitpore Road, they've lit that bonfire in my courtyard and are now howling round it like a lot of demented dervishes. Is that non-violence?"

The best statement of differences in the outlooks of these two great minds of modern India is given by Romain Rolland, who had the imagination to appreciate and interpret both. His words will bear repetition:

"The controversy between Tagore and Gandhi, between two great minds, both moved by mutual admiration and esteem, but as fatally separated in their feeling as a philosopher can be from an apostle, a St. Paul from a Plato, is important. For on the one side we have the spirit of religious faith and charity seeking to found a new humanity. On the other we have intelligence, free-born, serene and broad, seeking to unite the aspirations of all humanity in sympathy and understanding.

"Tagore always looked upon Gandhi as a saint, and I have often heard him speak of him with veneration. When, in referring to the Mahatma, I mentioned Tolstoy, Tagore pointed out to me —and I realise it now that I know Gandhi better —how much more clothed in light and radiance Gandhi's spirit is than Tolstoy's. With Gandhi everything is nature —modest, simple, pure—while all his struggles are hallowed by religious serenity, whereas with Tolstoy everything is proud revolt against passion. Everything in Tolstoy is violence, even his doctrine of non-violence.

"Yet it was inevitable that the breach between the two men should widen . . . At the time he (Tagore) was not only the 'poet' but the spiritual ambassador of Asia to Europe, where he had asked people to cooperate in creating a world university at Santiniketan. What an irony of destiny that he should be preaching cooperation between Occident and Orient at one end of the world, when at that very moment non-cooperation was being preached at the other end!

"Non-cooperation clashed with his way of thinking, for his mentality, his rich intelligence, had been nourished on all cultures of the world."

What Tagore feared was not Gandhi's spirit of exclusion—he knew that the Mahatma was above it— but that of his followers who would not scruple to inflame prejudice or passion to work up a fever of nationalism. He explained his misgivings to his students in Santiniketan some of whom had been swept off their feet by the Mahatma's appeal to non-cooperate. What does the boycotting of schools and colleges amount to? he asked. What sacrifice are the students called upon to make? Not sacrifice for more complete education but for no education. He was consistent in his opposition to drag students into the muddy waters of politics. More than a decade earlier when he himself was a leader of the Swadeshi movement in Bengal, a group of young students had come and told him that they were prepared to give up their studies if he asked them to do so. When he declined to do so, they went away in anger, doubting his patriotism.

Tagore's misgivings and protest against what he feared was "blind obedience" that might "crush, in the name of some outward liberty, the real freedom of the soul" were eloquently voiced in a public lecture in Calcutta which was later translated into English and published in the *Modern Review* under the caption, "The Call of Truth". "Tagore's noble words," comments Rolland, "some of the most beautiful ever addressed to a nation, are a poem of sunlight, and plane above all human struggles. And the only criticism one can make of them is that they plane too high. Tagore is right from the point of view of eternity. The birdpoet, the eagle-sized lark, as Heine called a master of our music, sits and sings on the ruins of time. He lives in eternity. But the demands of the present are imperious."

Gandhi replied to the poet's challenge in a powerful rejoinder published in his *Young India.* He hailed the poet as the "Great Sentinel" whose warnings against moral pitfalls must be listened to with respect; but—goes on the Mahatma— his misgivings were not justified. Finally, worked up to a moral passion, he admonishes the poet for fiddling when the house is on fire.

"The poet lives for the morrow, and would have us do likewise. He presents to our admiring gaze the beautiful picture of the birds in the early morning singing hymns of praise as they soar into the sky. These birds had their day's food and soared with rested wings in whose veins new blood had flown the previous night. But I have had the pain of watching birds who for want of strength could not be coaxed even into a flutter of their wings. The human bird under the Indian sky gets up weaker than when he pretended to retire. For millions it is an eternal vigil or an eternal trance. I have found it impossible to soothe suffering patients with a song from Kabir . . .

"Give them work that they may eat. 'Why should I, who have no need to work for food, spin?' may be the question asked. Because I am eating what does not belong to me. I am living on the spoilation of my countrymen. Trace the source of every coin that finds its way into your pocket, and you will realise the truth of what I write. Every one must spin. Let Tagore spin like the others. Let him burn his foreign clothes; that is the duty today. God will take care of the morrow."

"Dark and tragic words these!" comments Romain Rolland. "Here we have the misery of the world rising up before the dream of art and crying, Dare deny me existence! Who does not sympathise with Gandhi's passionate emotion and share it? And yet in his reply, so proud and so poignant, there is nevertheless something that justified Tagore's misgivings: *Sileat poeta,* imposing silence on the person who is called upon to obey the imperious discipline of the cause. Obey without discussion the law of Swadeshi, the first command of which is Spin!"

Unwilling to prolong an unnecessary and futile debate with a man whose character he deeply respected and whose advent on the scene he had hoped for and predicted, Tagore kept silent and retired to his favourite retreat in Santiniketan. Had he not earlier admonished himself: "If you cannot march in step with your compatriots in the greatest crisis of their history, beware of saying they are in the wrong, and you in the right! But give up your place in the ranks and go back to your poet's corner and be prepared to meet with ridicule and public disgrace." And so he went back —not to sulk, but to sing. In the darkness of defeat he saw a smile and heard a voice that said, "Your place is with the children, playing on the beaches of the world, and there I am with you." A series of beautiful child-poems were the result, which were later published in 1922 as *Sisu Bholanath,* lyrical interpretation of the child-mind, reminiscent of the poems he had written nearly two decades earlier which had been later published in English as *The Crescent Moon.*

The dejection from which he sought relief in these poems had in fact begun earlier in New York where he had felt a prisoner" in the dungeon of the Castle of Bigness." "My heart is starved," he had wailed. "Day and night I dream of Santiniketan which blossoms like a flower in the atmosphere of the unbounded freedom of simplicity . . . Here I feel every day what a terrible nightmare it is for the human soul to bear this burden of the monster of Arithmetic. It incessantly drivers its victims and yet leads them nowhere. It raises storms of battle which are for sowing broadcast the seeds of future conflict." In the Diary which he began keeping during his voyage to South America two years later, he has described how the suffocation he had suffered in America brought about in its reaction the mood in which these poems were born. The sight of monstrous accumulation of wealth, luxury and power and man's blind and smug belief that this accumulation will keep on piling and will last forever had invoked before his mind the image of Siva Bholanath, the god of supreme detachment and unconcern, whose divine dance makes and unmakes the universe, mocking at man's vanity. The very first poem in the book is an ode to this divine Sisu, the eternal child in Bholanath and to the eternal Bholanath in every child.

These poems are as exquisite as the poems of *Sisu* (*The Crescent Moon*) written nineteen years earlier, and have the same undercurrent of intuitive wisdom in the child's seemingly meaningless prattle with its mother.

" I sleep and awake, sleep again and wake. I often wonder why, mother. When you put me to sleep, you lose me, mother, and yet you do not lose me—except as the night loses the sun and the day loses the stars . . ."

"Were you not my mother, but some one else's, d'you think I wouldn't know you, mother? Wouldn't I still hide in your lap? What fun it would be to have two homes, one for the day and one at night! As the evening came I would creep up stealthily behind you, put my hands over your eyes and ask, 'Who am I?' And you would say, 'Surely some one I know, and yet I know not who . . ."

"Mother, you want to know where I would like to go? Where I came from, that's where I want to go. But where it is, I keep on guessing. I don't seem to remember it a bit. Seeing me perplexed, Father said laughing the other day, 'It's beyond the clouds, where the evening star resides.' And you say, 'It's beneath the earth from where the flowers spring.' And Auntie says, 'It's under the sea where in the dark cavern the pearl shines in secret.' But elder brother pulls my hair and says, 'You fool, that place is lost in the air. How can you ever see it?' Then it seems to me that it must be everywhere. Only the schoolmaster says, 'It is nowhere.'

"Monday, Tuesday, Wednesday, they come so soon, they must have airplanes at home. But why does Sunday come so late, mother? It seems to lag behind all others. Does he live farthest of all, as far away as the sky is, and is he the child of poor parents as you were, mother?"

And so on the poems trip and skip merrily in light and delightful metres, till one is lost in a world so simple and beautiful that one wonders why the adults have made such a hell of it. The poet said as much in a letter to his niece Indira: "I wrote these poems to give respite to my mind from its obsession with adult responsibilities. I have tried to express in them what had of late persistently recurred to my mind, namely, that the meaning of my life was summed up in its foreword which said that I was born as a child in the playground of this world. When with age we are caught increasingly in the fever of our sense of responsibility, we are inclined to look down upon play. We forget that thereby we malign the Creator of the universe, Who functions without toil, Who is supreme bliss because He is free of all obligations."

But the respite was brief and intermittent. Santiniketan clamoured for his attention. Pearson returned to the asrama on 26 September, after an absence of five years. With him came Leonard Elmhirst, the young Englishman whom Tagore had met in New York. He had accepted Tagore's invitation to help in organising a rural community welfare centre at Sriniketan and had brought with him adequate funds for the purpose made possible by the generosity of Dorothy Straight. Soon after, the French savant Sylvain Levi arrived as Visiting Professor to Visva-Bharati and thus was founded the first department of Tibetan and Chinese Studies in any Indian University. Tagore himself used to attend Levi's classes. On 23 December 1921, Visva-Bharati was formally inaugurated, and the land, buildings and other properties at Santiniketan were legally transferred to it by a trust deed. Tagore also made a gift to it of the copyright on his Bengali books published till then. The Nobel Prize money had already been donated by him to the school.

In the midst of these excitements he continued to brood on the political scene in the country until the subconscious churning of the mind found a dramatic expression in a symbolic play which he wrote in the early part of January 1922. The play which is in a sense a noble tribute to the personality of Gandhi and his campaign of non-violence, is named *Muktadhara* (Free Current). The background of the play is the political subjection of the people of Sivtarai to the neighbouring kingdom of Uttarakut. Muktadhara is the mountain spring whose waters come down the slopes of Uttarakut and irrigate the plains of Sivtarai. Wishing to bend the subject people more effectively to his will by controlling and manipulating the main source of their economic well-being, the King of Uttarakut has had a large dam erected to prevent the waters of Muktadhara from flowing into the plains below. Its engine-tower dominated the landscape and outsoared the trident of the temple of Siva on mountain peak. The play opens with the King and citizens of Uttarakut preparing to participate in a festival in honour of the Machine—very proud of their achievement and heedless of its consequences to the poor people whose lands would be deprived of water.

The Crown Prince, however, professes open sympathy with the subject people and rebels against the callousness of his own country. His character provides the main psychological interest of the play, his love of freedom and justice involving him in a conflict of loyalties. He determines to risk his life in an attempt to liberate the imprisoned waters of Muktadhara by forcing the dam at a point which he happened to know was weakly constructed. He succeeds. The leaping torrent of water breaks free and carries away the Prince's body in its turbulent sweep. The socio-political motif of the play, such there is, seems to dissolve at the end in an undefined sense of mystic exaltation, as in some of Ibsen's later plays.

The author has reintroduced in the play that remarkable character, the Ascetic Dhananjaya, prototype of Mahatma Gandhi, who first appeared in his drama *Prayaschitta* (Atonement), published in 1909. In that play as in the present one, Dhananjaya exhorts the subject people to resist the ruler's unjust claims-nonviolently and fearlessly. Perhaps no other play of Tagore expresses his political convictions with such directness and vigour— his abhorrence of exploitation, whether by a foreign or a native tyrant, and his faith that tyranny can be effectively resisted by non-violence and evil redeemed by voluntary sacrifice, The plot is simple and direct, unburdened with sub-plots or extraneous incidents, though anonymous passers-by and wayfarers come and go freely on the stage, as is usual in Tagore's plays; for according to him, the true stage is the world, and the world is full of common folk. Against the grim background of the towering menace of man's diabolical skill, symbolised in the Machine, pass and repass processions of men and women, tyrants and sycophants, idealists and humbugs, rebels and their servile agents and the multitude of anonymous folk, with their quaint humour and unsophisticated wisdom.

This remarkable play was never staged. The author read it out to a group of friends in Calcutta in January 1922, and later made preparations to stage it, but before the play could be staged, the news came in March of Mahatma Gandhi's arrest, trial and the sentence of rigorous imprisonment for six years. The preparations were abandoned and never revived.

East and West

All humanity's greatest is mine.

TAGORE's dream of making Santiniketan a nest where kindred spirits would gather from different parts of the world was coming true. Or so it seemed. What was originally planned as hermitage was becoming a cosmopolitan beehive. Whether this picturesque beehive produced more honey than buzzing, it is difficult to say. The atmosphere was certainly stimulating and the poet was susceptible to atmosphere and attached value to symbols. Much pioneering work was also done of which the benefit was reaped, not only by Visva-Bharati but by many other Universities.

The stimulus, however, was enough for the poet to imagine that the world was becoming one and that he had only to travel more to win men's hearts for his ideal. There is hardly any illusion more exhilarating than the belief that one is healing the world's wounds and Tagore was neither the first nor the last of great men to come under its spell. Nor need one cavil at the missionary zeal of one of the most sincere and eloquent protagonists of international understanding of the modern age who sought to achieve on the moral plane what the ill-fated League of Nations and its successor the United Nations have tried to achieve on the political. He risked unpopularity at home and suffered ridicule and jeers for his faith in One World long before that faith became a world-fashion.

A greater sacrifice was the risk he took in exposing his creative leisure and spiritual poise to the clamour of the market place. Would the glare of limelight help to blossom or to wither the sensitive plant so far nurtured in the protective shade of comparative obscurity? Would he ever again recapture the passionate and single-minded devotion to his Muse, the intimate dialogues with his Jivan-devata, the Beloved Lord within him, the rapture of communion with the seemingly commonplace sights and sounds, the simplicity of the reed waiting for "Thee to fill with music" which had once been his? The poet was losing to the prophet, the singer to the preacher, the devotee to the missionary. The "endless meaning in the narrow span of a song" was dissolving in the endless preaching over the wide span of the world. He was sensitive and sincere enough to be now and then haunted by an awareness of this predicament, as is evident in the following passage (which reads almost like a confession) from a letter to Andrews written from Chicago (26 February 1921):

"When I came to this world I had nothing but a reed given to me, which was to find its only value in producing music. I left my school, I neglected my work, but I had my reed and I played on it 'in mere idle sport.' All along I had one playmate, who also in His play produced music, among leaves, in rushing water, in silence of stars, in tears and laughter rippling into lights and shadows in the stream of human life. While my companion was this eternal Piper, this Spirit of play, I was nearest to the heart of the world. I knew its mother-tongue, and what I sang was caught up by the chorus of the wind and water and the dance-master of life.

"But now came the schoolmaster in the midst of my dream-world, and I was foolish enough to accept his guidance. I laid aside my reed, I left my playground, where the Infinite child is spending his eternity 'in mere idle sport.' In a moment I became old and carried the burden of wisdom on my back, hawking truths from door to door.

"Why have I been made to carry this burden, I ask myself over and over again, shouting myself hoarse in this noisy world where everybody is crying up his own wares? Pushing the wheelbarrows of propaganda from continent to continent—is this going to be the climax of a poet's life? It seems to be like an evil dream, from which I occasionally wake up in the dead of night and grope about in the bed asking myself in consternation: 'Where is my music?'

"The poet who is true to his mission reaps his harvest of love; but the poet who strays into the path of the good is dismissed with applause. So I founded my International University—a great work! But I lose my little song—which loss can never be made up to me. How I wish I could find my reed again and be contemptuously ignored by the busy and the wise as a hopeless ne'er-do-well!"

Would Tagore have been a greater poet if the Nobel Prize and the consequent blaze of fame and publicity had not invaded the obscurity in which his genius had so far matured? Would his spiritual insight have plumbed deeper depths if he had continued to churn the ocean of self instead of sailing over the oceans in missionary zeal to help men understand one another better? Who can say what might have been, if this or that had or had not happened? These are vain guesses: "With an 'if' you might put Paris in a bottle," is a wise French saying.

What is remarkable is that despite the many temptations, distractions, and occasional aberrations, he never strayed too far or for long from his true vocation, which was that of the poet and singer, a lover of nature and of men, a devotee who saw the divine in man and hailed the human in the divine. Indeed, one might even say that the western interludes and periodic spells of missionary fervour were distractions that served as healthy diversions enriching his spirit and enlarging his mental horizons. Whether because of it or in spite of it, the fact is that Tagore never ceased to be creative, in the best sense of the word, till the last day of his conscious life and continued to explore new fields and to reach heights unscaled before in Bengali language and literature. Even during his comparatively sterile periods he wrote enough and of such quality as to make many another writer famous.

It is true that at times the inspiration seemed to wane, the vitality to flag, and he drew less from life than from habit. At such times he tended to be prolix, repetitive and stale. Too frequent travel and repeated appearance on public platform, adulation of the unthinking multitude and a ceaseless crusade for lofty ideals (which also became a campaign for raising funds for Visva-Bharati) were a distraction hardly conducive to a mood of creative thought or of contemplative insight. Gradually he came to be surrounded by a flock of admirers, many of whom were little better than courtiers, sycophants and parasites who applauded whatever he wrote or said or did, and who were like a solid wall which stood between him and the real world. This is a danger which celebrities all over the world have to face, but nowhere it is more deadly than in India, the traditional home of idolators. The idol breakers become idols themselves.

That Tagore survived this hazard and himself smashed the idol that others had made of him, that he broke the fetters he had forged for himself, and went on discovering new areas of creative expression, surpassing his own earlier achievements, that nothing could keep him captive to a pinnacle however high or to a pasture however green and luscious, is the best evidence we have of the unfailing vitality of his genius, his untiring quest of the unknown, his intellectual vigour and spiritual integrity. But the evidence was yet to accrue.

Meanwhile in this phase of restlessness, even during the period Tagore was in India, he spent almost as many days outside Santiniketan as in it. The world had become his stage and Santiniketan an ideal studio for rehearsals. Its international character was emphasised by the students and staff celebrating the third centenary of Moliere's birth in February 1922. In July Tagore presided at Shelly Centenary Celebrations in Calcutta. In August and September a new musical sequence *Varshamangal* (Rains Festival) and a new version of his earlier drama *Saradotsav* (Autumn Festival) were presented on the Calcutta stage. These compositions which are an enchanting amalgam of poetry, drama, music and dance were written for community celebration of the seasons of the year and breathe of the open air and the simple joy of living. They were not built on any pattern, the folk and classical traditions intermingle in them as freely as do philosophy and frivolity, religious mysticism and a running commentary on contemporary affairs.

In September 1922 Tagore left for a long tour of western and southern India, visiting Bombay, Poona, Madras and a number of other important towns in the south, finally crossing over to Ceylon. Everywhere he was feted and the public thronged to hear him speak. On his way back he revisited Gandhi's asrama at Sabarmati in Ahmedabad. The Mahatma was in jail, and Tagore in his address to the students and inmates of the asrama dwelt at length on "the true meaning of sacrifice which Gandhiji represents." His simple and homely address is instinct with deep respect for the Mahatma's personality.

After spending about two months in Santiniketan, he again left for a tour of north and west India, going as far west as Karachi and Porbundar, the birthplace of Gandhi in Kathiawar. Returning to Santiniketan in April, he left soon after for Shillong to spend the summer in that lovely hill station of Assam. He had only to stay quiet to be creative, and so in Shillong he commenced writing a remarkable play, which he named *Rakta Karabi,* later translated and published in English as *Red Oleanders.*

This play, like the earlier one, *Muktadhara,* shows Tagore's increasing concern with the basic problems of modern civilisation. While the earlier play was concerned with the diabolical use of technological knowledge (symbolised in the Machine) for colonial exploitation, this one raises the more fundamental issue of the free spirit of life set against the more terrible machine of a highly organised and mechanised society which turns men into robots, reducing names to numbers. The age-old struggle between the individual and the State, between the liberative impulse and the compulsive will, between free intelligence and cold calculating intellect, which has assumed sinister proportions with the development of the "scientific technique," is the theme of this play. The treatment is characteristically Tagorean, half-realistic, half-allegorical, logic and mysticism diluting each other and making the dramatic conflict more suggestive than obvious, the conclusion more baffling than convincing.

The kingdom of Yakshapuri flourishes on gold mining and forced labour. Its King lives behind locked steel doors, veiled in mystery, awe and terror, literally and symbolically behind the iron curtain (long before Churchill thought of the symbol). In his name the Police Chief rules the land with a ruthless exercise of the whip and a judicious use of religious superstition. It is the same cord, says a victim, that makes the whip and binds the rosary. Into this " brave new world" comes a young and wilful girl,

Nandini, who fears no one and whose beauty charms every one. She upsets the whole order, not only making the workers rebellious but luring the King himself out of his hiding. When he sees what his henchmen have made of his people, he himself leads the revolt against his own generals—but not before Nandini's beloved companion, a brave and carefree youth, Ranjan, who refuses to be conscripted, is killed.

The zeal of a pilgrim-ambassador had possessed Tagore. Not content with touring in his own country, he now thought of visiting China. Nearly a thousand years had passed since the last band of Buddhist monks had carried their Master's message of compassion and peace to that land. Tagore wanted to restore the ancient cultural link between the two countries which had been snapped for so long. He did not succeed. He could not have, for China and India had in the meanwhile drifted too far away, and each land was seething in its own ferment. The Chinese intelligentsia had grown impatient of traditional values and virtues and were western-oriented. They were convinced that nationalist solidarity, materialist commonsense and a ruthless application of science and technology could alone lift their ancient country from the morass into which it had sunk. They were more amenable to the rational scepticism of a Bertrand Russell than the mystic insights of a Rabindranath Tagore. They looked upon the Indian poet as a reactionary idealist, a futile visionary and viewed his visit with indifference, if not with hostility. Tagore understood this mood and temper with some aspects of which he was familiar in his own country, and his lectures in China, delivered mostly extempore, show with what understanding and sympathy he approached the Chinese mind. He was personal, reminiscent and friendly, and though he was as usual blunt and forthright in his opposition to war, national rivalries and the fetish of indiscriminate worship of material progress, he soon disarmed hostile criticism and won over many a progressive intellectual.

Tagore returned to India in the latter half of July via Japan where he stayed for about six weeks and gave several lectures. His visit to China and Japan led to the first conscious attempt in the history of Asia to formulate the idea of Asian Unity by the organisation of an Asiatic Association in Shanghai in September of the same year. Reporting this event the *Christian Science Monitor* of Boston wrote: "There is on foot an important movement to establish Asiatic concord through the common culture of Asiatic nations . . . It has been stimulated by the recent visit to the Far East of Rabindranath Tagore, who preached the doctrine of idealism opposed to western materialism. The new feeling is shown in the formation of Asiatic Associations in the principal centres, the first of which is located in Shanghai . . . Inspiration for the movement is acknowledged to Tagore whose teachings permeate the issued declarations." As was aptly pointed out by the Calcutta *Hindustan Standard,* "This convention was thus a predecessor to the Asian Relations Conference held in Delhi 23 years later" in the year of India's independence. Surprisingly enough, no mention was made of Tagore at this latter conference held in his own land. Politicians have short memories.

Hardly two months at home, then again to the other side of the world. The occasion was an invitation from the Republic of Peru to attend the centenary celebrations of her attainment of independence. So in September 1924 he sailed for the New World, with Elmhirst, who had accompanied him earlier to China, again his companion. It was early autumn when he set sail in the Japanese boat Haruna-Maru, and the music of autumn stirred in the poet's heart. He forgot his mission and was once again the lover and the singer. Not sermons but poems poured out of his pen exquisite in their wistful tenderness. The 63-year old poet was entering the evening of his life and the mellow richness of the evening melody pervades these poems. As always in such moods, the memory of his first love haunts him.

I had said I would not forget, when
with tear-dimmed eyes you had looked into my face.
Forgive if I have forgotten.
A long time has passed since then...
Your dark eyes had inscribed on my soul
the first epistle of love, shyly, timidly.
Over that signature of your heart

Time has passed its brush in strokes of light
and shade, fitfully, again and again...
If in today's spring is hushed
the music of that earlier spring,
If from my lamp of pain the flame has departed
without a sound,
Forgive me.
This I know, because you had come into my life,
my life overflowed into such a harvest of songs,
to its abundance there is no end.

During the voyage near the Argentinian coast Tagore suddenly took ill and was obliged to disembark at Buenos Aires where a heart specialist advised complete rest for some time. Tagore did not know a soul in Buenos Aires, but fortunately the charming and talented Victoria Ocampo offered her hospitality and he was happy to find refuge in an attractive and secluded villa in San Isidro on the bank of the river Plate. The visit to Peru had to be cancelled on the doctor's advice. Nor was Tagore sorry about it, for on this voyage the poet had triumphed over the prophet and he was very content and happy to watch the river from the balcony of the villa and be looked after by so charming and devoted a hostess. It was a real devotion, the devotion of a young and ardent spirit to an ideal and not the "fussing" of a society lady eager to capture a lion. That this enforced holiday was fruitful in a truly creative sense is evidenced from the quality of poems exquisite and haunting in their playful and restrained tenderness which he wrote during his stay at San Isidro and for some time after. These poems were published in 1925 under the significant title, *Puravi,* which is the name of a lovely evening melody. The volume was dedicated to Vijaya (the Sanskrit parallel of Victoria) by which name Tagore used to address his hostess. "I am sending you," he wrote to her from Calcutta when he sent her a copy, " a Bengali book of poems which I wish I could place in your hands personally. I have dedicated it to you though you will never be able to know what it contains. A large number of poems in this book were written while I was in San Isidro . . . I hope this book will have the chance of a longer time with you than its author had."

How lovingly some of these poems written in San Isidro "encircle," to quote the author's own phrase, the memory of days spent with Vijaya, may be guessed from the following specimen (unfortunately bereft of the exquisite flavour of original):

> Laughing she came with her flowers of joy; I had nought else but the fruit of my sorrow. I asked her, "Who will be the loser if we exchange what we have?" Amused, the lovely one smiled, "Come, let's exchange! Take my flowers for your fruit of pain rich with tears!" I looked at her and knew that she was ruthless in her beauty.
>
> Lightly she picked up my load of fruit and clapped her hands and laughed. Her abundance of flowers I held to my heart. "I win," she said as she laughed and tripped away.
>
> The sun climbed to the mid-sky and the heat was great. At the end of the burning day, the wilted flowers had all fallen down.

Sixteen years later, shortly before his death, the memory was still fresh and the poet, now aged and ailing and waiting for the end, enshrined it in one of his last poems (*Sesh Lekha*):

> How I wish I could once again find my way to that
> foreign land where waits for me the message of love!
> The dreams of yesterday will wing their way back
> and fluttering softly build their nest anew,
> Sweet memories will restore to the flute its lost melody . . .
> Her language I knew not, but what her eyes said shall
> forever remain eloquent in its anguish.

On 4 January 1925 the poet and his companion Elmhirst bade goodbye to their hostess and sailed from Buenos Aires. He hurried away for he felt guilty that he should be happy and enjoying himself when his country needed him. But when he reached his own land he realised that this happiness had been creative, and that in the long run he did more good by being creative than by being merely helpful, He expressed this feeling very charmingly in a letter to Victoria Ocampo written from Santiniketan in August of the same year:

"You express regret in your letter that I could not continue to stay in that beautiful house near the river till the end of the summer. You do not know how often I wish I could do so. It was some lure of duty which drove me from that sweet corner with its inspiration for seemingly futile idling; but today I discover that my basket while I was there was being daily filled with shy flowers of poems that thrive under the shade of lazy hours. I can assure you, most of them will remain fresh long after the time when the laboriously built towers of my beneficent deeds will crumble into oblivion."

A few days after his return to his country Tagore's elder brother Jyotirindranath passed away. The death of this gifted brother who had been his friend and guide during the critical years of adolescence, moved him deeply, though he kept his feelings to himself. He had suffered so many bereavements that death had ceased to be a stranger. "Through death and sorrow," he said again and again, "there dwells peace in the heart of the Eternal."

In May of the same year (1925) Mahatma Gandhi visited him at Santiniketan, to try once again to convert him to his favourite thesis that the way to Swaraj lay through the charkha and khadi. Tagore received him, as usual, with great cordiality and respect, and when he led him to his room which had been tastefully decorated with fresh leaves and flowers, the Mahatma smiled and asked, "Why bring me to this bridal chamber?" The poet replied with a smile, "Because Santiniketan, the ever young queen of our hearts, welcomes you." Gandhi's visit both failed and succeeded in its purpose. If he had hoped to convince Tagore that the charkha was or could ever be anything more than one of the many necessary crafts in an undeveloped village economy, he must have disappointed. On the other hand, each such meeting and exchange of views, even if only a conflict of views, forged a deeper bond between the two. Whatever the seeming clash between their temperaments and their outlooks, their spirits always met as in a "bridal chamber".

Later Tagore explained and elaborated his viewpoint in an article, "The Cult of the Charkha," published in the *Modern Review* which provoked a rejoinder from the Mahatma in the *Young India,* under the heading "The Poet and the Charkha". Tagore wrote a personal letter assuring him that "even if you have hit me hard in the cause of what you think is Truth, our personal relationship based upon mutual respect will bear the strain." This assurance was borne out to the end and the deep affinity that linked the Mahatma and the Poet survived the many duels on the public platform. Twenty years later when Gandhi visited Santiniketan for the last time, four years after the death of Tagore, he said, "I started with a disposition to detect a conflict between Gurudev and myself but ended with the glorious discovery that there was none." The glorious discovery was mutual.

In the winter of 1925, Mussolini eager to woo the Indian poet sent two distinguished orientalists, Carlo Formici and Giuseppe Tucci, as Visiting Professors from Italy to Visva-Bharati, with a collection of valuable Italian books as a gift to the University. Before the year ended Tagore presided over the first session of the Indian Philosophical Congress in Calcutta where he spoke on the philosophic significance of the folk cultures and folk religions of India. Soon after, in the beginning of the new year, he went to Locknow to attend the All India Music Conference. In the midst of the music festival came the news of the death of his eldest brother, Dwijendranath, the gentle and amiable philosopher-mathematician. One by one the links with the past were snapping. Dwijendranath was a true philosopher who took even his own vast learning and talents philosophically and neither paraded the former nor made much of the latter. He was Borodada (eldest brother) not only to Rabindranath but to all, including Gandhi and Andrews who were much attached to him. "Borodada's death," commented the Mahatma, "means the withdrawal of a great sage, philosopher and patriot from our midst." He was the more dear to Gandhi because, unlike his younger brother, he believed wholeheartedly in the Mahatma's programme of the spinning wheel.

At the invitation of Dacca University, Tagore delivered a series of lectures and also visited several towns in East Bengal. Returning to Santiniketan he wrote a prose-drama *Natir Puja* (Worship of the Dancing Girl), based on an old Buddhist legend which he had earlier used in a poem. This is one of Tagore's simple and straightforward plays, deeply moving and free from symbolic abstractions and intellectual sophistications which make some of his other plays at once puzzling and fascinating. The main action centres in a simple religious emotion which rises to a high pitch as the story ends in a tragedy of martyred devotion.

The Buddha had challenged the infallibility of the Vedas and the hierarchy of the Hindu caste. Worship of the Divine cannot be the monopoly of this caste or that, nor can its expression be for ever imprisoned in one particular Vedic pattern. True worship is the surrender or dedication of the best we have to the call of Truth. The sage dedicates his learning, the man of action his deeds, the poet his songs, and the humble Nati her dance. Thus the dancing girl by her sincerity and devotion redeems the so-called degradation of her calling and vindicates by her death the innate majesty of her spirit.

One other point of interest to note about this play is that it has no male characters. The introduction of the Buddhist monk in the Prologue was a later addition to enable the author to satisfy the public clamour for his appearance on the stage. There was a deep-rooted prejudice in the Indian society, whether Hindu or Muslim, against the public appearance of women on the stage. With the staging of this play in Calcutta in January 1927, Tagore made a bold assault on this prejudice by recruiting the entire cast from among girl students of his own university and ladies of good families, all of whom he himself trained and rehearsed. He also brought non-professional dancing on the stage. Since then the old prejudice has disappeared and the pendulum has swung to the other side, and not only is dancing on the stage accepted as a respectable form of public entertainment but is valued as a medium of interpreting traditional Indian culture.

Pilgrim–Ambassador

Praise shames me, for I secretly long for it.

PARTLY flattered by Mussolini's courtship and partly curious to see for himself this colourful personality and its impact on an ancient and lively culture, Tagore accepted an invitation from Italy and sailed for Naples on 15 May 1926. As he himself put it, "It is for me to study and not criticise from outside. I am glad of this opportunity to see for myself the work of one who is assuredly a great man and a movement that will certainly be remembered in history." That Fascism will be remembered in history, there is little doubt. That the Duce was "a great man" was an illusion which Tagore temporarily shared with many shrewd and seasoned politicians of the time.

On arrival in Naples he was received by the chief officials of the city with a message of welcome from Mussolini. On 7 June the Governor of Rome held a public reception in the capital where he conveyed to the poet the greetings of the Eternal City. On the following day Tagore delivered his first public lecture on "The Meaning of Art" with Mussolini among the audience. He was also received by King Victor Emmanuel III and attended a performance of his play *Chitra* in Italian. But more than the King or the Duce, Tagore was keen on meeting the philosopher Benedetto Croce who was at that time virtually home-interned in Naples. Some common friends, however, took the risk of bringing him over clandestinely to Rome where the two met.

While he was being feted in his almost royal tour of Italy, he did not realise that garbled and distorted versions of his speeches and interviews were being headlined by the Italian press to boost the fascist regime. It was only when he crossed over to Switzerland to rest for a few days in Villeneuve that he came to know from Romain Rolland how the Italian propaganda machine had made a dupe of him, twisting and distorting his words to suit their end. Tagore was disillusioned and found it painful to reconcile what he now heard with what he had just seen. In Zurich he met Signora Salvadori who gave him a first-hand account of fascist atrocities witnessed by herself, corroborated by Modigliani in Vienna. Profoundly shocked by what seemed unimpeachable evidence, Tagore wrote a letter to the *Manchester Guardian* explaining his visit to Italy and condemning Fascism in no uncertain terms. This exposed him to bitter revilement in the Italian press.

He felt hurt and humiliated at this fiasco and confessed in a letter to Elmhirst: "Somehow I have the unenviable knack of getting myself entangled in responsibilities that should have been avoided and I regret that I ever allowed myself to pay this last visit to Italy." Then immediately recovering his light-hearted good humour, he added: "Can you lend me an aeroplane if you have one at your disposal? I want to fly back to Uttarayan (name of his house at Santiniketan) immediately, for the rain clouds of July have gathered about our asrama and are wondering where the poet could have gone who was to greet them with his grateful songs in return for the music of rain."

But the music of human adulation seemed to have become sweeter for the time being than "the music of rain," for he continued his stay in Europe for five more months. The German tour was once again hectic and he received large ovations everywhere and was received by President Hindenburg. Tagore's friendship with Albert Einstein began with this visit. After a week's stay in Prague where his play *The Post Office* was staged in Czech, he went via Vienna to Budapest where he was obliged to take rest in a sanatorium on the lake Balaton, his health having broken down under the strain of the prolonged excitement of the tour. The linden tree he was made to plant in the park attached to the sanatorium is still cherished as a relic of his visit. But he could not stay for long and had soon to resume his tour.

After crowded receptions and lecture engagements in Belgrade, Sofia, Bucharest and Athens where the Greek Government decorated him with the "Order of the Redeemer," he visited

Cairo. The Egyptian Parliament, then in session, was adjourned in his honour and King Fuad presented him with a set of Arabic books for Visva-Bharati. In December he returned to his own land.

One would imagine that after this long and hectic tour during which his health had broken down more than once, the poet would have been content to enjoy the seclusion and peace of Santiniketan for which he had longed so much. In a charming poem of *Puravi,* called "Asha" (Hope), he had expressed his wistful longing for a quiet nook in a secluded corner of the earth, with only one distraction, "not wealth nor honour, only a little love." But though one side of his genius throve "under the shade of lazy hours," another constantly drove him to attempt "laboriously built towers of my beneficent deeds." Peace and glory are rarely found together and when they meet they soon part company.

It is not without significance that his poetical and musical compositions of this period revolve round the concept of Nataraja, the Divine Dancer holding the universe in the whirl of his cosmic dance. He embodied it in a song-and-dance sequence called *Nataraja Riturangasala* which was produced in Santiniketan in February. In march he went on another tour of western India during which he presided over a Hindi literary Conference held in the then princely state of Bharatpur.

He spent the summer in the pleasant hill-station of Shillong in Assam where he began what might have been his biggest novel, *Teen Purush* (Three Generations). He had planned it on an ambitious scale, as the title indicates, and he began it superbly, in the best traditional manner of story-telling, unburdened with sophistication or affectations. The loving observer of his people, the story-teller and the social psychologist have combined to achieve a consummate work of art which makes some critics acclaim this novel as "the most satisfying of all the novels Tagore has written." But Tagore was no Tolstoy or Balzac and could not live long at a stretch in one fixed world even though peopled by his own creations. The poet, the singer and the teacher constantly meddled with the novelist and lured him away from concentration on one plot or one set of characters. And so, having planned this saga as a trilogy, he gave it up after completing the story of one generation only and the novel was published two years later under the altered title *Yogayog* (Cross Currents).

Almost all the major novels of Tagore depict the inevitable conflicts and contradictions of the Indian (chiefly Hindus) society in transition. Although the conflict is almost always and basically social and cultural, the aspect analysed differs from novel to novel. In *Gora* it was the religious and intellectual ferment, and in *Ghare Baire* (the Home and the World) it was the political. In *Yogayog* it is the rise of a new economic class that results in an inevitable conflict between values nurtured in an old family of landed aristocrats which has lost its wealth but not its pride and the aggressive claims of a self-made tycoon who thinks that money can buy anything. Kumudini, the lovely and gentle daughter of the former, is married to Madhusudhan, the go-ahead millionaire, crude, vital and assertive, one of the few flesh-and–blood male characters made by Tagore. Accustomed to imposing his will "on his human and mechanical tools," he imagines he can posses Kumudini merely because she is his wife, but soon discovers that though he can possess her body, the real she eludes his grasp.

The psychological interest of the novel lies in the gradual and almost imperceptible transformation in the husband's feelings towards her. At first brutal, violent and exultant, they are gradually inhibited by sudden spasms of tenderness and awe which he cannot understand, having never experienced them in any other sphere of life. The bullying, blustering boss loses his self-confidence and fumbles clumsily reaching out for what his hands cannot grasp. The end of this novel is, unfortunately, weak—a failing which many other novels of Tagore share. It is as though he suddenly tires of continuing the narrative and wants to finish it somehow so as to attend to the demands of some other Muse in his harem, or that he gets squeamish and afraid of a character getting the upper hand and going its own way in defiance of the author's moral and social inhibitions.

Even as he was writing this novel and probing the spiritual hollowness of mere success, he was himself getting restless for fresh fields to conquer. The missionary zeal once again proved stronger than the creative, and in July 1927 he set out on his ninth foreign tour, this time to the neighbouring lands of South East Asia. After visiting Singapore, Malacca, Kuala Lumpur, Ipoh, Taiping and Penang, attracting crowds and receiving ovations everywhere, he sailed for Indonesia, composing on the way a beautiful long poem on Java which he read out (in English rendering) at a banquet given in his honour in Jakarta. In Java he met, among others, the late President Soekarno, then a compartively unknown revolutionary youth. In Java and Bali Tagore was deeply impressed by their affinity with the traditions in his own country. His visit was fruitful in restoring a cultural link that had been snapped for centuries and attracted many Indonesian students to Visva-Bharati University and led to the adaptation by Santiniketan artists of the Indonesian technique of *batik* designing and dyeing which has since spread to many parts of India. After a short visit to Thailand where he delivered a lecture on Education at the University in Bangkok, he returned to India in December, in time to preside over the annual celebrations at Santiniketan.

Once again he prepared to leave for abroad on receipt of an invitation from Oxford University to deliver the Hibbert Lectures, but the voyage had to be abandoned as he fell ill on arrival in Madras. After a week's rest at Adyar as the guest of Annie Besant and a few more days in the pleasant climate of Coonoor, he sailed for Ceylon hoping to recoup his health sufficiently to take a boat from there to England. On the way he landed at Pondicherry to visit Sri Aurobindo Ghosh whom he had known in his earlier days of revolutionary political activity. Recording the impression, the poet wrote as he resumed his voyage, "Years ago, I saw Aurobindo in the heroism of his early political struggle and I said, Aurobindo, accept the salutation of Rabindra. Today I saw him seated in the poise of calm wisdom, and I repeated in silence, Aurobindo, accept the salutation of Rabindra."

He stayed in Colombo for ten days, but as there was no visible improvement in health, he gave up all hope of sailing for England

and returned to the mainland, resting for three weeks in Bangalore as the guest of his old friend, the learned philosopher Sir Brajendranath Seal, Vice-Chancellor of the Mysore University. Having given up the voyage, he was no longer restless and fretful. The old poise returned and with it the creative mood. During this brief stay in Bangalore he not only completed the novel *Yogayog* but also finished another which he had begun during his recent voyage to Colombo, *Sesher Kavita* (Last Poem).

This novel which is almost half poetry is very popular among Bengali readers and stands in a class by itself. Its modern setting, its playful mocking tone, its challenging style, the author's trick of introducing himself as the butt of the hero's merciless criticism, the scintillating wit of the dialogue and the final tragic note voiced in the beautiful poem at the end which gives the book its title—all these won for it an immediate popularity with the young readers. Nor has it failed to win generous praise from mature and discriminating critics. *Sesher kavita,* says Prof. S.K. Banerjee, "is a novel written in a more consistent poetic strain and on a more purely poetic theme than perhaps any other novel in the world's history." Dr Sukumar Sen describes it as "a love story written as if to end all love stories." It is interesting to recall that the author completed this and the other novel, *Yogayog,* almost simultaneously— and no two novels could be more dissimilar, in theme, style, treatment, mood or language.

The hero is an amusing specimen of the ultra-modern Bengali intellectual of the twenties whose Oxford education has not only given him a superiority complex but induced in him a craze for consciously cultivated originality which results in a deliberate and frivolous contrariness to all accepted opinion and convention. His aggressive self-complacence, however, receives a shock when he accidentally encounters and falls in love with a quite different product of modern education—a highly intelligent girl of fine sensibility and deep feelings. This experience is so utterly different from his previous excursions in flirting that it comes as a shock, releasing his submerged depth of sincerity which he finds hard to adjust to the habits of sophistry and pose practised so long. In the process he manages to strike a new romantic attitude.

The struggle makes of him a curiously pathetic figure—one who is being worked against his grain. The idol-breaker has become a worshipper so ardent that the girl understands that what he is in love with is not herself but an idealised image of her to which she could never correspond. Sensing the tragedy, she releases him from his troth and disappears from his life. The last poem in which she takes farewell of her lover is a testament of the depth of feeling of which she was capable. Here is a stanza shorn of its superb cadence in the original.

No loss is yours in losing me,
an image of clay.
If of that mortal dust
you have fashioned a goddess,
let the goddess remain for you to adore
with the evening star.
No gross touch of the actual me
shall disturb the play of your worship,
no hot breath of ardour passion-lit
sully its flowers, sacred, fragile . . .
What I gave to you
is yours by right everlasting.
What others receive
are the daily driblets the heart yields
to tender importunity.
O my princely, my peerless friend,
what I gave to you was your own gift—
fuller your acceptance, deeper my debt,
my friend, farewell !

The ageing poet was reliving in imagination his romantic youth. The embers were burning out and needed artificial blowing to work them into a flame. His younger contemporaries, charmed by his latest Novel, begged him to make an anthology of his love poems and add a few new ones.The suggestion was enough to stimulate a mind that needed no more than a prod. As he himself put it lightly, he was like an automobile engine which kept on running, once the self-starter was released. So instead of compiling a selection he wrote a completely new volume of verses, mostly love poems, which he named *Mahua,* after the strong scented Indian flower of spring which yields a native heady wine. The title was appropriate, for these poems, some of them very tender and exquisite, were not born of the anguish of a living experience but were induced by an artificial stimulus, as but intoxication. Not quite artificial, for the poet was always in love with love, an impersonal love.

It was during the rainy season of this year, 1928, that Tagore introduced two seasonal festivals, Vriksharopana (Tree-planting) and Hala-karshana (Ploughing) at Santiniketan and Sriniketan respectively. These picturesque festivals with their simple and artistic ceremonials accompanied by music, dancing and Vedic chanting, invoking nature's fertility and symbolising its ever-recurring youth, are still celebrated annually and attract crowds of visitors from the neighbouring countryside, and from Calcutta. Tagore, the lover of forests, who had long bewailed the ruthless deforestation of the countryside, sought to introduce a practice which would catch the popular imagination and make people plant trees for the love of them. He succeeded. Not only is Santiniketan, which was once a wasteland of corroded soil, now a miniature garden town, but the tree-planting ceremony initiated by him is now an all-India festival actively sponsored by the Central and State Governments. One of his most characteristic volumes of verses is named *Vanavasi* (Voice of the Forest), a collection of poems on trees, shrubs and flowers and on the various seasons with which their life is linked.

1928 was indeed a fruitful year, thanks partly to the fact that his health obliged him to stick to his own soil. It was in this year too that Tagore began his experiments in an entirely new and unforeseen medium of creative expression, painting. He had always been drawn to this art and had occasionally cast furtive and longing glances at it, ever since as a young boy he had seen his elder and versatile brother Jyotirindranath draw. Later, when his nephews Abanindranath and Gaganendranath discovered their talents for painting he encouraged them in their pursuit and helped in founding what was once hailed as the modern renaissance in Indian Art and which, since the connotation of the word "modern" has changed radically, is now dubbed as the Bengal or Revivalist School of Indian Painting. He himself never took the brush in hand.

But though he did not wield the brush, he doodled freely with his pen. His manuscripts bear ample and fascinating evidence of these playful exercises interwoven with his verses. Most of these lineal exercises were induced by what he has called "casualties in my manuscripts," deletions and erasures which he hated to leave alone as desultory scratches on his pages. They seemed to him like "widowed gypsies" in frantic search of mates, calling to him piteously to rescue them from their irrelevance as outcasts; and so he would work on them with the self-same pen and connect these various "solitary incongruities" into some kind of rhythmic pattern, fanciful or grotesque.

From now on he painted not to provide rhythmic patterns to the erasures in his writing, but as he liked. He let himself go, delighted with his new play like a child with a new-found toy. Fortunately, he had had no training and no reputation at stake as a painter, and so he painted without inhibition, without affectation. The only unfortunate part of it was that not taking his art seriously he drew on whatever paper was at hand and with any instruments and colours, with the result that the preservation of these paintings many of which are of high quality is presenting a serious problem. He painted fast and with a sure hand, in between the intervals of his literary activity, finishing each picture at one sitting, and has left behind nearly 3,000 paintings and drawings, all done during the last thirteen years of his life —a remarkable achievement, considering that during the same period he also published a large number of volumes of literary writing, poetry and prose.

He himself described his paintings as "my versification in lines" and confessed in a letter that he was "hopelessly entangled in the spell that the lines have cast all round me." There is no doubt that many of these drawings are marked by a strong feeling for rhythm, but apart from this affinity there is little in common between his poetry and his painting. In fact, it would seem that some other self of his, if not deeper, at any rate more hidden, were seeking expression through this new medium. In his literary writings Tagore is a conscious artist, a finished craftsman with perfect control over his tools and his medium, so that he is able to say what he wants to say and in a manner which he approves. What he says is therefore necessarily selective and, as in all great art, beautiful and striking, often so much more than merely beautiful as to make one wonder how far it is the voice of Rabindranath the individual and how far of something much bigger and transcending him —maybe, the spirit of India or of his people, or of humanity, or of life and nature, or of something far more mysterious and divine, comprehending and surpassing them all. He writes as one dedicated consciously and impelled subconsciously to a higher purpose. But when he paints, it is rather like somnambulist walking, sure of his step without seeing, driven by an urge of which the direction is outside his control. The grotesque, the bizarre, the cruel, the sardonic, all that he scrupulously kept out of his writings peeps out of his drawings. Not only Angels and Ariels but Pucks and Calibans too have their full play on his canvas.

On I March 1929 Tagore sailed for Canada at the invitation of the National Council of Education of that country. Invitations had been received from several Universities in the United States, and so from Canada the poet sailed for Los Angeles.On arrival in Los Angeles his passport was unfortunately lost and he felt irritated by the formalities to which he was subjected by the Immigration Officers some of which he considered too humiliating. He therefore cancelled his engagements in the States and sailed for Japan. This was not the first occasion when an accident intervened to mar his appreciation of the United States. On a previous visit too he had been rubbed the wrong way. It was unfortunate indeed that his high expectations received repeated rebuffs in a country known for the exuberance of its hospitality and friendliness.

He spent nearly a month in Japan. He loved this country and its brave and disciplined people and was filled with unhappiness as he watched their minds being steadily warped by a deliberately engineered hysteria of imperial ambition. With his usual courage he warned them in a public address against "the ghosts of ideals which no longer have a living reality," which merely serve to alienate nations from one another. After a pleasant halt in Saigon, then French Indo-China, where he was warmly received, Tagore returned to India in July— in time to welcome with songs, as he used to say, the rain-laden clouds over the Santiniketan sky.

In January 1930 Tagore visited western India and gave lectures in Baroda on "Man the Artist,"returning to Santiniketan in early February. In March he sailed for Europe to keep his engagement for the Hibbert Lectures at Oxford which ill-health had prevented him earlier from keeping. Lecture engagements were a convenient excuse; the compelling reason was his own restlessness, this time made more imperious by the prospect of his paintings being exhibited in Paris and of his seeing once again his charming Argentinian hostess Victoria Ocampo who had come all the way to Paris to organise the exhibition which opened at Galerie Pigalle in early May. The paintings were well received by Paris critics, who described them as "pure paintings, absolutely sincere and wholly uninfluenced by our studio customs."

The Hibbert Lectures delivered in Oxford later in the month were published in the following years as *The Religion of Man*, dedicated to Dorothy Elmhirst. After an exhibition of his paintings in Birmingham and London, Tagore left for Berlin in July. This visit deepened his affection and regard for Einstein with whom he had long discussions, a gist of which is recorded in an appendix to *The Religion of Man.* His pictures were exhibited at Gallery Moller in Berlin and a civic reception was accorded to him in the ancient Town Hall of Munich. He visited many places in Germany, including Oberammergau where he witnessed the Passion Play. "How like our Prophet!" whispered the audience as they saw the Indian poet.

That the Passion Play left a deep impression on his mind can be guessed from the theme of his poem, *The Child*, which he wrote soon after during his stay in Germany, the only poem he ever wrote directly in English. This remarkable pros-poem, a product of Biblical inspiration and Hindu imagination, embodies a basic attitude of Tagore's thought, namely, his reverence for life. The symbolism is as relevant to the story of Jesus as to that of Gandhi as later events were to prove. The poem is too long to quote, but here is an excerpt to give an idea of it.

...The Man of faith moves on a long pitiless paths
strewn with flints, over scorching sands...
They follow him, the strong and the weak,
the aged and young...
Some grow weary and footsore, some angry
and suspicious,
they ask at every dragging step,
How much farther is the end?...
It is night.
The travellers spread their mats on the ground...
A gust of wind blows out the lamp
and the darkness deepens like a sleep into a swoon.
Someone from the crowd suddenly stands up
and pointing to the leader with merciless finger
breaks out:
False prophet, thou hast deceived us !
Others take up the cry one by one,
women hiss their hatred and men growl.
At last one bolder than other's suddenly deals him a blow.
They cannot see his face, but fall upon him
in a fury of destruction...
suddenly they become still and gasp for breath
as they gaze at the figure lying dead.
The women sob out aloud and men hide their faces
in their hands.
a frew try to slink away unnoticed,
but their crime keeps them chained
to their victim.
They ask each other in bewilderment,
Who will show us the path?

The old man from the East bends his head and says:
The Victim...
And they all stand up and mingle their voices and sing,
Victory to the Victim !...

After nearly a month's rest in Geneva, Tagore left for Moscow, at the invitation of the Soviet Government. Fortunately, he kept a record of his impressions in a series of letters he wrote home, which were later published as *Rashiar Chithi* (letters from Russia).These letters testify to one of the most significant qualities of the ageing poet, namely, that as he grew older in years, he seemed to become younger in spirit. He was less conservative and more tolerant in his old age than during his manhood. Strange as it may sound, he even looked more handsome in old age than as a young man— this is borne out, not only by his photographs but by those contemporaries who had seen him at both the ages. No man could have said more truthfully than he:"Grow old along with me; the best is yet to be, the last of life for which the first was made." Whatever wrinkles age furrowed in his face there were none in his mind.

Like Gandhi he discovered with the years that truth was higher than any religion and human good more important than any philosophy. Were it not so the author of *Gitanjali* and the great exponent of India's spiritual heritage could hardly have looked upon his visit to the Soviet land as a pilgrimage. "If I had not come to Russia," he wrote in a letter,"life's pilgrimage would have remained incomplete. Before judging the good and bad of their activities here, the first thing that strikes me is: What incredible courage ! what is called tradition clings to man in a thousand different ways; its numerous apartments, its innumerable doors are guarded by sentries whose number is legion; its treasury rises mountain high, filled with taxes gathered over the centuries. Here in Russia, they have torn it up by its roots; there is no fear, no hesitation in their minds."

He had heard many contradictory reports about this country and had been told of the pitiless violence of the Bolshevik regime. Many friends had tried to discourage his visit by painting lurid pictures of the lack of "civilised" comforts and amenities in that land, had warned him of the coarse food and the crude ways of the people and had added that in any case whatever he would be shown would be "mere window-dressing". But "I was thinking within myself that in the very courtyard of western civilisation, so triumphant in the display of wealth Russia has raised the seat of power of the dispossessed, totally ignoring the frowns and curses of the entire western world. If I do not go to see such a sight, who will? They are striving to destroy the power of the powerful and the wealth of the wealthy. Why should we be afraid of that? And why should we be angry? We have neither power nor wealth. We belong to the hungry and the helpless underdog class of the world."

Tagore was anything but a believer in communist ideology. Marxism or the philosophy of dialectic materialism was alien to his mental make-up which sought for harmony and cooperation rather than contradiction and conflict in the process of history. His faith in the validity of the individual conscience and in the "infinite personality of man" biased him against any technique of political action aimed at wholesale and violent suppression of opposition. He had a horror of the machine dominating the man and knew that the party machine did it more ruthlessly than any other kind. He believed that inhumane means were capable of perverting the most humane ends. He was by no means a blind admirer of whatever he saw in the Soviet Union. He was aware of the ruthless nature of the party dictatorship and of the many moral limitations of the Soviet experiment. But these limitations did not make him lose his perspective and miss the wood for the trees.He knew that a certain element of barbarism was inevitable in a Revolution, as in a War, but he trusted the great creative urge behind the Russian upheavel as evidenced in their enthusiasm for educating and uplifting the masses.

Returning to Germany, Tagore left for the United States, his last visit to the rival wonderland of modern civilisation, where on 25 November a public banquet was given in his honour by 400 leading citizens of New York. A reception was also organised for him at the Carnegie Hall where he spoke on Education. Ruth

St.Denis who admired him gave dance-recitals to raise funds for his school, but as her own country had been recently hard hit by an economic crisis, the poet handed over the proceeds for the benefit of the unemployed in New York. An exhibition of his paintings was held in New York and Boston, and in Washington the poet was received by President Hoover. American opinion was breaking away from the British fetters, for at one time President Wilson had not even deigned to acknowledge his cable from India. Tagore was also happy to meet Will Durant whose book, *The Case for India*, had been banned by the British Government in Bengal. Inscribing the book to Tagore,Will Durant had written, "You alone are sufficient reason why India should be free."

In January 1931 Tagore returned to India via London where he had a long talk with Bernard Shaw at a luncheon which the *Spectator* gave for him in Hyde Park Hotel. It had been a long and tiring tour but rich and fruitful in experience. He had seen the western world in its different phases and had left behind a trail of memory which, though it soon faded as all memory must, was not altogether lost. He did not know then that this was his last visit to the west, that his sun in the western sky had set.

Last Harvest

When I go from hence let this be my parting word,
that what I have seen is unsurpassable.

ONE might ask why he who welcomed, despite his repugnance to violence, the stormy upheaval in Russia did not show the same enthusiasm for the non-violent mass movement which the Mahatma was leading nearer home. As a matter of fact, Tagore keenly sympathised with the political and social upsurge in his own country—had he not partly inspired it himself?—and held the Mahatma in higher esteem than he did any other leader or personality, Indian or foreign. On the other hand, he recoiled from what he felt was a medieval and reactionary element in the Mahatma's mental make-up and social ideology which he feared would be misused by his followers. The Mahatma could rise above the limitation of his own biases but would his followers do so? How far his misgivings were justified may be left to the verdict of history.

He himself had passed, at the turn of the century, through a phase of patriotic fervour when he had harped on the glory of India's heritage and had imagined the mannerisms of her tradition to be the language of her spirit. But he was soon sobered by the innate lucidity of his mind and learnt to distinguish the mask from the face and came to realise that India, for all her uniqueness, was but a part of humanity like any other part and must march with the rest. The spirit of the age was a better guide than the ghost of the past and love of truth and reverence for life the true religion of man. Gandhi made the same discovery when he said, "If it is possible for the human tongue to give the fullest description of God, I have come to the conclusion that God is Truth. Two years ago I went a step further and said that Truth is God."

In his beautiful poem on Shahjahan, Tagore had said that

even greater than his achievement in building the Taj Mahal, was its builder's glory in leaving it behind. India too can surpass her past by leaving it behind and not by getting buried in it as in a mausoleum. The humblest cradle holding a new-born babe is a better vindication of man's immortal heritage than the noblest mausoleum brooding over the dead. In his paintings Tagore had completely turned his back on tradition. In his poetry and prose he went on steadily discarding the very perfection he had himself achieved. In his themes he continually harped on the new as he grew older. His very first production after his long foreign tour was a music-and-dance sequence called *Navin* (The New).

Meanwhile India was passing through hard times. Hundreds of brave Bengali youths, the flower of the people, were languishing in concentration camps on mere suspicion of their hidden sympathies with the revolutionary underground movement for freedom. In one such camp at Hijli two youths were murdered in cold blood by the guards. When the news of this outrage leaked out, Tagore was greatly perturbed and gave vent to his feelings at a mammoth public meeting held in Calcutta. Earlier he had sent a message of greetings in a poem to the prisoners in another concentration camp at Buxa. To the callousness of the rulers was added the ravage of nature caused by floods in north Bengal. In aid of the flood-stricken victims he staged in Calcutta *Sisu-tirtha,* a dramatised version in Bengali of the poem, *The Child,* which he had written in English the previous year in Germany.

The Rabindra Jayanti which had been organised by the citizens of Calcutta at the end of the year to mark the seventieth birthday of the poet, was suddenly cut short at his insistence on 4 January 1932 when the news was received of the arrest of Mahatma Gandhi within a week of his return from London where he had been invited to participate in a Round Table Conference. The poet who had still some faith left in the British professions of justice and fair play sent a cable to the Prime Minister, Mr Ramsay Macdonald, protesting against "the policy of indiscriminate repression... causing permanent alienation of our people from yours."On 26 January he issued a statement which the Government censorship or press did not allow to be fully published. The poet, hurt and mortified, expressed his feelings in poem, called "Prasna" (A Question), addressed to God: You have sent your messengers from time to time who have preached forgiveness and love of all mankind. They were noble souls and worthy of our reverence, and yet today their message seems a mockery and I want to ask you, Are you yourself, O Lord able to forgive and to love these creatures of yours who have poisoned your air and darkened your light?

The dejected poet sought retreat for a few days in a quite villa on the Ganges at Khardah where he composed a number of poems directly inspired by paintings, some his own and some of other Indian artists. These were later published as *Vichitrita* (Variegated) and dedicated to the artist Nandalal Bose.

Age and claims of a strenuous life were telling on Tagore's health and his straight back and stately shoulders were getting bent. When he had come to the regretful conclusion that he would no longer be able to undertake another foreign tour, came an invitation from the King of Iran, Reza Shah Pehlavi, to visit his country. "It would hardly do to refuse" an invitation from the august head of a neighbouring and friendly nation, he noted in his Dairy. And so on II April 1932 he left for Persia, accompanied by his daughter-in-law Pratima Devi, who looked after him in old age with the devotion of a loving daughter. To avoid the strain of a long and arduous journey they travelled by air.

From Bushire he travelled by road to Shiraz, the land of Hafiz and Sa'adi, where Tagore was happy to pay his respects at the graves of the two celebrated poets. After a brief halt at Ispahan, the party reached Teheran on 29 April where the Indian poet was overwhelmed with honour, both official and popular, the newspapers hailing him as "the greatest star shining in the eastern sky." His birthday was celebrated, while he was still in Teheran, with great éclat and the poet was deeply moved by the affection and honour showered on him with oriental lavishness, both by the Shah and by the people, and expressed his feelings in his farewell speech. On his way back to India he broke his journey at Baghdad where he was received by King Feisal of Iraq. He also spent a day in Bedouin camp—a long cherished desire since the days of his youth. Oh that I were a Bedouin!— he had exclaimed in one of his early poems.

Tragic news awaited him on his return from the land of roses and nightingales. His only grandson, Nitindra, delicate, sensitive youth of much promise, whom he had sent to Germany for training in book-printing, was seriously ill with galloping phthisis. Nitindra died in Germany on 7 August. The death of his only grandson in a far-away land was a severe blow. But the poet had known many bereavements, and from each great sorrow he had emerged more chastened in spirit and firmer in his faith in life. "From afar you seemed terrible and invincible in your pitiless majesty," he wrote in a fine poem. "With trembling heart I stood before you, in dread of your ominous frown. Then came the blow. I shivered and asked in fear: What more? Is the final thunderbolt yet to fall? It fell. Could this be all? I asked. Nothing more? My fear fell from me. When your thunderbolt loomed above, you seemed so much bigger than I. When you came down to strike me, you shrunk to my level and I ceased to shrink. Big you may be, but not bigger than death. It's I who am now bigger than death. Let this be my last word."

Whatever the affliction—and Rabindranath had his full share—he never succumbed to morbidity which he considered as a disease of the mind worse than any disease of the body. Sorrow and defeat were part of life and must be accepted with manly dignity. The cult of growling when balked or of whining like a beaten cur in which some poets have vented their pride or sought their solace was repugnant to his nature. Such sentimentalism as he sometime indulged in was provoked by his pity for others, pity for life, but rarely by self-pity. His most dominant feeling was his love of life, his philosophy was but an affirmation of it. The joy of living and exercising his sensibilities was to him a gift divinely dispensed for which he never ceased to be grateful. Even while he was grappling with his private sorrow he wrote:

> Once again I wake up. The night has waned and the
> world's petals unfold. This is a wonder without end . . .
> On the bark of this noble tree are inscribed

the signatures of centuries. Many a royal crown
it has seen roll in the dust. Today I sit under
its shade for one more day;
And I know that through this day revolves
unseen and unheard the wheel of time.

The music of this wheel revolving and rolling onward, invisibly, inaudibly, had never ceased to fascinate him. He looks back on the past, and there she stands, his beloved Muse, the ever varied, ever-beckoning Guardian Angel of his life. She had led him on, through smiles and tears, along many paths and by-paths, rough and smooth, and through many phases; and all the harvest of his life he has poured at her feet. Why is she now smiling and holding a basket in her hand at this end of the day? Must he still keep on pouring himself out and be emptied completely?

This and many other poems, some reminiscent, some pensive, some exultant, including the angry one named "A Question", referred to above, written on a variety of subjects and instinct with mellowed wisdom that come from conquered sorrow, were published as *Parisesh* (The End) in 1932. As the title indicates, he thought that they marked the end of his creative career. But in fact they marked only the end of a phase which had begun eighteen years earlier, in 1914, with, *Balaka*. It was a majestic phase which had begun and ended splendidly. But it was by no means the end. Another phase was to begin of which he had had a premonition in the poem cited above where he saw his Muse, the smiling lady half-veiled, waiting with an empty basket in her hand.

As though the ageing poet had suddenly recovered his prime of life, he was seized with passion to explore new ground, to strike music out of prose, to exploit the rhythmic possibilities of this pedestrain, utilitarian medium. However hard, rugged and uneven the ground, he would make his Muse trip over it as gracefully and with as much abandon as over the loveliest meadow. This he did superbly in the four volumes: *Punascha* (Postscript, 1932), *Sesh Saptak* (Last Melodies, 1935), *Patraput* (Plate of Leaves, 1936), and *Syamali* (The Dark Green One, 1936). He did not altogether discard his earlier love and published several volumes in conventional verse too, free or rhymed, but in all that he wrote from 1932 to his death nine years later, the evidence was clear and unmistakable that his poetic genius had revealed a new peak. His normal spiritual poise seemed to be maintained at a higher level and his eyes watch with even greater sympathy and understanding than before whatever passed before them, coaxing the commonplace to reveal its inmost beauty.

Fortunately for him, the adulation of the western world had considerably paled and had almost faded, and his name was becoming little more than hazy memory of a once dazzling meteor. The urge to preach and to reform the world was also cooling down. "The preacher is the professional dealer in particular ideas," he had once written. "His customers come at all hours of the day and put questions to him. His answers, which he gets into the habit of producing, gradually lose their living quality and his faith in his ideas runs the risk of being smothered under the deadness of his words. I believe that such a tragedy is more common than people suspect, especially with those who are good and therefore are ever ready to sign their cheque of benefit for others without waiting to see if the cash has had time to accumulate in the bank. This makes me think that it is safe to be nothing better than a mere poet. For poets have to be true to their best moments and not to other people's requirements."

Such golden moments were waiting for him to gather and it was lucky for him and his readers that he was henceforth to be confined to his home soil and thrown back on his native resources. This proved to be a great boon. Years ago he had sung:

> I have dived into the ocean of forms
> in the hope of getting the pearl of the Formless.
> I shall wander no more from one landing place
> to another in my worn-out boat.

Ceasing to wander he could now dive deeper than ever and get his pearl.

Many discerning Bengali critics believe that Tagore's greatest poetry was written in the last decade of his life. This may or may not be so, depending on the reader's mood, taste and personal predilection. What is undisputed is that he scaled many peaks in his long career, each different from the others, and as one watches him atop any one of them, it seems the highest peak. And since the peak scaled last was the nearest to his readers and its conquest was the more arduous and heroic because it was climbed in old age and failing health, it is no wonder that its scaling should seem to many other things besides writing poetry, some of them too must claim attention.

On 20 September 1932 the nation was stunned by the news of Mahatma Gandhi resorting in jail to a "fast unto death" as a protest against the British Prime Minister's decision known as the Communal Award, which aimed at dividing the Hindu community into separate electorates of caste and outcaste Hindus. At 3 a.m. of the day on which he was to begin the fast the Mahatma wrote to Tagore: "Dear Gurudev, this is early morning 3 o'clock of Tuesday. I enter the fiery gate at noon. If you can bless the effort I want it. You have been to me a true friend because you have been a candid friend often speaking your thoughts aloud... If your heart approves of the action I want your blessing. It will sustain me." But even before the letter was despatched he received the poet's wire: "It is well worth sacrificing precious life for the sake of India's unity and her social integrity. Our sorrowing hearts will follow your sublime penance with reverence and love."

On 24 September, Tagore, unable to keep away, left for Poona to visit the Mahatma in Yeravda Jail. The British Government having in the meanwhile conceded the main demand and accepted the compromise formula, the Mahatma broke his fast on the 26th, the poet seated by his bedside in jail. "The fast taken in the name of God," said the Mahatma in a public statement, "was broken in His name in the presence of Gurudev . . . The breaking was preceded by the Poet singing one of his Bengali hymns." The hymn sung was the original of the *Gitanjali* poem: "When the heart is hard and parched up, come upon me with a shower of mercy . . ."

Tagore had been persuaded by the University of Calcutta to

accept the Chair of Bengali, in which capacity he now delivered a series of lectures. He also organised a project, under his direct personal supervision, for compiling a glossary of technical and scientific terms in Bengali, a subject in which he had shown interest more than half a century ago when he was in his youth. In the midst of many public activities which included several important lectures, he wrote two new plays, *Tasher Desh* (The Kingdom of Cards), a delightful satire based on an earlier short story, and *Chandalika* (The Untouchable Girl), a short drama with only two characters on the stage, based on a Buddhist legend. The naive plot of the popular legend, showing how the psychic power of the Buddha had saved his devotee from the lust of a chandal girl, has been transformed by Tagore into a psychological drama of great spiritual significance. It is no longer the story of a wanton female bent on seducing a holy man, but of a very sensitive and proud girl, condemned by birth to a despised status, who is suddenly awakened to a consciousness of her destiny as a human being as good as any other, and to an awareness of her heart's hunger and capacity for love.

Both these plays, *Tasher Desh* and *Chandalika,* were staged in Calcutta in September. Soon after the performances, which were followed by a lecture on *Chhanda* (Prosody) at the Calcutta University, Tagore left for Bombay with a party of Santiniketan students and artists to participate in a Tagore Week organised there by his admirers led by the poetess Sarojini Naidu. From Bombay he went to the pleasant University town on sea, Waltair, where he was received by Dr Radhakrishnan, then Vice-Chancellor. The lectures delivered at the Andhra University were later published as *Man.* After a visit to Hyderabad where he was received by the Nizam who had earlier given a handsome donation to Visva-Bharati for a Chair of Islamic Studies, Tagore returned to Calcutta at the end of December to deliver his famous address at the Senate Hall on "Bharat-Pathik Rammohun" (Rammohun the Indian Pilgrim.) Before the year was over two new novels and a drama in prose were published, *Dui Bon* (Two Sisters), *Malancha* (The Garden) and *Bansari* (after the name of the main heroine in the play). It was indeed a fruitful year in literary activity, despite the many distractions of public engagements and political happenings.

Dui Bon is a short novel, mainly psychological in interest, dealing with the usual triangle, in this case two sisters in love with the same man. It is as if the author is trying to show that a man seeks in woman both mother and sweetheart. Lucky the man who can find both in one. But human nature and society being what they are, a man cannot always have both and love is at best only a partial fulfilment. A heart that is alive cannot escape frustration. The situation in this novel is further complicated by the two rivals being sisters, both of them equally admirable, each in her fashion.The author has tried to face boldly the psychological dilemma caused by a conflict of loyalties, loyalty to married love and loyalty to love, free and unfettered—without sentimentalising and without moralising.

Malancha is shorter in length but more dramatic in situation. The novel is mostly in dialogue and one wonders why the author did not write it as a play. The theme is almost similar to that of *Dui Bon,* two women and a man, though the rival in this case is not the wife's sister, but the husband's cousin. The psychological interest of this novel is, however, of a different nature.

Niraja was happily married to a florist who was passionately devoted to his nursery garden. She grew to share this devotion– in the usual feminine way, for only by sharing his interests could she possess her husband fully. The husband doted on her and their happiness was the envy of friends. Because she was happy she was generous. But the fates were jealous and after ten years of unblemished happiness, she suddenly became a bed-ridden invalid with no hope of sharing her husband's work in the garden. She could only watch from a window by her bed the scene of her past happiness.

This consolation, poor enough, turned into a source of bitterness when her husband sent for his young cousin Sarala to help in the garden. Seeing another woman, younger and healthy, take her place by her husband's side in the garden, Niraja assumed the worst and was wild with jealousy. Her very suspicions, which she took no care to hide, provoked fate and brought about what she most feared. More tragic than her physical misfortune was its effect in warping her mind. She who was generous when happy became unjust and vindictive. Aware of this self-degradation she tried to fight it but was helpless.Hers is a double tragedy. Deprived of health and then of love, she succumbed to the poverty of spirit which paralyses our capacity to love and to forgive.

Bansari is a witty play, sparkling with brilliant dialogue. It depicts the sophistication of high society in Calcutta, their high-brow pretensions and snobberies. The capacity for love is dissipated in intellectual flirtations resulting in a tragedy presented as a comedy. The play was never staged by the author, though he once planned its production—probably because the author was not sure of its effectiveness on the stage. His own acquaintance with the life and types of characters he was depicting was remote, largely derived from hearsay and gossip. Tagore was too old and famous to mix freely with the social types that were emerging and had no opportunities of observing them closely, himself unobserved. His treatment of love was becoming more and more intellectualised, bolder in thought but less potent in conveying its feeling. Not only the flesh and blood but perhaps the heart, too was getting old, only the mind was active and in full armour.

Returning to Santiniketan at the beginning of January 1934, he received, a fortnight later, Jawaharlal Nehru and his wife, Kamala. The poet who admired Jawaharlal Nehru for his patriotic courage and intellectual integrity, his rational outlook and international sympathies, held a public reception to welcome him and his wife. Meanwhile on 15 January, north India was rocked by an earthquake of great severity,causing great damage to life and property in several towns of Bihar. Gandhi who was at that time touring south India said in a public statement that this calamity was a divine chastisement for the sin of untouchability. "A man like me cannot but believe that this earthquake is a divine chastisement sent by God for our sins . . . For me there is a vital connection between the Bihar calamity and the untouchability campaign."

Tagore was shocked to see the Mahatma resort to such a characteristically priestly tactic of exploiting the conception of sin to din fear in the minds of the people and said in a public statement: "It has caused me a painful surprise to find Mahatma Gandhi accusing those who blindly follow their own social custom of untouchability of having brought down God's vengeance upon certain parts of Bihar, evidently specially selected for His desolating displeasure. It is all the more unfortunate because this kind of unscientific view of phenomenon is too readily accepted by a large section of our countrymen." Gandhi, however, reiterated his faith in an article in his English weekly, *Harijan.* "To me the earthquake was no caprice of God, nor a result of a meeting of blind forces," he wrote. "We do not know the laws of God nor their working." Jawaharlal Nehru's comment on this controversy is worth recalling:" During my tour in the earthquake areas, or just before going there, I read with a great shock Gandhiji's statement to the effect that the earthquake had been a punishment for the sin of untouchability. This was a staggering remark and I welcomed and wholly agreed with Rabindranath Tagore's answer to it. Anything more opposed to the scientific outlook it would be difficult to imagine."

The poet was restless—athirst, as ever, for the far-away. He was ageing and was no longer able to travel as he would have wished to. More harassing than the problem of age was that of money. While the income from the ancestral estates might have been adequate for his personal and family needs—he lived simply and despised ostentation or luxury—it could hardly suffice to meet the expenses of his school and university as well. The royalties from his Bengali publication were meagre— poetry is rarely a profitable vocation and the buying capacity of the very limited reading public of his country was pitiful. For a few years after the Nobel Prize the income from his English and other foreign publications was a welcome windfall, but much of it was spent on his many foreign tours and in Germany where his books had sold most the phenomenal inflation reduced the value of his royalties to almost nothing.

By 1934 Tagore had become in the west more a memory than a living voice and his royalties had considerably dwindled. On the other hand his university at Santiniketan had grown so indiscriminately that it threatened to become a white elephant which every one was willing to admire but no one ready to feed. The poet who had given to his people great and lasting riches which few legacies could equal was reduced to the pitiful position of begging for doles to keep his university from starving. The university which was his pet child had become a prodigal, a source of constant headache and humiliation to the last years of a life otherwise free and glorious. Begging was a humiliation to this aristocratic mind;nor was it of much avail in a country where the moneyed classes pour offerings either in the lap of priests or in the pockets of politicians.

The only way left to the ageing poet was to earn money by making the school itself productive. This he could do by training troupes of actors and dancers who would stage his plays and ballets in different towns and help to raise money. This was not, of course, the only reason. The artist in him itched to see his own creations on the stage. Unlike his other written works, the songs had to be sung to be enjoyed, the ballets staged to be appreciated. Moreover, these two aspects of his creative activity, along with his paintings, were the only ones which all his countrymen, even those who did not know Bengali—and they were the vast majority—could appreciate and enjoy. And so the country was regaled with the unusual spectacle of the venerable poet and seer escorting a band of performing artists, singers and dancers all over the country. Whatever this man who has been rightly called an artist in life did became somehow creative and educative, and these tours, apart from their other aspects, became a mission of considerable educative importance, creating a taste in the public for aspects of Indian culture hitherto ignored or despised.

The first of these cultural tours, apart from the earlier one to Bombay, was in Ceylon for which charming island Tagore had always had a warm corner in his heart. It was during his stay in Ceylon that Tagore completed what was to be his last novel, *Char Adhyay* (Four Chapters). In this short and powerful novel, which has since been successfully dramatised for the stage, he returns to the theme he had discussed earlier, in a different setting, in *The Home and the World*—human values and political ideals. The setting is the underground revolutionary movement in Bengal; against its heroism and its terrorism are depicted the frustration of love and the gradual debasement of human values. The author's analysis of the motives that inspire and condition political heroism is marked by deep psychological insight in this tragic drama of frustrated idealism and is expressed in language of great vigour and beauty. the novel aroused a storm of controversy in Bengal and the author was mercilessly reviled. He had uttered too many home truths.

During the five years from 1932, despite the many tours he undertook within the country and one outside India to Iran, Tagore published seven volumes of poetry, two novels, a drama, and composed music for, a directed the production on stage of five dance-dramas: *Sapmochan* (Redemption), *Chandalika* and *Tasher Desh* in 1933, and *Chitrangada* and *Syama* in 1936. Except for *Tasher Desh* (The Kingdom of Cards), which was based on a shrt story written much earlier, the themes of the other four were drawn from of Hindu and Buddhist legends which he had earlier retold in verse. What Tagore had taken from the ancient lore were skeletons to which he gave new life by filling the dry bones which flesh and blood not ony of music and dance but of dramiatic interest and deep psychological and moral significance. Since then this form of dance-drama which is neither a ballet proper nor an opera has gained considerable vogue in India.

The two novels *Malancha* and *Char Adhyay* (both 1934), the drama *Bansari* (1993) and two books of verse *Parisesh* (1932) and *Vichitrita* (1993) have already been referred to earlier. Of the five remaining volumes of poetry, four were of prose-poems, a form in which he had occasionally experimented earlier but which he now took up in earnest. He began it with *Punsacha* (The Postscript), published soon after *Parisesh* in 1932. Introducing these poems he said that a prose-poem is not one which merely ignores or flouts the prosodic rules of metre and rhyme but which while seeming to follow the uninhibited freedom of prose succeeds in creating a new rhythm of poetry thereby widening tis horizon. The urge to exalt the possiblities of this pedestrain form was also the reflection of his current mood of lingering lovingly on the commonplace incidents and objects of everyday life.

The very first poem "Kopai" seems to indicate this. Kopai is a rivulet that flows not far from Santiniketan. The poet contrasts its modest and unassuming charm with the awesome majesty of the river Padma on whose bank he had spent so many years of early manhood." The proud river has her name in the venerable texts; through her veins runs the sacred current of the Ganges." When she swelled during the rains, hundreds of homesteads were submerged. The river was pitiless in her pride. But in his old age the poet is content to have Kopai as his neighbour."Her speech is the speech of the humble home, not the language of the learned . . . Its cadence fails not the Santal boy lazily tramping along with his bow and arrows; it times itself to the lumbering market cart loaded with straw; to the panting breath of the potter shouldering earthenwares in a pair of hanging baskets tied to a pole, his pet pariah dog fondly following his shadow; it moves at the pace of the weary steps of the village schoolmaster worth three rupees a month, holding an old torn umbrella over his head."

There is a large variety of themes and moods depicted in this and the three volumes of prose-poems which followed, some playful, some serious or even metaphysical, some frivolous, some sad, some narrative, some lyrical, some sentimental and some devastating in their irony. Many of them are reminiscent and some in the first person singular, though what is in first person singular need not always be reminiscent or autobiographical. Three main characteristics mark these poems: a recurring reminiscent mood, a need to look back on the long path strewn with memories; a widening horizon of thought and a deepening sympathy with what is commonly ignored, discarded despised, uninhibited by moral or social bias; and a restless urge to explore to the farthest limits the possibilities of Bengali diction and rhythm and to draw uncanny music out of the seemingly discordant.

It would be wrong to imagine that these four books of prose-poems, remarkable as they are, mark, whether as an aberration or a further development, a stage of no return, where Tagore ceased to be what he had always been. As a matter of fact, even while he was writing these prose-poems, he was also writing other verse of less unorthodox kind as well as pure traditional lyrics in the form of songs. Though he went on outgrowing his past and trying out new forms and media, basically he did not cease to be what he always was, namely, a lover of nature, lover of earth, lover of life, lover of death, and lover of the mystery that unites life with death. It is this love that enabled him to identify himself—often in a manner that seems uncanny—with every aspect and mood of nature, and which explains his intuitive humanism, his universal sympathies and his overflowing tenderness for his fellow beings or for whatever is nurtured in the lap of our earth. This love is a recurrent theme in all his writings spread over a period of more than six decades.

In the poems of the last decade of his life, when the world had so radically and violently changed from the world he had been born and grown into, this love instead of recoiling from life and the world grown menacing and mocking, and retreating into its shell, became even more all-embracing, more tender, more frankly avowed than ever. "I have loved. How much or how well I could not know. This earth I loved. With eyes entranced I have gazed on it. Midst its hungers and thirsts, I've tasted its nectar. In its dust I found my true fulfilment, and among the dishonoured the degraded my liberation." This is said, not by way of socialist bravado, but with deep humility and feeling, as though what he had sought in heaven, he now found lying discarded on earth.

He had been brought up in the religion of his father, a kind of devotional theism which sought God in the heart and not in any concrete visible image. His religious poetry (his poetry includes songs where his lyricism is at its purest and perhaps at its best) thus began as an intimate *tete-a-tete* with his deity whose image invisible though it was and remained, went on changing and assuming different aspects until, one might say, it almost ceased to be independent of what he saw and heard and felt. His God became everything, and everything, however seemingly ugly or terrible, was lit up with divinity.

This wisdom, such at it was, came to him through sorrow. As he put it, in the deepest cavern of the being there is such utter darkness that one can only catch a glimpse of what is hidden there with the torch of sorrow. This wisdom was primarily of the heart and not of the head, much less the wisdom gleaned from scripture and philosophy. It helped to release him from bondage to any formal faith, creed or tradition and committed him only to love of this earth and what is sustained by it, or as he chose to put it, he was content to be good-for-nothing and glad."Over the play of light and shade outside this window, let my consciousness float away—no thinking, no disputing, no learning—until it merges into the great ocean where death awaits life."

His humanism came to him more directly and with greater certitude from this wisdom of the heart than from the subtle speculations of the Upanishads or from the Vaishnav lyrical mysticism or from the liberal humanism of western thought. In one of the poems of *Punascha* he tells an anecdote which well illustrates his characteristic feeling and attitude. It is about a *rangarejini* or the daughter of a Muslim dyer. Shankarlal was a learned Court Pandit renowned for his erudition and power of debate. Once he had to face the challenge of a celebrated Pandit from the south. Noticing that the turban he proposed to wear at the contest was soiled, he took it to Jaseem the local dyer. Jaseem asked his young daughter Amina to take the turban to the near-by stream and wash it.Having washed it,when the cloth was spread on the grass to dry, Amina noticed a verse inscribed in one corner of it: *Tōmār sripada mōr lālāte biraje* (Your sacred feet rest on my forehead). Amina fetched from her cottage some coloured thread and stitched another verse below it: *Parash pāi ne tāi hridayer mājhe* (That's why their touch is missing in the heart). When the Pandit came to fetch his turban he noticed the second verse and stared at the dyer's daughter. Then he said, "Maiden, you have transformed the arrogance of my intellect into wisdom of the heart. I cannot now go back to the royal court. My way lies elsewhere."

Punascha was followed by *Sesh Saptak* (Last Melodies). Even after adding the Postscript he found he had much to say, he needed to think and feel aloud—at any rate on paper. He was in a pensive mood, musing and recalling, and thought that these would be his last melodies. The very first poem is full of regrets that he failed to appraise her worth (Whose? his wife Mrinalini's?) when she was with him . He took her love and devotion for granted. But now by his suffering he has gained her truly. On his birthday (25 Vaisakh by Bengali calendar) he reviews his long life during which he has died and has been reborn again and again, a garland woven of many Rabindranaths. He looks back on the world's past and sees nothing but broken ruins of pomp and glory and pride. All around are the shifting sands of impermanence, and in the midst of it all "I feel in the throbbing of my heart the stillness of the infinite."

Sitting in the dark one evening in his lonely room, he misses her who was once his playmate and had brought so much joy to his life. Suddenly there was a rustle and he could feel her presence and almost a touch of her breath. "Have you come back to your old haunt—from the other world?" He heard an inaudible voice: "To whom shall I come back?" He replied, "Why, am I not there? Can you not see me?" The voice said, "He who was my own and ever-young playmate on this earth, him I do not see in this room any more." I asked, "Is he nowhere then?" There was a soft whisper: "He is there where I am. Nowhere else." Needless to say, not all the poems are pensive or reminiscent in this strain. The fare is varied and lively.

Two other remarkable collections of prose–poems came in quick succession in 1936: *Patraput* which means a cup or vessel made of tree leaves, and *Syamali,* meaning the dark green one (feminine gender), the title of a magnificent ode to earth and also the name he gave to the mud hut specially built for him, which became his favourite residence in his last years and where Mahatma Gandhi also stayed when he visited Santiniketan later. Many of the poems in these two volumes are exceedingly beautiful and in them Tagore's power of expression is at its best. As usual, some of them are lyrical, whether playful or pensive, some philosophical or abstruse, some narrative or reminiscent, and some give vent to his passionate protest at the ominous and ugly happenings in the world outside. One of them is addressed to

Africa and is an indictment of the centuries-old White atrocities on the Blacks.

With-man-traps stole upon you those hunters
whose fierceness was keener than the fangs of
your wolves...
Your forest trails became muddy with tears and blood,
while the nailed boots of the robbers
left their indelible prints
along the history of your indignity.
And all the time across the sea
Church bells were ringing in their towns and villages,
the children were lulled in their mother's arms,
and poets sang hymns to Beauty.

In another he explores the extreme of humanism and defiantly challenges all prescribed formulae of religion. He has no need of God if He is not in the light of the sun and in the heart of the untouchable and beyond all barriers. For him the primal mystery of creation is in the eflgence of light and its final mystery in the nectar of love. He belongs to the trible of spiritual outcastes.

They are the outcastes, the uninitiates in the sacred chant,
the dealers in religion keep them outside the temple doors...
A poet, I am of their clan,
I Have no caste, no sacred chant,
My offerings do not reach the Deity
imprisoned in his Temple.
The priest comes out and asks smiling,
"Have you been inside and seen the Deity?"
"No, "I reply
Dumbfounded he asks, "Don't you know the way in?"
"No, "I say.
"Have you no caste?" he asks.
"No."...
Ignored by the multitude
I have hungered for Man's comradeship,

Man round whose meeting place no walls are raised,
and no sentries stand on guard . . .
I missed Man within enclosures
and found him beyond all frontiers
that divide nation from nation,
land from land.

In between *Sesh Saptak* and *Patraput* was published in 1935 *Bithika* (The Avenue), a book of poems in rhymed verse, including some songs. This form was his oldest love and he reverts to it again and again, whatever his experiments and explorations of other modes. Some of the poems are very beautiful and as usual represent a large variety of themes and moods. He looks back on the long avenue of the past he has traversed and left behind and although he cannot get back what is lost, he has learnt to gaze at life's mystery and has experienced"the joy that comes of forgetting all loss and gain, all sorrow and happiness." Many are love poems but it is a bodiless, objectless love, without passion and without a concrete object. The poet is in love with love and cannot forget the love he has known. He can only console himself. "It is there and yet not there, and so there is no burden. One has to do without it and therein lies its value." But there is a real passion of grief in one poem addressed to "Durbhagini", the ill-fated one. It is dated 6 August 1932. The poet's only surviving daughter was in Germany by the bedside of her only son who died the following day. Tagore must have had a premonition of the impending tragedy and imagines her daughter standing before him and he cannot look her in the face. Her eyes have been drained of tears and there is only a persistent question in them: Why, O Why?

Unable to travel about freely, the poet took to changing his dwelling place, from house to house. He now took it into his head that he must live in a mud cottage. So a mud hut had to be built, next to the house he was then occupying. Day after day he watched the walls of the new hut rising under the nimble hands of Santal women—immortalised in an exquisite poem included in *Bithika*.

The Santal woman hurries up and down the gravelled path under the *shimool* tree; a course grey sari closely twines her slender limbs, dark and compact; its red border sweeping across the air with the flaming red magic of the *palash* flower.

Some absent-minded divine designer, while fashioning a black bird with the stuff of the July cloud and the lightning flash, must have improvised unawares this woman's form; her impulsive wings hidden within, her nimble steps uniting in them a woman's walk and a bird's flight.

Before the year was over two of his plays were staged, *Saradotsav* (Autumn Festival) in Santiniketan, and *Arupratan* (Invisible Jewel), a modified version of *The King of the Dark Chamber,* in Calcutta the poet appearing in both of them. It was not only that the public clamoured for his appearance on the stage; he also loved to act. After delivering three lectures on Education in Calcutta in February 1936, he was absorbed in preparing a musical version of his early drama, *Chitrangada,* himself conducting the rehearsals of the ballet. His daughter-in-law, Pratima Devi, was the chief collaborator in the preparation of his ballets.

The dance-drama (*Nritya-natya,* as the author described it) is perhaps the most popular of all his ballets. It was successfully staged in Calcutta, winning high praise, and was then taken by the poet on a tour of north India. After earning more applause than money in several big towns, it was staged in Delhi in the last week of March. Gandhi who happened to be in Delhi was much perturbed that the aged poet in failing health should be obliged, for want of funds for his university, to undertake such arduous tours, and immediately sent him a letter enclosing a bank draft for Rs. 60,000 as an offering from "Your humble countrymen". "Now," wrote the Mahatma, "You will relieve the public mind by announcing cancellation of the rest of the programme." Tagore was deeply touched and grateful, though at the back of his mind was passing regret that he would miss the excitement of taking his troupe around, for there is no doubt that he thoroughly enjoyed putting his creations on the stage, himself seated in a corner, like a silent and motionless conductor, or, as a critic once put it, like an authentic signature to his own work.

As the Delhi visit made memorable Gandhi's generous and loving solicitude for the poet's health, it made notoriously manifest the British government's ungenerous arrogance. Delhi was then the imperial capital and the authorities had long chafed at Tagore's forthright condemnation of the Government's repressive polices. How unimaginative the imperial bureaucracy could be was demonstrated when the Delhi Municipality's proposal to give a civic reception to Tagore was vetoed by the Government.

Returning from Delhi Tagore did not sit back and relax, as the Mahatma would have wished him to do. He continued to preside over public meetings in Calcutta—a much greater strain than watching his own dramas. After paying a graceful tribute to the Mahatma at a special service held in the Santiniketan Mandir on the occasion of Gandhi's birthday on 2 October, he set to work on a new dance-drama based on an earlier poem,"Parisodh" (Retribution), which he renamed *Syama* (after the name of the heroine). This was staged in Calcutta later in the month, the author, as usual, present on the stage.

The theme is the tragedy of love's blind egoism which does not scruple to sacrifice every other happiness to its own, only to find that it has thereby lost its right to happiness. Syama, the city's beautiful courtesan, is in love with Vajrasen, a foreigner, who is falsely arrested for a crime he did not commit and is sentenced to death. Syama saves his life by persuading one of her many admirers to sacrifice himself in Vajrasen's place. The greatful foreigner gladly turns Syama's lover, but when he comes to know of her inhuman conduct by which she procured his freedom he is filled with disgust and shame and leaves her. The moral law working through him brings the nemesis, the inevitable retribution, to the unfortunate Syama, so devoted to her lover, so guilty to humanity.

In February 1937, Tagore delivered the Convocation address of the Calcutta University, a landmark in the history of that university, for it was the first occasion in the eighty years of its history when a private citizen was offered this privilege hitherto reserved for British Viceroys and Governors. It was also the first occasion when the address was delivered in Bengali, and no in English. Tagore used the occasion for a magnificent plea for the use of the mother tongue as the medium of education.

After two more public addresses of importance, one to the Bengali Literary Conference, the other to the Parliament of Religions held in Calcutta to mark the birth centenary of the Indian saint, Ramakrishna Paramahamsa, Tagore inaugurated at Santiniketan the Cheena Bhavan (Department of Sino-Indian Studies), the first of its kind in India and still a leading centre of Chinese studies in the country. The summer was spent in the pleasant Himalayan resort, Almora, where he wrote *Visvaparichaya,* an introduction to modern science for Bengali readers. Tagore had no academic education in science or for that matter in any other discipline. But ever since as a young lad he had accompanied his father on a visit to western India and to Dalhousie in the Himalayas and had received practical lessons in astronomy under the clear star-lit sky, he had developed an interest in the physical sciences which he continued to satisfy by desultory reading. In his school at Santiniketan the study of nature and the teaching of science were important items in the curriculum, and his own favourite reading-hobby till his last years were books on higher physics which dealt with the mystery of the universe around us. This was the theme of the book *Visvaparichaya* which he wrote for Bengali readers. It incorporates no original research but is with out doubt an original and fascinating exposition for the benefit of Bengali readers of the results of the latest researches in the physical sciences.

Returning from Almora, he addressed a public meeting in Calcutta to protest against the ill-treatment of political prisoners in the Andamans who had gone on a hunger strike. In September 1937 he composed and directed the production of *Varsha-Mangal,* a song-and-dance sequel celebrating the rainy season, which was staged in Calcutta, with him seated on the stage. He loved nature in all its moods, and every season of the year, including the tropical summer with its extreme heat and terrific dust-storms, had been celebrated by him in poems and songs. But he loved most of all the rains. The very first jingle he had learnt as a child was the Bengali nursery rhyme, "The rain patters, the leaf quivers..." The verbal jingle as well as nature's jingle as the rain patters and the leaf quivers had never ceased to delight his ear.

The autumn, with its clear, rain-washed sky and stray clouds "floating uselessly" was also a season very dear to him. But the autumn of 1937 had a grim experience in store for him. On the evening of 10 September, as he was seated in his usual chair, he suddenly lost consciousness. There had been no warning of an impending ailment and no diagnosis of the comatose condition which persisted for fortyeight hours could be had until a team of doctors arrived from Calcutta. There was no telephone at Santiniketan in those days and it took time before the message for medical aid could reach Calcutta. Meanwhile the unconscious poet hovered between life and death. Fortunately he recovered his consciousness and was gradually restored to normal health

Beneath the stupor of coma, the seemingly suspended consciousness must have been active underground, for the experience of the borderland where he hovered between life and death survived very vividly and was described by the poet in a series of poems, which comparatively short and only eighteen in number, mark one of the highest peaks in his poetic achievement. Born of a profound travail in the subconscious, a kind of shock therapy administered by Fate's own skilled hand, they are compact and tense and bear in them the powerful impress of a deeply felt experience. Far from the ravings of a sick mind, there is no hint in them of fear or pain or complaining. The mind is more concentrated and vigorous than ever and the consciousness is surcharged with the anguished elation of a perilous and exciting adventure, of having been hijacked, as it were, to the fantastic borderland where the familiar world is blotted out and the soul is forced to peer into the void of the Great Beyond, at once dark and luminous, where there is no night, no day. They were published in 1938 with the appropriate title, *Prantik* (The Borderland).

"With stealthy steps the messenger of death came creeping out of the lightless cavern of the universe," was how the poet described the sudden onslaught in the first poem he wrote after regaining conciousness." All the layers of fine dust that had accumulated in the enveloping spaces of the mind were dissolved and washed clean in the corrosive acid of pain, and behind the heavy curtain of a deep swoon was carried out silently a ruthless scouring of the soul..." The metaphor changes from poem to poem," I saw–in the dusk of my wearied consciousness–my body float down the murky river, loaded with its tore of feelings and its multiple pains. . . . The body fades into a shadow, melts into a point and loses itself into darkness without end. . ." And again: "When one by one the lights went off the stage and the auditorium emptied, my mind was stilled as though at the command of Silence, like a sleep whose dreams are wiped out by the ink-black hand of darkness. All the make-up I had devised for my prolonged appearance on the stage since the curtain went up came to nothing; all the attitudes I had struck, the colour I had flaunted to impress the multitude were wiped out. . ." But there is no regret, for the has seen the farthest limit of being and is struck with wonder.

Not all the poems are self-exploratory or introspective. The last two in this slender sheaf show an acute awareness of the tragedy that was hovering over Europe and was soon to engulf it. As he put it in one of them which he himself later translated into English:" When my mind was released from the black cavern of oblivion and woke up into an intolerable surprise, it found itself at the crater of a volcanic hell-fire that spouted forth a stifling fume of insult to man. . . On its one side a defiant savagery and the growl of homicidal drunkeness, on the other timid power tied to the load of their carefully guarded hoardings. . ." He is angry and would like to hurl an "imprecation upon this cannibal whose gruesome hunger spares neither women nor children. . ." But cursing is not normal to his nature, in fact it is alien, and he knows that such wrath is itself savage and futile. He would like to utter words of peace and love and compassion, but is afraid they would sound even more futile. And so in the last (and shortest) poem of *Prantik* written on the Christmas day of 1937 he said:

> All around the serpents hiss and spread
> their poisonous fumes,
> Sweet words of peace will seem like hollow mockery.
> Let me, before I take my leave,
> hail those who are getting ready in many homes
> to battle with the Demon.

And yet only a little later he was to write that though he had seen enough evil and pain in the world, had seen the spirit of man being poisoned by man's own hand, he had also listened to the music of harmony that is in the heart of the universe, had heard amidst the dust and din of the storm the eternal voice of peace. Tagore's poetry would not be what it is but for these contrary voices and conflicting affirmation to which it owes much of its richness, variety and never-failing vitality. He was true to each mood and phase as he experienced it, and this passionate sincerity which enabled him to challenge and surpass himself again and again was his most consistent virtue, as it was of Mahatma Gandhi.

While the poet was convalescing he had been taken for further treatment to Calcutta where Gandhi and Nehru who happened to be there for a political conference called on him. By January 1938 he was well enough to receive Lords Lothian and Brabouren who visited him at Santiniketan. Soon after, as the spring came, he was seized with the recurring frenzy of song and he began working on a music-and-dance version of his drama *Chandalika* (The Untouchable Girl). This is one of his most moving and powerful dance-dramas and was successfully staged in Calcutta in March, the author seated in a corner of the stage at the last performance. Gandhi happened to be in Calcutta again and called on him. With his deep insight and sympathy the Mahatma understood that it was no use expecting the poet to stick to his earlier assurance that he would not risk his health by attending stage performances of his plays in cities. The raising of funds for his school and university was merely an excuse or at best a stimulus; the real need was of the artist to create and to witness his own creation on the stage.

The summer was spent in Kalimpong, the charming little town nestling in the eastern Himalayas where his son had a house. There on his birthday he wrote a magnificent poem with which began a new book of poems published later in the year as *Senjuti* (Evening Lamp). He is still haunted by his experience of the Borderland, though the enchantment of life was beginning to regain its hold on him. A few lines are quoted below in the poet's own English rendering;

My birthday!
With Death's passport in hand
it has emerged from its dive into the
    chasm of nothingness
to breathe a while on the outskirts of existence.
From the worn-out chain have dropped
    the beads of the past years
and with this newest birthday
begins the counting of the days
of a new-born life.

He is aware of the inestimable value of this boon, this temporary reprieve, and prays·

Grant me, mother earth,
that my life's mirage born of burning thirst
may recede in the farthest horizon
and my unclean beggar's bowl empty into the dust
its accumulated defilements;
and as I start my crossing to the unrevealed shore
let me never look back with longing
on the last leavings of the feast of life.

From Kalimpong he went to Mungpoo, a nearby hillside in Darjeeling district, to be the guest for a few days of a young poetess, an ardent admirer and devotee whose husband was the

Director of the Government Cinchona plantation (from which quinine is extracted). There he wrote, besides some poems, a treatise on Bengali language, later published as *Bangla Bhasha Parichaya* (An Introduction to Bengali Language). Study of Bengali language, its structure and sound system, its folk reserves and literary usages were an old hobby of his and his explorations in this field bear ample evidence of his remarkable critical insights. With him poetic exuberance and critical analysis, romantic idealism and objective appraisal of cold facts went hand in hand. Something of the dashing adventurism of his romantic grandfather as well as the severe and practical idealism of his father had survived in him, although assuming vastly different colours.

He always responded warmly to feminine solicitude and care, and both at Kalimpong where his daughter-in-law looked after his needs and comfort and at Mungpoo he was relaxed and at ease. His Mungpoo hostess has recorded with almost Boswellian fidelity his conversations and his light-hearted banter with her and other members of the household, and her memoir which was published later is a charming and unfailing humour and his warm-hearted responses.

Returning to Santiniketan in early July, in time to welcome the rains he loved so much, he had a painful exchange of letters with the Japanese poet Yone Noguchi whom he had once admired and who had been earlier accorded an affectionate and ceremonial welcome at Santiniketan. Yone Noguchi had pleaded with him to believe that what Japan was doing in China was for Asia's "liberation". Tagore was provoked to reply: "You are building your conception of an Asia which would be raised on a tower of skulls. I have, as you rightly point out, believed in the message of Asia, but I never dreamt that this message could be identified with deeds which brought exaltation to the heart of Tamerlane at his terrible efficiency in manslaughter . . . The doctrine of 'Asia for Asia' which you enunciate in your letter, as an instrument of political blackmail has all the virtues of the lesser Europe which I repudiate and nothing of the larger humanity that makes us one across the barriers of political labels and divisions."

Tagore had loved Japan very much and it was for him a source of deep anguish and humiliation that a nation which he had once hailed as the new sunrise in Asia should behave as a scourge of the East. What a mockery of the Buddha was its militant bravado and its blood-thirsty heroism! In this anguish he wrote a poem bristling with pained mockery from which a part of a stanza is quoted below in his own English rendering:

> They pray for success;
> for they must raise weeping and wailing
> in their wake, sever ties of love,
> plant flags on the ashes of desolated homes . . .
> and so they march to the temple of the Buddha
> the Compassionate,
> to claim his blessings,
> while loud beats the drum rat-a-tat
> and earth trembles.

Tagore had a multi-track mind on which different wagons plied almost simultaneously. All through 1937, before and after his encounter with death which was an experience so profoundly traumatic that some of the utterances of that period read as though written in heart's blood, he was also painting weird grostesque, mocking or fantastic scenes and figures, and penning humorous and deliciously frivolous verse sparkling with fun and mischief and full of folk rhythms and idiom, which are a delight for young and old, for the simple as much as for the sophisticated. A series of such volumes were published in 1937: *Khapchhada* (Nonsense Rhymes), *Chhadar Chhabi* (Pictures in Rhymes), and a book of tales and fantasies in prose, named *Shey* (He)—all in one year. These were followed by *Prahashini* (The Smiling One) 1939, humorous poems, playful and mocking, many of them teasing the modern woman for her affectations. Tagore loved to prattle with children and he had a sense of the absurd and the fantastic which was an unfailing source of delight and wonder to the young for whom he wrote a large number of nursery and nonsense rhymes as well as fantasies in prose. They are impossible to render into another medium, but some idea of what he did in this line could be had from the following English translation by Humayun Kabir of a poem he wrote for the young pupils of his Santiniketan school:

One night I dreamt a strange dream. Binu was calling to me, "Wake up and see what is happening."

I sat up and saw Calcutta shuffling along with uncertain steps as thousands of beams and rafters knocked against one another. The brick-built houses marched ahead like rhinos, while doors and windows banged and clanged. The streets moved like huge pythons and on their back clattered trams and carriages. The shops and markets bobbed up and down while roofs hit one another on the head in a drunken orgy. The Howrah bridge crawled like a giant scorpion and Harrison Road trailed behind. The Monument reeled, as if a mad elephant was waving its trunk in the air. Our school was rushing forward madly, with arithmetic and grammar books running fast. The maps were fluttering on the wall like birds flapping their wings. The bells tolled ceaselessly and without break, with no heed of the hour.

Millions cried,"Stop this madness, for where is it you want to go and whence ?"

Drunken with movement, Calcutta paid no heed, for the lure of dance had made even pillars and walls restless.

I thought to myself,"What does it matter if Calcutta goes straight to Bombay? If she prefers Delhi, Lahore or Agra all we need do is to put a turban on her head and horned shoes on her feet. Or if she wished to rush off to England, all the people will become hatted coated and booted Englishmen!"

Suddenly there was a bang and I woke. Calcutta was as always in Calcutta.

Three volumes of serious verse followed in the wake of *Senjuti* discussed earlier: *Akashpradip* (Lamp in the Sky). 1939, *Navajatak* (The New-Born) 1940 and *Sanai* (The Flute) 1940. These poems lack the sombre grandeur of *Prantik*, for the memory of the Borderland and the haunting sense of the terror and beauty that lay beyond it had weakened and the poet was once more nestling in the soft arms of his beloved earth. The sense of the awesome sublime would return later when his utterance would again attain the same if not higher, heights of sombre exaltation.

Meanwhile he was content to relax and watch and savour what simple delight of sight and sound were still left for him on earth. Not much was left of the old familiar joy living. What was the use of lighting a lamp in a house that was empty? He would rather lift up the lamp skywards where old memories had lost their way among the stars which had watched over him all his life. May be, the lamp will draw the memories down. That's how he explains the title of the book in the first poem. His joy and solace lie in recollecting. Many of the poems are thus reminiscent, but they are free of morbidity or self-pity of any kind.

He is sipping his morning cup of tea in the month of *Chaitra* when the mango trees begin to bear fruit. He sees three unripe mangoes fall down on the ground and his mind flies back to the days of his boyhood when unripe mangoes were "the golden key that opened the door to the secret chamber of daylong joy." She loved unripe mangoes and he had won access to her presence by picking them secretly and bringing them to her. It was for bidden to climb the tree. So he would patiently wait until a strong gust of wind brought the unripe mangoes down. The first time he took them to her, she said, "Who asked you to bring them? No one, he replied crest fallen, and leaving the basket at her feet, slunk away. Another day, while picking them, he was stung by a bee. She chided, "You don't have to do this." He remained silent. But in the end he won her friendship. A gold ring she gave him one day with something sweet inscribed on it. While bathing in the Ganges it slipped from his finger and was lost. The unripe mangoes still fall from the tree, but he has no heart to pick them. "The lock is not there, and the key does no fit."

He recalls the nursery rhyme his grandmother used to recite to him: "The bride comes in the palanquin, with strings of pearls round her neck and anklets of gold round her feet!" Ever since then he had looked for that bride who, on her way to him, was lost among the stars.

The next volume of poems, *Navajatak* (The New-Born), express a very different mood, more masculine and vitally concerned with what was happening around him in the contemporary world. Introducing these poems he wrote that his poetry had changed its season from time to time, often without his being aware of it. These poems were his *tete-a-tete* with the new age that was taking birth all around him. It needs to be pointed out that these various volumes were not written as separate bunches, each at a stretch and representing a uniform mood or phase. Many poems published in separate volumes were actually written almost simultaneously. The very first poem, for example, of *Navajatak* in which he hails the new age was written in August 1938, though the volume was published in 1940. His transition from mood to mood, even from whim to whim, was often very swift and sometimes occurred many times in one day. These varying moods were expressed in widely differing poems which were later sorted out and published in different volumes. The poems of *Navajatak* are comparatively less subjective in mood and reflect his keen interest in the world around. The very themes and metaphors employed indicate this objective concern: the radio, the railway train, the station, the aeroplane, Hindustan, Rajasthan,etc.

The poem referred to earlier, mocking the Japanese militarists praying to Buddha, the Compassionate, is from this collection and was written in January 1938. The climate of menace and aggression in Europe and in Far East and the misuse of the aeroplane as an engine of destruction has biased him against this invention of man. In the poem entitled "Bird-Man" he laments that this evil emissary of aggression should have invaded the space which God had reserved for birds. The poem ends with: "Listen to this prayer of the sad earth— Let the dark green forests be joyous again with the songs of birds!"

On the other hand, relaxing in his easy chair at Mungpoo in the mild chill of a Himalayan morning he is enchanted with the music that the radio brings him from across the seas. "A foreign girl sings in a foreign voice." The music is wafted over mountains, rivers and seas, and to the incorrigibly romantic heart of the ageing poet seems like a new *Meghaduta* bearing the message of a love-lorn heart. The poem is called "Half-past Nine."

A night-train, in a poem of that name, seems to him an image of life, crawling into darkness, the compartments jammed with sleeping forms, the anonymous moving towards the anonymous, driven by someone anonymous. "Some say, it's only a machine, nothing else. And yet to that blind hand they entrust their life; not knowing it, they trust it, and make their beds and sleep and dream of a distant morning." In another poem called "Station" he is fascinated by the comings and goings of bustling passengers on the platform. Some catch a train, some miss it and wail, and some wait patiently. It's like a painting in perpetual making and unmaking, born with one stroke and wiped out with another, some images floating in form this end, and some floating out at the other. That, too, is like life.

In another poem, beautiful and powerful, he asks what purpose there could be in the stupendous and seemingly meaningless waste of energy in the cosmos, as also in the life and mind of man. And in the end will everything disappear and melt into the great void, like a discarded pot when the meal is over? Why? There is no answer, and the poet offers no consolation or palliative and leaves the question as it is, in the void, as it were. The poem is appropriately named "Why?"

The volume of poems named *Sanai* (The Flute), which followed in quick succession is very different in theme, mood and diction. The Sanai is a sophisticated Indian flute capable of a haunting melody, and so are the poems and songs in this volume sweet and haunting, raising a strange nostalgia. Some "modern intellectual" Bengali critics have found fault with the poet for being so "soft" at his age; some others equally modern and intellectual have marvelled how the poet could utter such lovely lyrics quivering with youthful longing at such an age. Tastes differ! But even in these moods when the poet has almost deliberately laid aside his role of the prophet or priest or the modern intellectual, and wishes to savour the simple delights of sight and sound and to lose himself in his dreams, he cannot avoid for long the rude knockings of the tempest raging outside. This mockery he brings out in a dramatic and startling fashion in a poem he wrote in Kalimpong in the summer of 1940. He is contemplating the gentle, somnolent beauty of rural scene in Bengal. It is evening, the wind is low, a hay-stacked bullock-cart is creeping along a deserted field, a young calf trailing behind it. Banamali Pandit's son is still angling in the pond, a flock of wild geese are flying towards the big lake in search of worms, two young friends, one of them newly wed, have met after a long time and are sauntering over the wet grass, happy in their endless chatter, wild flowers raise their heads on all sides, from amidst the branches of the jarul tree the cuckoo is crying itself hoarse with its monotonous wail. "Just then comes the telegraphed news that Soviet bombs have rained over Finland smashing it." The poem is ironically named "Accident".

Meanwhile the war had broken out in Europe. The first world war of 1914 had caused him great agony and had hustled him into the public arena to preach the message of peace. He had at one time believed fondly that there was enough goodwill and wisdom in the Christian civilisation of Europe to prevent the repetition of the tragedy. The disillusionment was very painful and he gave vent to it in a poem of which the last stanza he rendered into English on the Christmas day of 1939:

> Those who struck Him once
> in the name of their rulers
> are born again in the present age.
> They gather in their prayer halls in a pious garb,
> they call their soldiers,
> "Kill, kill," they shout.
> In their roaring mingles
> the music of their hymns,
> while the Son of Man
> in His agony prays,
> "O God, fling, fling far away
> this cup-filled with the bitterest of poisons."

The Sunset

In the mind rings the refrain:
It is not far, not very far.

THE year 1940 began auspiciously as well as ominously. In February Mahatma Gandhi and Kasturba came to Santiniketan –the last meeting of the Mahatma and the poet. Tagore held a ceremonial reception in their honour in the picturesque mango-grove and paid his homage to one whom he had earlier described as "this great soul in a beggar's garb," and said, "We accept you as our own, as one belonging to all humanity." The Mahatma, gracious as ever, said in his reply, "Even though I call this visit a pilgrimage ... I am no stranger here... I feel as if I have come to my home... I have received Gurudev's blessings and my heart is full to the brim with joy."

On 5 April C.F. Andrews passed away in Calcutta. The death of this devoted friend was a deeply felt personal bereavement to the poet. At a special memorial service held at Santiniketan he said, "In no man have I seen such triumph of Christianity." Earlier he had said that he could not harbour an ill-feeling against the British people, if for no other reason than that Andrews was one of them. There was a time when Andrews was very close to him and was one of his chief associates, advisers and friends. To no one else did Tagore ever write so many letters in English, full of such open-hearted confidences, as though he had needed a trustworthy friend to whom he could think and feel aloud. Some of these letters were later edited by Andrews and published under an aptly descriptive title, *Letters to a Friend.* Andrews, on his part, loved and adored the poet. He had been a living link between Tagore and Gandhi, whom also he had loved and adored, though differently. Andrews was a true servant of humanity, a friend of the distressed whoever and wherever they were, and was rightly known as Deenabandhu. Christ's Faithful Apostle, was how an Indian admirer had interpreted the initials of his name, C.F.A. Being what he was, his presence was needed in many places, in India and outside, far away from Santiniketan and Tagore's presence. And so the active contacts between the two had of late diminished, though the old bond had survived.

Tagore could be exuberant, and sometimes even loquacious, in his literary expression, but in personal relations he was very reticent and seemed, not unoften, aloof and remote, even when his heart was full of affection. And so, although he must have felt deeply the loss of so old and trusted a friend, he kept the grief to himself except for the homage he paid to his memory at the memorial service at Santiniketan. A few days later, when he was at Mungpoo, he recalled to his hostess how Andrews, whenever he was at Santiniketan, would come in the morning and embrace him daily, and went on to add: "What an unmixed wonderful love he had! How much he has done for us, unending labour, absolutely selfless and without asking for fruit! He was not in the least proud of all that he had done—a true Christian!"

Part of the summer was spent, as in the year before, at Mungpoo and Kalimpong. It was while he was at Mungpoo that the news was broken to him of the last great bereavement of his life. His dearly beloved nephew Surendranath had died in Calcutta. Suren and Indira the two children of his elder brother Satyendranath had been his playmates when he had first visited England as a student more than sixty years earlier. Since then the affection had deepened and both brother and sister had been very close to him till the end. He sat quietly without uttering a word when the news was broken to him. He did not speak the whole day and in the evening expressed his feelings in a short and moving poem. Both Andrew's death and this death must have reminded him that it would not be long before he too would go the same way. As he had so often put it, he was sitting by the river steps, waiting for the ferry to take him to the other shore.

The news of Surendranath's death had been received the previous day which was the poet's birthday and was for that reason kept back from him. The observance of his birthday in that little mountainous village had a simple and austere dignity which could hardly have been possible in a bigger place like Kalimpong, much less in a city like Calcutta. In Mungpoo there were no social and literary celebrities to crowd round him, obscuring the sad solemnity of his last but one birthday on this earth. In the morning an old Nepali Buddhist from the village came to wish him. He sat on the ground, burnt an incense and chanted an invocation to the Buddha. The poet was moved and expressed his feeling in a poem he wrote the next day. Listening to the hymn addressed to "the supreme man whose birth made this earth holy and gave meaning to man's life," he felt that his own birth had been blessed, for 'entering the world of men eighty years ago, I too have shared the supreme man's legacy."

In the evening his hostess invited the hillmen from nearby villages to a feast. They brought flowers, heaps of them, for the poet. This simple gesture of affection from humble, illiterate folks who had never read anything of him, touched him deeply. He could only express his thankfulness in a poem. It seemed to him that when after centuries of fiery penance on her bare rocky seat, the earth had received the boon of flowers, it was to greet the advent of man in her lap. Was there such manifestation anywhere else in this vast universe of myriad suns and planets?

He must have been led to brood in his solitary meditation on the wonder and mystery of creation, for a longer and more magnificent poem was also written the same day.

As I enter the eightieth year of my life
my mind is struck with wonder—
millions and millions of stars and suns
filling the endless void with light
rushing silently at inconceivable speed—
beneath this impenetrable, endless firmament
I suddenly happened
like an instant's spark from the sacrificial
fire of creation without end.

He went on to describe the birth of the primordial life from the womb of the sea and the gradual unfoldment of human consciousness and its drama on the world's stage.

I too am one of its *dramatis personae*,
dressed for my part,
I have helped to raise the curtain,
and that for me is a great wonder.
Blessed this earth, the soul's mortal abode,
wrapt round with sky, light and wind
carrying the seas, mountains, the under-earth,
what deep purpose impels it to wheel round the sun!
Linked by this mysterious cord I came here
eighty years ago
and shall depart some years hence.

But not "some years" some months only were left of his sojourn on this earth.

Shortly after his birthday at Mungpoo, Tagore left for Kalimpong where his son and daughter-in-law were waiting for him. Meanwhile the Nazi hordes were let loose over Europe like a pack of hungry wolves, and it was becoming increasingly painful for him to listen to the news of what was happening to the countries he had visited, loved and admired. He expressed his horror, puzzlement and anguish in two poems he wrote there in the latter half of May. Why do men seemingly civilised turn suddenly into dangerous maniacs? Are they, he asks, the agents of Fate enraged at man's accumulated pile of centuries-old crimes, men turned into their own bitter enemies to expiate sins of the past? He is hurt, humiliated and unhappy, but does not fume or curse. He is in a chastened, meditative mood, inclined to view his fellow-men's misdeeds in the wide perspective of history. He will not give up hope altogether.

The drums sound,
signalling time for change
of the storm-tossed age.
A new chapter, heartless, will begin,

or else why this pitiless waste,
this dragging down of injustice
by its own ghost, the herald of future?...
What will vanish of this battered
age and what will remain?
Now is the time to know
this polished dross for what it is—
and so the drums sound.

But however dismal the present, the poet cannot give up hope for the future. Faith in the ultimate perfectibility of man, in the essential divinity of his spirit, is the desperate need of Tagore's own soul. This faith he affirms in the other poem.

When this hideous game climaxes
in the terrible dance of death
and this sinning age ends,
Man, penance-driven, austere
and untroubled by greed,
will take his seat on the ash-bed
of the funeral pyre, to meditate
a new creation.
Today's roar of the cannon
heralds this news creation.

Having vented his anguish and affirmed his faith in the only medium of which he was master, he was not content. His own country was in a sulky and frustrated mood and on the verge of a desperate decision. Old infirm and ailing (he had been running a temperature for some time now), he felt he must do something to voice his nation's protest. And so on 15 June, while still at Kalimpong, he sent a letter to President Roosevelt of the U.S.A. bemoaning India's helpless predicament as a British colony at a time when the free world elsewhere was faced with a life-and-death struggle. A free India would be an asset to the free world, an enslaved India merely a burden and a liability.

On 7 August 1940 the University of Oxford held a special

Convocation at Santiniketan for the purpose of conferring on Tagore its Doctorate (*honoris causa*). The citation referred to him as "Most dear to all the Muses." Sir Maurice Gwyer, then Chief Justice of India, Dr Radhakrishnan and Mr Justice Hendersen of the Calcutta High Court represented the Oxford University. "The University whose representative I am," said Sir Maurice Gwyer, "has, in honouring you, done honour to itself." Twenty-eight years earlier the same University had declined to recognise the Indian poet. To quote Rothenstein: "Fox-Strangways wanted Oxford or Cambridge to give Tagore an honorary degree. Lord Curzon, when consulted, said that there were more distinguished men in India than Tagore. I wonder who they were; and I regretted that England had left it to a foreign country to make the first emphatic acknowledgement of his contribution to literature."

Before the year ended three short stories—his last contribution to this form—were published in a volume entitled *Teen Sangi* (The Trio). These stories, "Ravivar" (Sunday), "Sesh Katha" (Last Word) and "Laboretori" (The Laboratory), are very different from his earlier ones. The poet has hardened into an intellectual, the superb story-teller has turned into a commentator, the Himalayas have shrunk into a tableland of skyscrapers. Tagore the perfectionist was never content with perfection if it became static, for then, according to him, it ceased to be perfection. Having scaled the highest peak he left it behind for other heights which though lesser had the merit of being fresher.

And yet in the same year was published *Chhele Bela*, reminiscences of his boyhood days, written in a style simple, lively and unaffected, and utterly different from the manner and mood reflected in the three stories cited above. Tagore thought and felt and reacted creatively at different levels, almost simultaneously, as though he could control many wave-lengths and could switch off one and switch on another at will. Perhaps not quite at will, for he was himself subject to the mood that happened to seize him at the moment. The following excerpt from the English translation (*My Boyhood Days*) by Marjorie Sykes will give some indication of the ease and simplicity with which he penned these recollections. There was an old and discarded palanquin lying in one of the rooms of the family mansion which had belonged to his grandmother, and in which the child Rabi sought refuge in the afternoon when the servant in charge of him had retired for his own meals and rest. Between the discarded palanquin and the neglected child there was a secret fellow-feeling and comradeship. The child would sprawl within its closed shutters safe from all prying eyes and give full rein to his fancy.

"My palanquin, outwardly at rest, travels on its imaginary journeys. My bearers, sprung from 'airy nothing' at my bidding, eating the salt of my imagination, carry me wherever my fancy leads. We pass through far, strange lands, and I give each country a name from the books I have read. My imagination has cut a road through a deep forest. Tiger's eyes blaze from the thickets, my flesh creeps and tingles. With me is Biswanath the hunter; his gun speaks—Crack!Crack!—and there, all is still. Sometimes my palanquin becomes a peacock-boat, floating far out on the ocean till the shore is out of sight. The oars fall into the water with a gentle splash, the waves swing and swell around us. The sailors cry out to us to beware, a storm is coming. By the tiller stands Abdul the sailor, with his pointed beard, shaven moustache and close-cropped head. I know him, he brings *hilsha* fish and turtle eggs from the Padma for my elder brother."

Three days after the Oxford University's special Convocation on 7 August (a significant date on which eight years earlier his grandson Nitindra had died in Germany and on which he himself would pass away a year later) Tagore gave a public address on the cultural significance of the *Ramayana* and paid a tribute to the memory of the great poet Tulsidas whose Hindi rendering of the Indian epic has been called the Bible of the Hindi-speaking world. On 3 September he presided over the Festival of Rain at Santiniketan—for the last time. A fortnight later he was in Calcutta for a medical check-up, and on 19 September went up to Kalimpong to recuperate in the glorious autumn of the eastern Himalayas.

Only a week's enjoyment of the autumn he loved so well was granted to him, the very last week in which he relaxed completely, sitting in his chair, bathed in the golden light of autumn, watching the blue of the sky mingle with the blue of the mountains.

> The sky claps its hands in silent glee,
> my joy is full with colour and sound,
> Is Kalimpong aware of it? . . .
> The golden bell of morning rings ding dong,
> Is it heard by Kalimpong?

This was written on 25 September. On the following day he was suddenly taken ill and lost consciousness, as he had done three years earlier in the same month of September. Once again "with stealthy steps the messenger of death came creeping out of the lightless cavern of the universe." As during the previous crisis, no adequate medical help was readily available, and Kalimpong was even farther from Calcutta than Santiniketan. Pending the arrival of Indian doctors from Calcutta, the British Civil Surgeon from Darjeeling was frantically begged to come. He came reluctantly and having examined the patient, gruffly inquired if he understood English. No sadder instance can be cited of the rapidly increasing alienation of the British ruling class from the people of the land. He diagnosed kidney infection and insisted on performing then and there a drastic surgical operation, if the unconscious patient's life was to be saved. Fortunately he was not allowed to do so and the medical escort from Calcutta arrived in time to take him there.

Two days after his removal to his ancestral home on 29 September, Gandhi's secretary Mahadev Desai arrived to convey to him the Mahatma's deep concern. The patient had not yet fully recovered his power of hearing and fluency of speech. He looked helplessly at Mahadev Desai and the tears streamed down his cheeks. Recording the scene the poet's daughter-in-law who was present wrote: "This is the first time I saw tears flow from his eyes. He was always so self-controlled that even in the hardest bereavement and sorrow I had never seen him break down. Now it seemed as though the banks had given way."

He was never to recover the full use of his faculties, but was soon able to sit up in bed and to talk. His hand was not steady enough to hold the pen, but since words and rhymes kept on buzzing in his head, he had to dictate his poems. A few lines from one such early poem are quoted below in Amiya Chakravarty's faithful and fine rendering.

> In this Great Universe
> the giant wheel of pain revolves;
> stars and planets split up;
> sparks of fiery dust, far-flung,
> scatter at terrific speed
> enveloping in network primordial
> the anguish of existence.
> In the armoury of pain
> spreading on the stretches of consciousness, aglow,
> clang the instruments of torture;
> bleeding wounds gape open.
> Small is man's body,
> how immense his strength of suffering.
> At the concourse of creation and chaos
> to what end does he hold up his cup of fiery drink
> in the weird festival of the gods
> drunk in their titan powers—O why
> filling his body of clay
> sweeps the red delirious tide of tears?

The poet does not pretend to know the answer and will not console himself with pious hopes. Nor would he let his will be broken or his faith defeated by his personal experience of physical suffering. He knows that man can draw nectar from the crucible of sorrow.

> To each moment he brings endless value
> from his unconquerable will.
> Man's sacrificial offering

his burning physical agony—
can anything compare,
in the whole fiery dedication of the suns and stars?

As health gradually returned, the poet recovered his usual liveliness of mind and his delight in the little, trivial sights and sounds. In the early morning of II November, he dictated a charming poem, tender and delightful, addressed to a little sparrow that used to peck at his window, then enter, hop about, wag it saucy tail, twitter and "enquire if there is any news."

When the sleepless night of pain drags on,
I wait for your first pecking
to bring me the simple and fearless message
of life and of the light of day
calling to me,
O my sparrow of early morn!

Equally tender and charming were the many poems addressed to his devoted attendants who were by his sick bed, day and night, by turns. He had obstinately refused to be attended by professional nurses. He needed the warm and friendly touch of those who loved him and whom he could tease, chide and pet as he wished.

When at dead of night
in the phantasmal light of the sick-bed
I am suddenly aware of your wakeful presence,
it seems to me
that the countless suns and stars
bear eternal assurance of my little life . . .

In another poem dictated in a lighter vein he playfully mocks at his own helplessness that he has to listen to such commands– "Be quiet", "Don't talk so much", "You must eat a little more"– from one who was only the other day playing with her dolls in the nursery.

Soon he was brought to Santiniketan where the sight of the open spaces, the blue sky and the trees, and the happy laughter of school children helped him to recover his zest for life.

Throw open the window,
let the bare blue sky
and the eager smell of flowers
enter my room,
and the first rays of the sun bathe my whole being.
That I am alive—
let me listen to this message of welcome
in the murmur of the leaves...

These and many other poems of varying quality and depicting a variety of moods and feelings were published at the end of the year in a volume named appropriately, *Rogasajyay* (On the Sick-bed, 1940). This was followed by another published in early 1941, *Arogya* (Convalescence). As the title indicates, the author was recovering from the acute stage of the illness (he never fully recovered), and could sit up in arm chair and be wheeled about. The anguish of pain has lessened, "the phantasmal light of the sick-bed" is brightened, if not replaced, with the sunlight from the window, and the poet is able to indulge once again in his favourite reminiscing or meditative moods. He loved the sun, and most of the poems in this volume and in the previous one were dictated in the early hours of the morning or the day. In the evening the fever would return and he felt too weak and worn-out for any exertion. The very first poem of the new volume is a reaffirmation of his old faith.

Honey-sweet is the world,
and honey-sweet the dust of this earth—
this great truth I have accepted
as my heart's hymn . . .
When I take my leave of this earth,
I shall say to her: On my forehead
I wore the caste-mark of your dust,

through the veil of *maya*
I glimpsed
the glory of the eternal,
saw the beauty of truth take image in your dust,
knowing this I leave behind my reverence.

He is grateful for the blessings of beauty and grace he has had in this life. "In the vessel of man's affection" he has tasted the divine nectar. Sorrow, hard to bear, has only shown him the unhurt, unconquered soul—"this memory let me leave in grateful words."

Lying in this sick-bed he had, in a poem of *Rogasajyay*, compared his state to that of a cast-off flotsam of dried sticks forming a tiny island in the middle of a river,"circling round itself away from the main current." Pain and suffering "in the closed sky of the invalid's room" had forced his thoughts to revolve round himself. Tagore was, as always, hard on himself in his self-judgement. Those who were attending on him have testified to his amazing capacity for bearing pain without showing it, and to his constant concern to those around him amuse by composing humorous verses and with his light-hearted comments. He could see pain reflected in their eyes, and to spare them their pain, he did everything to hide his own. All his life he had trained himself to stoical endurance of physical pain, and when he was younger and healthier, he had attained a high degree of self-discipline in this respect. He has himself related how once, many years earlier, when he had occasion to sleep alone in an unused ground-floor room of their old ancestral house in Calcutta, he was woken up at dead of night by an excruciatingly sharp pain in one of the toes which had been stung by a large scorpion of a vicious kind. Few experiences are more immediately painful than a scorpion sting. There was nothing to be done, and he would not wake up any other member of the house for his own sake. So he tried to bear it. But the pain went on increasing and when it became unbearable, he concentrated all his will on separating his consciousness from his body. What was in pain was that body stretched before him. He was not that. By a supreme effort of concentrated will, he succeeded in establishing this duality between his self and the body, and the moment he did so, the pain ceased completely. This strange experience of an abrupt and total cessation of acute pain by an effort of will was never repeated, but whenever he was again in any physical pain or discomfort he always recalled his earlier experience and tried his utmost to disembody his consciousness.

He was never without pain or discomfort now, even after his return to Santiniketan, but was better able to forget it, particularly in the morning and during part of the day, before the temperature returned in the afternoon or evening. And when the spring came in early February, he had almost recovered his old robustness and could rejoice in the glory of nature and the joy of life, and was once again deeply concerned with the world of men. In one such mood he dictated a remarkable poem on 13 February in which "floating on Time's leisurely stream," he casts his mind back on the panorama of his people's history. What he sees is a great emptiness across which shadow-pictures pass— of empire-hungry Pathans followed by the Moghuls, "victory's chariot-wheels raising patterns of dust." He looks again and finds that "no trace of them remains today". Another shadow-picture passes, that of the English "along iron-bound roads in fire-breathing chariots." They too will pass and "leave not a sign behind." What remains is "the blue space at morning and eve," and the common folk who toil and labour to sustain life on this earth.

They, ever,
pull the oars, keep holding the helm,
sow seeds, cut the corn,
they go on working,
the toilers.
The kingly sceptre breaks, the war-drums no longer resound;
columns of victory gape, stupidly oblivious of their own meaning;
blood-stained weapons, and blood-shot eyes and faces
hide their annals in children's story books.
They go on working
the toilers

in Anga, in Banga, in Kalinga's seas and river-ghats,
in Punjab, Bombay and Gujarat...
Sorrows and joys unceasing
blend in chant raising the mighty hymn of life;
on the ruins of hundreds of empires
they go on working,
the toilers.

Some well-meaning admirers have read in this poem the ageing poet's increasing affiliation to their socialist credo. In their wishful thinking, the best homage they can pay Tagore is to make him out to be a poet of the proletariat. But Tagore was not a "committed" poet in the sense in which the word is used nowadays. He was committed only to his love of life and his reverence for its common joys and sorrows, and this poem is in fact only a "mighty hymn of life," to borrow the poem's words. He had loved and felt for the common man all his life, long before it became a fashion to do so. Nearly half a century earlier when he was living in the country and looking after the family estates his letters bear testimony to his very deep feeling and concern for the lowly folk, the peasant and the toiler. This concern was humane, a normal expression of a healthy moral sensibility, and not derived from any ideology.

Nor is there anything particularly original or revolutionary in the statement that while empires fall, the common man continues to maintain life on earth. It is the way it is said that makes the poem so memorable. A discerning Bengali professor has complained that the poem's "sheer technical perfection has often been overlooked." He goes on to say, "His mastery is so perfect and effortless that we almost feel and hear the very rhythm of the poet's serene and sober contemplative spirit." And adds, "Tagore remains true to his genius and does not bow before fashions in literature, though he is quick to catch the slightest change in the world around him."

What Tagore loved and admired was the man in man, irrespective of his status in society, be the status common or uncommon, low or high. In this respect, too, he and Gandhi were akin. Indeed, only a few days earlier, on 13 December 1940, he had dictated a poem on the Mahatma which, though in a folk rhyme and composed in a mood half grave and half light, is fairly indicative of his general attitude and the normal habit of his mind.

Followers of Gandhi Maharaj,
some rich, some destitute,
we all have one thing in common:
We neither fill our bellies by robbing the poor,
nor bend our knees to the rich,
nor ever turn pale with fear.
When the bully raises his fist or his baton,
we smile and say,
"Your blood-shot glare
may scare babes out of sleep,
but how frighten those who refuse to fear?"

Arogya was followed by *Janmadine* (On Birthday), a volume so named because many of the poems are reflections or recollections occasioned by his previous birthday, and all are pervaded by a pensive awareness that "the days of birth and death face each other." In one of them he recalls his visit to China in 1924 when his birthday in May was observed there with great warmth.

Once I had gone to China,
those whom I had not known before,
they put on my forehead a mark
which said, "We know you."
The stranger's garb slipped from me
revealing the inner man who is always the same.
. . . A Chinese name I took, wore Chinese clothes,
and I realised,
wherever I find a friend, there I am born afresh.

Some poems were written on his last birthday at Mungpoo, to which a reference was made earlier. One of the finest among them was dictated at Santiniketan on 21 January 1941. Reviewing his own achievement as a poet, he is aware of the gaps in it and with touching modesty acknowledges the limitation as a failure. How vast and varied is this world and how little he knows of it! His mind dwells in a small corner of this immense expanse, many a vast area of land and life outside his direct awareness. What he has learnt of it is from books and from others.

> I am a poet of the earth,
> Its many voices and sounds
> evoke response in my reed,
> but my reed's notes have a limited range,
> and great gaps are left beyond their reach...
> Most difficult of access is man hidden within man,
> with no tangible measure in space and time,
> knowable only when mind
> communes with mind.
> Not everywhere have I had this communion,
> the fences raised round my life's path
> have barred my entry to many a door.
> The tiller ploughing the field,
> the weaver at his loom,
> the fisherman casting his net—
> on their varied toil, spread far and wide,
> the world is sustained.
> Banished to a high pedestal of fame,
> seated in a small corner by a small window,
> I have now and again approached the outer precincts
> but have lacked the courage to enter their homes.
> When communion is lacking between life and life,
> the value of song is vitiated,
> and so I admit the charge
> that my singing has remained incomplete,
> that my poetry, having traversed many ways,
> could not reach everywhere.

Having confessed to his limitation, he hails the poet of the future who will be close to the soil, who will share the tiller's life and be his comrade, who will be a poet of dumb, obscure men, give voice to their hidden sorrow, and bring joy and song to this dry and desolate land. He prays that the new poet may be true to his faith, that his "words and deeds may achieve true concurrence," that he may not merely flaunt the badge of pretended sympathy for the poor. To such a poet he offers his salutations. But beware of the counterfeit!

He did not know that very soon this sympathy for the dumb and down-trodden will become a cult and a fashion and the literary world will be swamped with poets wearing badges. Or did he anticipate it and hence the warning? In any case, though the admission of his limitations was candid and showed how high and noble was his conception of a poet's role, he need not have been unduly apologetic about his own. Where is a poet whose range of vision will cover with equal sympathy and understanding everything on this earth and in the lives of its myriad men? Those who sing passionately of the dispossessed seem to have little sympathy for anything else. This poem, as also the one discussed earlier where he talked of empires falling and the toilers sustaining the world, does in no way indicate that the aged poet, face to face with death, had suddenly changed his faith and turned a "fellow-traveller". Rather it illustrates that as he grew older, his range of awareness widened, his sensibilities deepened, his understanding of the contemporary predicaments became fuller, and his faith in man's destiny and his own vocation as a poet more eloquent and fervent.

Along with serious verse, he was also dictating nursery rhymes as well as tales and fables told as grandfatherly yarns and prattle full of such gay fancy and quaint humour that one would hardly imagine that they were the voice of one who was in extreme physical pain and almost on death-bed. The latter were published in 1941 as *Galpa-Salpa* (Tales and Trifles). One of them, called "Big News," is a parable of today and alludes to the contemporary dilemma of the industrial society in the guise of an imminent conflict between the oars that labour and the sail that claims to lead the boat while seeming to do nothing. And that is the big news, that the world is in need of a drastic adjustment. It is told to little Kusmi by her Dadamashai (Grandfather) whom she is always asking, "What's the big news today?" But Kusmi can make nothing of this "big news" and thinks that her Dadamashai is pulling her leg.

> "Your big news, is it so small as this? You are joking."
> "Joking it may seem to be," said Dadamashai,
> "but soon this news will become big indeed."
> "And then?"
> "Then your Dadamashai will practise keeping time
> with the strokes of those oars."
> "And I?"
> "Where the oars creak too much, you will pour a drop of oil."
> "True news," continued Dadamashai, "appears small, like the seeds. And then comes the tree with its branches and foliage. Do you understand now?"
> "So I do," said Kusmi. Her face showed that she had not understood. But Kusmi had one virtue: she would not admit to her Dadamashai that she did not understand.

This book of parables and tales as well as the volume of poems *Janmadine* discussed earlier were published in April 1941. The Bengali new year begins in the middle of this month and its celebration at Santiniketan used to be (and still is) combined with the observance of Tagore's birthday (which actually falls about three weeks later, on 7 May), to enable the students to participate in the joint festival before they dispersed for the summer holidays which began soon after. On that day (14 April 1941) was delivered the poet's last public address, published as *Sabhyatar Sankat* (Crisis in Civilisation). Too weak to deliver it himself, it was read for him in his presence. Both his own people in India and the peoples in Europe and the Far East were passing through a period of great travail, in different ways and for different reasons. What was happening was a crisis in civilisation and Tagore's address is both a testament of faith and of its frustration. He began by recalling how his faith in modern western civilisation had grown with his admiration of its humanistic tradition as revealed mainly through English literature and British liberal institutions. He recalled how as a young student in

London he had listened with rapt attention to the speeches of John Bright in the British parliament. "The large-hearted radical liberalism of those speeches, overflowing all narrow national bounds, made so deep an impression on my mind that something of it lingers even today, in these days of graceless disillusionment." He went on to analyse how this "graceless disillusionment" was the result of the cynical disregard by the British rulers of the very values which were the pride of western civilisation. "The wheels of Fate will one day compel the British to give up their Indian empire. But what kind of India will they leave behind, what stark misery? When the stream of their two centuries' administration runs dry at last, what a waste of mud and filth they will leave behind them!"

But even in the darkest gloom Tagore's testament could not end in a note of despair. "As I look around I see the crumbling ruins of a proud civilisation strewn like a vast heap of futility. And yet I shall not commit the grievous sin of losing faith in Man. I would rather look forward to the opening of a new chapter in his history after the cataclysm is over and the atmosphere rendered clean with the spirit of service and sacrifice."

How genuine was his faith in the destiny of Man (whether ill- or well-founded, who can tell?) is even more fervently expressed in a new song composed by him and sung for the first time on the same occasion. A few days earlier his grand-nephew Saumyendranath Tagore had come from Calcutta to see him and had begged him to give a new song which could be sung in chorus to hail the advent of the new man, the real man, the free man who will vindicate man's true destiny and not be a mere cog in a social or political machine. The suggestion was like a seed which took no time to sprout and flower.

The Great One comes,
on earth the blades of grass shiver in anticipation,
in the heavens the trumpets sound . . .
the dark night's fortress crumbles into dust,
over the crest of dawn is proclaimed
the assurance of new life: " Fear not"—
and the great sky resounds with the hymn

of victory to the coming of Man.

The last three months were filled to the brim with suffering. His own physical suffering, the burden of a body tormented with pain, with little or no respite. His unhappy country becoming like a vast prison camp, the leaders in jail, the people cowed and sullen, the spectre of hunger stalking the land. Deeply as he loved his people, his sorrow was not only on their account. He brooded over the gruesome scene in Europe ravaged by war, with Hitler's armies advancing in Russia, and felt intensely for the fate of the innocent millions of all nations who had been dragged into the war as its victims or its tools, for no fault of their own. Though his own sympathies were with the Chinese, Russians and the Allies, he did not think of the Germans and the Japanese as the sole and unmitigated villains in the drama. The world—he had not tired of repeating— was caught in a vicious trap of its own making, where isms of diverse kinds merely helped to make its stranglehold more vicious, and where the greedy merchant, the crafty priest and the power-hungry politician exploited the passions of the common people, their capacity for hatred and heroism, to serve their own ends.

In the midst of this suffering, physical and mental, and his literary preoccupations, his thoughts would now and again wander to his beloved Santiniketan and the little children in the school. The school was his first love which he had somewhat ignored when the glamorous Visva-Bharati came on the scene. Now the old solicitude returned. "Who is teaching Bengali in the school these days?" he suddenly inquired. "I hope some one who loves literature and has a feeling for the language, and not a mere erudite Pandit. The children must catch the feel of the sound from the teacher's voice." He went on to recall how he used to lose himself in joy when teaching children. His voice was thick as he added, "But I can no longer teach them myself, nor supervise."

He saw to it that jars of lozenges and boxes of chocolates were always kept at hand for the little ones who never went into his room without coming out with something in their hand o mouth. A pariah dog, not to be left out, managed to make itself an honoured inmate of the house by the simple process of seeking shelter under his reclining chair. Each morning it would come and doggedly stand near him until the poet touched its head with his hand when it would sit down near the chair, moving to another corner if visitors turned up. One of the poems of *Arogya* is on this nameless dog whose sad and mute devotion must have touched the heart of the convalescing poet. Later, when his condition worsened and he had to be confined to bed and could no longer sit in the chair, he expressed the anguish of "the empty chair" in a very moving poem part of which is quoted below in Amiya Chakravarty's translation. This chair was very dear to him. In this chair he had spent many happy hours, seemingly futile but creatively rich, at San Isidro as the guest of Victoria Ocampo more than sixteen years ago. Seeing how relaxed and restful he had felt in that chair, his hostess had insisted on the chair accompanying him when he sailed from Buenos Aires. Since then it had been his favourite seat of repose at Santiniketan where it is still preserved in the Museum.

> The sunlight blazes hot,
> this lonely mid-day.
> At the empty chair I glance,
> no trace of consolation is there.
> Filling its heart
> words of despair seem to rise in lament,
> the voice of emptiness
> laden with compassion
> whose inmost meaning cannot be grasped.

His fortitude and his kindly sense of humour remained with him till the end. Those who attended on his sick-bed treasured as their greatest reward the pleasantries and witticisms he constantly exchanged with them. He could not get over his amusement at being fed on Glaxo and would refer to himself as "Glaxo baby." As he could take nourishment in very small quantities only, which would be gradually increased, he was much amused when told one day that he was being given the dose for a two-month old baby. Since then each time Glaxo was brought, he would inquire, "How many months old am I today?"

The trees were perhaps his oldest love. As a little boy he had been fascinated by the ancient banyan at which he gazed from a window of his ancestral home where he was kept confined within a chalk circle by the servant who kept guard on him. Immobilised again in his last months, he would watch with wistful tenderness the graceful *shimool* outside his cottage in Santiniketan. During the summer drought he was distressed at the fate of the trees in the asrama. The trees must be saved at all cost. "Have you a *mahua* tree in your garden?" he would suddenly inquire of a visitor. "If not you must plant one. When it grows, you will see how Santal women will gather under it to pick the flowers from which they make their wine." Reluctant to taste the most carefully prepared delicacies made to tempt his palate, he would nibble, eagerly and excitedly like a child , at a wild *jambu* berry when a bunch of them was brought to him. He kept the bunch near his bed and would tempt the visitor, "Just try one and see how sweet my *jambus* taste. From my own tree at the back of Syamali !"

Three days before his birthday which by Bengali calender was due to be observed on 8 May, he dictated the last song (words and music) he was to compose. He never had recourse to notations but would sing the song as the tune came to him, and some one else had to catch the tune from him and give the notation. In this last song of his, which was first sung on his last birthday and is still sung on each anniversary of his birthday, he invoked the Ever New to reveal itself afresh.

> May you be revealed as the Sun
> is revealed dispersing the veil of mist,
> may the unending wonder of the Endless
> be made manifest,
> proclaiming Life's victory !

The poem he dictated on the morning of 6 May is deeply

touching in its appeal and humility. In the midst of the seeming festivity of the coming birthday he feels like one lost. His bag is empty, he has given away all he had. Utterly beggared and denuded, he longs for the touch of human warmth and wants as his parting gift

man's affection, man's forgiveness,
to take with me
when in my last ferry I cross over
to the wordless festival of the End.

As is not uncommon with poets, the change of mood had always been swift with him. But in these last months when the anguish of living had been intensified, the transition from mood to mood was even more abrupt, from elation to depression, from faith to questioning, from tenderness to detachment. Each mood as it came was felt intensely and expressed with utter sincerity and often with great power and beauty, without frills or ornaments, bared of all superfluities. When uncertain and pensive:

All around the grey dusk descends —
the mind says, let me go home,
but where the home is, it does not know.

When faith asserts its robustness:

Death, like Rahu,
only casts its shadow on life,
the squeeze of inertness
cannot drain life of its heavenly nectar—
this I know for certain.

Faith was a source of strength, the staff in hand as also the beckoning light to guide the way in darkness. It was not a blind for self-deception. He will not shut his eyes to the hard reality of suffering on this earth, to the seeming indifference of Providence and Nature to what happens to individual life. He will not deceive himself with false hope. Nor will he, in the bitterness of frustrated arrogance or self-pity, deny or repudiate the terrible beauty of truth. In a poem of *Rogasajyay* he addresses Providence as the Primordial Ascetic (feminine):

> Today in the unrelieved darkness of suffering,
> I can see in my mind
> you seated in the absolute blackness
> of Time's first cycle,
> dumb and blind, in terrible loneliness,
> contemplating creation.

A week after his birthday he muses again on the mystery of creation, looks steadily, without blinking. He awoke, he says, on the bank of Rup-Narain—which is the name of a river in Bengal and also means the world as the visible manifestation of God.

> This world, I knew
> is not a dream.
> My own being I saw
> written in blood,
> through hurt after hurt,
> pain after pain,
> I came to know myself.
> Truth is hard,
> that hardness I loved,
> it never deceives.

And so the months of May and June dragged on, the blazing hot sun of summer sucking the earth dry outside and the scorching heat of pain squeezing out what little strength had lingered in the poet's body.

> Sluggish is the flow of life
> by my sick bed,
> with weeds and moss it fashions
> little shapes—no great value they have . . .

Such was his own modest estimate of the poems he dictated

in his last days. But there are many Bengali critics, discerning, mature and sophisticated, who believe that in these last poems, brief, tense and compact, was born "a terrible beauty" such as is not to be found in his earlier poems, superb and almost perfect as some of them are. These poems dictated before his death were published posthumously as *Sesh Lekha* (Last Writing).

The daily toll of suffering went on rising, the fever rose higher each evening and the nights were increasingly restless. The team of leading physicians and surgeons who came periodically from Calcutta insisted on his removal to Calcutta for a major operation. The decision upset the patient who had little faith in allopathic claims and resented the idea of physical mutilation perpetrated on him in the name of scientific surgery. But he was helpless. Even Gandhi had to yield and submit to an operation. "Why can't I be allowed to die in peace?" he protested. "Haven't I lived enough?" With his surer instinct he knew that the end was near, that it was "time for the bird to fly." as he had said earlier in one of his poems. "Momently I feel the time draws near for me to leave." But those around him were adamant. They would miss no chance, however feeble, of saving a life so valuable, And he could not reject the importunities of the dear and near ones. So he yielded—most reluctantly and against his better instinct. He would have liked nothing better than to breathe his last at Santiniketan, surrounded by those he loved best, men and women, children and the trees, his very own, as it were. It was July and the rain clouds had gathered in the sky to greet him and cheer him as of old. He was unhappy to leave the site he had cherished so dearly and where almost every tree had grown under his care. "Perhaps I shall not see these trees again," he murmured.

On 25 July he was taken to Calcutta. It was so ordained, and perhaps it was right, that he should spend his last days under the same old ancestral roof where he had spent his first. Two days later he dictated a poem whose brevity, concentrated strength as of a mantra and daring of thought match the best in the Rig Veda. It is quoted in Amiya Chakravarty's fine rendering.

The first day's sun
asked
at the new manifestation of being—
who are you,
No answer came.
Year after year went by,
the last sun of the day
the last question utters
on the western sea shore,
in the silent evening—
Who are you,
He gets no answer.

It might be asked if this utterance, so lofty and majestic in its intellectual detachment, does not indicate that Tagore's last affirmation was one of doubt rather than one of faith. An answer either way would be naive, too simple to be true. Tagore's is really an affirmation of a truth that is beyond faith and doubt, or is inclusive of both doubt and faith. What the poet uttered was the stark truth that of the ultimate mystery of life and the universe he has no knowledge. What he really is beneath and beyond the body, he does not know. No one has ever known. The bare statement—"No answer came"—reflects,not the poet's nihilism but his truthfulness. Truth, he knew, was hard, and Truth was what mattered. But he was not a materialist or a nihilist as the words are normally understood. He believed that life is bigger than death and the spirit of man bigger than life, and that life, nature and the world of matter are linked together and governed by a universal law whose principle is not mechanical but spiritual, so that the way to its understanding, however partial, is through the heart and not through the head, through love and not through ratiocination.

Basically a man of faith, his faith was brave and true, for it had been tested in the fire of suffering. It did not rest on the artificial props of borrowed beliefs but was founded in the experience of sorrow and shone through it. He had indeed inherited or imbibed in his young age many beliefs, but what in them was unreal or assumed gradually dropped off or was discarded. Only what had been burnt into him and had melted into his being remained with him to the end. The last two poems (quoted in Amiya Chakravarty's rendering) which he dictated as he lay on what became his death-bed are a testament, at once sombre and shining, tragic and sublime, of his faith's climax. The first is dated 29 July, four days after his arrival in Calcutta.

Sorrow's dark night, again and again,
has come to my door.
Its only weapon, I saw,
was pain's crooked pretence;
fear's hideous gestures
preluding its deception in darkness.
Whenever I have believed in its mask of dread,
fruitless defeat has followed.
This game of defeat and victory is life's delusion;
from childhood, at each step, clings this spectre,
filled with sorrow's mockery.
A moving screen of varied fears ...
Death's skilful handiwork wrought in scattered gloom.

The surgical operation was performed the following day. In the early hours of the morning before the patient was carried to the operation table, he dictated his last poem, his final offering to his Muse, the last of his many *tete-a-tetes* with his beloved God, and perhaps the most intimate and heart-wrung of them all.

Your creations's path you have covered
with a varied net of wiles,
Thou Guileful One.
False belief's snare you have
laid with skilful hands
in simple lives.
With this deceit have you left a mark
on Greatness;

for him kept no secret night.
The path that is shown to him
by your star
is the path of his own heart
ever lucid,
which his simple faith
makes eternally shine.
Crooked outside yet it is straight within,
in this is his pride.
Futile he is called by men.
Truth he wins
in his inner heart washed
with his own light.
Nothing can deceive him,
the last reward he carries
to his treasure-house.
He who has easefully borne your wile
gets from your hands
the unwasting right to peace.

Normally he read what he had dictated and often corrected and revised the text. But in this case he had no chance to do so. Before he could recover from the after-effects of the operation his condition worsened and he gradually lost his consciousness, never to recover it again. On 7 August at ten minutes past midday he breathed his last in the same old Jorasanko house where he had first opened his eyes eighty years and three months earlier. It was the day of the full moon of *Sravana*, the month of rains so often celebrated in his verse and song.

He had earlier written a song which he had desired should be sung at his death. It was. It is still sung at each anniversary of the day.

In front lies the ocean of peace,
launch the boat, Helmsman,
you will be the comrade ever. . .

And so the poet set sail on his last voyage, with his Beloved at the helm, towards the Great Unknown he had always sought in the known. More than three decades earlier he had sung in *Gitanjali* :

> Let all my songs gather their diverse strains into
> a single current and flow to a sea of silence in
> one salutation to thee.

The strains were indeed diverse and became more so during the thirty intervening years and while seeming to stray farther and farther from one another, met again and again in a single current. A few months before his death the prayer was repeated in a poem:

> Let the veil of "I" fall apart
> and the white Light of Consciousness
> break through the mists
> revealing the everlasting face of Truth.

In a song:

> May the bonds of earth snap,
> may the great universe take him in its arms,
> and may he know in his heart, bereft of fear,
> the Great Unknown.

With him, it seemed, passed away an age, an epoch which despite the fact that India was in subjection to a foreign rule, will nevertheless be remembered as a golden age in Indian history, for it laid the foundations of India's unity and freedom on which the present and future generations are free to raise a superstructure of their choice. It also gave to her two of her greatest sons of all time. One of them did not live to see his country free, the other was shot to death by an ungrateful countryman. But do they die who leave behind a deathless legacy?

Bibliography

This is a very brief and select bibliography of books (in English) on the life and works of Tagore. As some of them (nos, 7,8,12 & 14) carry at the end fairly complete bibliographies of Tagore's published works in Bengali and English, and one of them (no. 8) includes, in addition, bibliographies of translations in many Indian and foreign languages as well as of books on Tagore, it has not been found necessary to append a separate bibliography of Tagore's work to this volume. The interested reader can find what he needs in any of the titles listed below and quoted above.

It needs to be pointed out that no bibliography of Tagore's published works can be complete for some time yet, as volumes of his Bengali letters (many of them unpublished before) are still being regularly brought out by Visva-Bharati. They are a very valuable source-material not yet fully utilised. Besides, new English translations of his writings are also coming out.

1. *Rabindranath Tagore: A Biographical Study.* By Ernest Rhys. Macmillan & Co., London, 1915.

2. *Rabindranath Tagore: The Man and his Poetry.* By Basanta Kumar Roy. Dodd, Mead & Co., New York, 1916.

3. *Rabindranath Tagore: Poet and Dramatist.* By Edward Thompson. Oxford University Press, London, 1926. (2nd ed. revised 1948).

4. *Rabindranath Tagore: His Personality and Work.* By V. Lesny. George Allen & Unwin, London, 1939.

5. *Tagore: A Study.* By Dhurjatiprasad Mukherji. Padma Publications, Bombay, 1943.

6. *On the Edges of Time: Recollections of his father by Rathindranath Tagore.* Orient Longman, Bombay, 1958.

7. *Rabindranath Tagore: 1861-1961: A Centenary Volume.* Sahitya Akademi, New Delhi, 1961.

8. *Tagore Centenary Exhibition 1961.* Lalit Kala Akademi, New Delhi, 1961.

9. *A Tagore Reader.* Edited by Amiya Chakravarty. The Macmillan Company, New York, 1961.

10. *Tagore by Fireside.* By Maitreyi Devi. Rupa & Co., Calcutta, 1961.

11. *The Later Poems of Tagore.* By Sisir Kumar Ghosh. Asia Publishing House, Bombay, 1961.

12. *Rabindranath Tagore: A Biography.* By Krishna Kripalani. Oxford University Press, London, and Grove Press, New York, 1962.

13. *The Lute and the Plough: A Life of Rabindranath Tagore.* By G.D. Khanolkar. The Book Centre Private Ltd., Bombay, 1963.

14. *An Artist in Life: A Commentary on the Life and Works of Rabindranath Tagore.* By Niharranjan Ray. University of Kerala, Trivandrum, 1967.

INDEX

Printed at : Compudata Services, New Delhi - 20